Adobe® GoLive® 6 For Dummies

C000049648

Shortcut Keys in GoLive 6

Windows Keys	Mac Keys	What It Does
Shift+Ctrl+Tab	Shift+Control+Tab	Toggles current palettes on- and offscreen
Ctrl+Alt+1	⌘+Option+1	Opens most recent site
Ctrl+Alt+F	Option+⌘+F	Lets you edit font sets
Shift+Alt+Ctrl+I	Shift+Option+⌘+I	Shows document statistics
Alt+Ctrl+Y	Option+⌘+Y	Displays site settings when in the Site window
Alt+Ctrl+L	Option+⌘+L	Removes link from the selected linked text or graphic
Shift+Ctrl+G	Shift+⌘+G	Left-aligns text
Shift+Ctrl+M	Shift+⌘+M	Center-aligns text
Shift+Ctrl+R	Shift+⌘+R	Right-aligns text
Ctrl+A, Ctrl+right arrow	Ctrl+A, Ctrl+right arrow	Opens all folders in the site
Shift+Alt+Ctrl+ K	Shift+Option+⌘+ K	Displays all keyboard shortcuts

The Site Toolbar

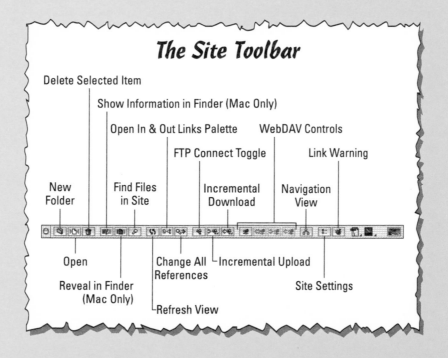

Delete Selected Item

Show Information in Finder (Mac Only)

Open In & Out Links Palette

FTP Connect Toggle

WebDAV Controls

Link Warning

New Folder

Find Files in Site

Incremental Download

Navigation View

Open

Change All References

Incremental Upload

Site Settings

Reveal in Finder (Mac Only)

Refresh View

For Dummies: Bestselling Book Series for Beginners

Adobe® GoLive® 6 For Dummies®

Cheat Sheet

The Color Palette

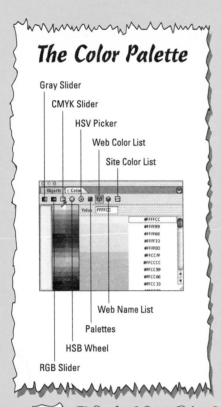

- Gray Slider
- CMYK Slider
- HSV Picker
- Web Color List
- Site Color List
- Web Name List
- Palettes
- HSB Wheel
- RGB Slider

The Objects Palette

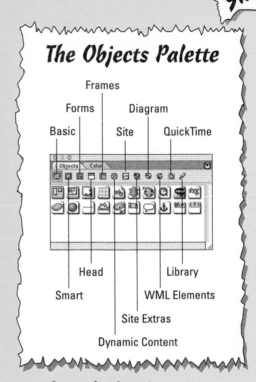

- Frames
- Forms
- Diagram
- Basic
- Site
- QuickTime
- Head
- Library
- Smart
- WML Elements
- Site Extras
- Dynamic Content

The Text Toolbar

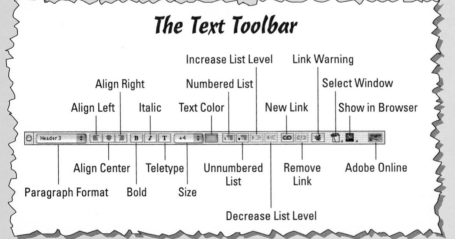

- Increase List Level
- Link Warning
- Align Right
- Numbered List
- Select Window
- Align Left
- Italic
- Text Color
- New Link
- Show in Browser
- Align Center
- Teletype
- Unnumbered List
- Remove Link
- Adobe Online
- Paragraph Format
- Bold
- Size
- Decrease List Level

Hungry Minds™

For Dummies: Bestselling Book Series for Beginners

Adobe® GoLive® 6

FOR

DUMMIES®

Adobe® GoLive® 6 FOR DUMMIES®

by William B. Sanders

Hungry Minds™

Best-Selling Books • Digital Downloads • e-Books • Answer Networks • e-Newsletters • Branded Web Sites • e-Learning

New York, NY ◆ Cleveland, OH ◆ Indianapolis, IN

Adobe® GoLive® 6 For Dummies®

Published by
Hungry Minds, Inc.
909 Third Avenue
New York, NY 10022
www.hungryminds.com
www.dummies.com

Library of Congress Control Number: 2002100100

ISBN: 0-7645-1629-9

Printed in the United States of America

10 9 8 7 6 5 4 3 2 1

1B/SX/QS/QS/IN

Distributed in the United States by Hungry Minds, Inc.

Distributed by CDG Books Canada Inc. for Canada; by Transworld Publishers Limited in the United Kingdom; by IDG Norge Books for Norway; by IDG Sweden Books for Sweden; by IDG Books Australia Publishing Corporation Pty. Ltd. for Australia and New Zealand; by TransQuest Publishers Pte Ltd. for Singapore, Malaysia, Thailand, Indonesia, and Hong Kong; by Gotop Information Inc. for Taiwan; by ICG Muse, Inc. for Japan; by Intersoft for South Africa; by Eyrolles for France; by International Thomson Publishing for Germany, Austria and Switzerland; by Distribuidora Cuspide for Argentina; by LR International for Brazil; by Galileo Libros for Chile; by Ediciones ZETA S.C.R. Ltda. for Peru; by WS Computer Publishing Corporation, Inc., for the Philippines; by Contemporanea de Ediciones for Venezuela; by Express Computer Distributors for the Caribbean and West Indies; by Micronesia Media Distributor, Inc. for Micronesia; by Chips Computadoras S.A. de C.V. for Mexico; by Editorial Norma de Panama S.A. for Panama; by American Bookshops for Finland.

For general information on Hungry Minds' products and services, please contact our Customer Care Department within the U.S. at 800-762-2974, outside the U.S. at 317-572-3993 or fax 317-572-4002.

For sales inquiries and reseller information, including discounts, premium and bulk quantity sales, and foreign-language translations, please contact our Customer Care Department at 800-434-3422, fax 317-572-4002, or write to Hungry Minds, Inc., Attn: Customer Care Department, 10475 Crosspoint Boulevard, Indianapolis, IN 46256.

For information on licensing foreign or domestic rights, please contact our Sub-Rights Customer Care Department at 212-884-5000.

For information on using Hungry Minds' products and services in the classroom or for ordering examination copies, please contact our Educational Sales Department at 800-434-2086 or fax 317-572-4005.

For press review copies, author interviews, or other publicity information, please contact our Public Relations Department at 317-572-3168, or fax 317-572-4168.

For authorization to photocopy items for corporate, personal, or educational use, please contact Copyright Clearance Center, 222 Rosewood Drive, Danvers, MA 01923, or fax 978-750-4470.

Hungry Minds is a trademark of Hungry Minds, Inc.

About the Author

Bill Sanders has written more than 30 computer-related books, including his most recent, *Creating Learning-Centered Courses for the World Wide Web*. He has worked with the Web since its inception and developed sites with virtually every component in Web pages. He is now a professor in the interactive technology program at the University of Hartford.

Dedication

This book is dedicated to the memory of Bogee and the celebration of WillDe.

Author's Acknowledgments

Developing this book was aided and eased by the work the people at Adobe Systems, Inc. Many different engineers, software developers, and project coordinators offered help no matter how simple or complex the questions. As GoLive 6 went from Alpha to Beta builds to the final product, improvements were constantly introduced and Adobe's assistance was in high demand. I want to thank the following people at Adobe: John Kranz, Frank Nießen, Eve Kosol, Adam Pratt, Lynn Grillo, Nils Hausig, Veronika Schlick, Jens C. Neffe, Claus Heitmann, Gerd Hamann, Lance Lewis, Sebastian Dimpker, and Erik Cottrell. I've likely left out some of the people whom I never was in direct contact with but who came up with an answer to questions I had or in some other way aided my efforts, and to them I am most grateful as well.

Along with a supportive team at Adobe, the alpha and beta groups who tested, critiqued, and enhanced GoLive 6 were a great bunch. Everyone offered help at one time or another. Kirk Samuelson and Roman Martinez Allende helped me test the workgroup server, and Roman set up a WebDAV for me to use for testing the GoLive 6 WebDAV capabilities. Rob Keniger and Adam Fishman helped on working through the use of extensions on GoLive, and Jennifer Smith helped to locate a technical editor. Most others on the alpha and beta discussion groups helped out at one time or another, and I am most grateful to them as well.

The support from Hungry Minds has been constant. Rebecca Whitney patiently saw the project through the different phases and was also helpful. Bob Woerner got the project off the ground and supported it through different transitions. Margo Maley-Hutchinson at Waterside Productions was efficient and helpful in moving the project into this edition.

The University of Hartford's interactive information technology program is a general source of inspiration as a talented group of students keep me on my toes. On many occasions, their ideas, queries, and willingness to push the envelope have found their way into my writing. And so I am most grateful to them and the generally supportive environment that the University of Hartford affords exploring new ideas and ways of thinking about the potential and promise of the Internet.

My wife, Delia, is always an inspiration, and my dog, WillDe, takes me for walks. They are both essential to getting a book written.

Publisher's Acknowledgments

We're proud of this book; please send us your comments through our Hungry Minds Online Registration Form located at www.dummies.com.

Some of the people who helped bring this book to market include the following:

Acquisitions, Editorial, and Media Development

Project Editor: Rebecca Whitney

Acquisitions Editor: Bob Woerner

Technical Editor: Sally Cox

Editorial Manager: Constance Carlisle

Media Development Supervisor: Richard Graves

Editorial Assistant: Amanda M. Foxworth

Production

Project Coordinator: Erin Smith

Layout and Graphics: Jackie Nicholas, Jeremey Unger

Proofreaders: TECHBOOKS Production Services

Indexer: TECHBOOKS Production Services

General and Administrative

Hungry Minds Technology Publishing Group: Richard Swadley, Vice President and Executive Group Publisher; Bob Ipsen, Vice President and Group Publisher; Joe Wikert, Vice President and Publisher; Barry Pruett, Vice President and Publisher; Mary Bednarek, Editorial Director; Andy Cummings, Editorial Director

Hungry Minds Manufacturing: Ivor Parker, Vice President, Manufacturing

Hungry Minds Marketing: John Helmus, Assistant Vice President, Director of Marketing

Hungry Minds Production for Branded Press: Debbie Stailey, Production Director

Hungry Minds Sales: Michael Violano, Vice President, International Sales and Sub Rights

Contents at a Glance

Cartoons at a Glance

By Rich Tennant

"Mary-Jo, come here quick! Look at this special effect I learned with the new GoLive software."

page 355

"You know, I've asked you a dozen times not to animate the torches on our Web page!"

page 7

"Well, shoot—I know the animation's moving a mite fast, but dang if I can find a 'mosey' function anywhere in the toolbox!"

page 301

"You know kids — you can't buy them just any Web design software"

page 155

"I can't really explain it, but every time I animate someone swinging a golf club, a little divot of code comes up missing on the home page."

page 239

Cartoon Information:
Fax: 978-546-7747
E-Mail: richtennant@the5thwave.com
World Wide Web: www.the5thwave.com

Table of Contents

Introduction

*E*very time I turn around, I see more great tools for creating Web pages
and Web sites. At the same time, World Wide Web art and technology
advance at a rate that's astounding. A few years ago, people were impressed
by animated images bouncing up and down on their page or by happily
blinking text. Now, Web pages and sites are castles of art and design with
liquid pages that respond to your touch and remember your name.

Welcome to GoLive 6 For Dummies! Anyone from a novice to a professional
designer can use this book to create great-looking, sophisticated sites. Want
to learn how to use GoLive 6 without a degree in computer science? This is
the book for you. You get what you need, when and where you need and want
it. In no time, you'll be creating sites that you never thought you could create.
You may even start your own business on the Web.

If you've ever wondered how Web designers accomplish these major feats,
let me give you a tip: *Do not look at the source code.* Both Netscape Navigator
and Internet Explorer have source code views built into their browsers, and
when you look at a site's code, it can be scary — it's a mass of JavaScript,
Cascading Style Sheet tags, calls to files named .swf, maybe some applets,
plus loads of mind-boggling HTML.

I'll let you in on a secret. The Web designer didn't put in all that code. She
may have tweaked it a little, but you can bet your neighbor's dog that she
used a page-development tool. It wasn't some little freeware tool downloaded
from the Web — it was a full-tilt-boogie, site-crunching, code-making, image-
enhancing, big, bad site-development tool.

Here's the best part. If that tool was Adobe GoLive 6, the designer didn't
have to spend lots of time on the great-looking site. She may have had to
patiently consider a navigation system, with lots of help from the GoLive 6
design-planning tools, and she had to develop and gather images and
content. However, after those chores were done, all the pieces were
organized, updated, optimized, and synchronized by GoLive 6. Those
really cool rollovers, the integrated color scheme, and the nifty floating
boxes were all coded, loaded, and floated by GoLive 6.

At this point, the only question should be "How can I learn to use GoLive 6?"

About This Book

This book is a user's book. By that, I mean that you don't curl up in bed with it, like you would with a copy of *Great Expectations*. You use this book with Adobe GoLive 6 loaded on your computer and ready to go. You can use the book to find out about GoLive 6 from scratch, or you can use it as a reference when you want to look stuff up on the fly. Keep it handy, and flag those sections you use often.

Each chapter deals with a logical chunk of GoLive 6. If you want, you can read the book from beginning to end, but (unlike your high school English teacher) I'm not telling you that you have to. If you want to find out about a certain aspect of GoLive 6, you can flip to a chapter to immediately see a list of what the chapter covers. You don't have to read the previous chapters, either. If you want to learn how GoLive 6 deals with frames, just go to the appropriate chapter and follow the guidelines. Like I said, this is a user's book — so use it.

You can find a wide range of material about GoLive 6 within the pages of this book. It is organized so that the basics are near the front, including a chapter on design and HTML. You will find how to create and control frames, windows, and floating boxes and use them together on a Web page. You find out about using the special GoLive windows, dialog boxes, toolbars, and palettes to outline, create, and maintain an orderly Web site and navigation system. Matching colors between the Web and a graphic on the page is explained along with using the GoLive 6 grid to make creating designs a simple task. Even a built-in FTP (File Transfer Protocol) application makes it easy to load your pages to a Web host server while maintaining all the links you established on your own computer.

A brand-new feature introduced with GoLive 6 is the workgroup server. The server software that comes with GoLive allows you to set up your computer to act as a server while at the same time being used to develop a Web site. You can work with developers and designers in the same building or with other team members around the world. (I personally tested it with a site connecting Argentina and Connecticut.) Site-development team members can work on the site together by checking elements in and out, and then others can add to, change, or remove page features. The server is worth the price of the GoLive 6 software alone, but you get it included at no additional cost.

How to Use This Book

You may have noticed the detailed table of contents and index in this book. They're tools to be used. Typically, when you want to know something about GoLive 6, you don't expect to pick up the book and begin on page 1 for a topic on page 253. You look up the chapter or a key word in the index and then go directly to the part you want.

You can take or leave the tips, warnings, and technical explanations, but you'll probably find them useful. Here's a tip you can take or leave: Go down to your local office-supply store and get a set of those sticky tabs you can put in your book. Use a different color for each topic that interests you. That way, you can quickly look up information you've tagged. (See? You can take it or leave it, but there it is.)

The book has detailed instructions on how to get something done with GoLive 6. At times, the instructions may appear to use material from earlier chapters or even earlier sections of the book that you know well. However, that's the whole point: You don't have to carefully read Chapter 1 before you can use the information in Chapter 7. Usually, I give you more than one way to perform a function with GoLive. For example, to put a graphic image on a page, I tell you to drag it from the Site window, use the Point-and-Shoot button to place it, or use the Browse window. Likewise, I give you both the menu path to a tool and the keyboard shortcut, just in case you prefer using the keyboard.

The book contains some HTML and JavaScript code (but not a great deal of it) that you can enter yourself. GoLive generates the great bulk of the code on a GoLive 6 page. What little code there is looks like this:

```
function goFigure() {
var taxrate=parseFloat(document.calculate.tax.value);
var ship=parseFloat(document.calculate.shipping.value);
var stuff=parseFloat(document.calculate.item.value);
var combine=(stuff + ship +(taxrate * stuff));
document.calculate.total.value=combine;
}
```

Although I don't present much code, what there is clearly stands out using a monospace font, as shown in the preceding code. As in the rest of this book, you use just what you need. (You don't need to program a single line of code to use GoLive 6, but if you like to add your own code, doing so is easy.) Whenever I want you to type something, I present it in a **bold** typeface.

What You Don't Need to Read

If you don't have access to and never plan on using WebDAV with GoLive, don't feel obligated to read the material on WebDAV. On the other hand, if you bought this book because it does cover using GoLive with WebDAV, just read the material on WebDAV and nothing else. There's probably much more information here than you want to know about, and that's fine. A book's value is measured by what you do get from it; not by what you didn't want to waste time reading. Read what you need — from cover to cover or just those parts when and if they help you get done what you need done. In addition, if the paragraphs marked by those little Technical Stuff icons start to give you a headache, skip those, too.

Foolish Assumptions

I assume that you know how to install GoLive 6 on your computer and how to use either the Windows or Macintosh operating systems to launch a program. I assume that you are not a computer programmer and that you do know what the World Wide Web is and have used an Internet browser, such as Internet Explorer or Netscape Navigator. (This statement further assumes that you know what a Web page is.) You don't have to know how to create Web pages. I just assume that you know what a Web page is when you see one. Otherwise, this book assumes that you want to find out how to use GoLive — and little more.

How This Book Is Organized

This book is arranged into five parts. Each part organizes related chapters based on either the level of complexity or their common elements. The chapters' order within each part is not as important as the order within each chapter. Some features require foundational knowledge. Chapter 1 is important if you're new to GoLive 6 because it introduces the way you use GoLive 6 as a tool. You'll see that the user interface (or UI, for the totally cool) is unique compared to other applications you may have used. However, each chapter is self-contained, and you can use the chapters and sections to get just what you need when you need it.

Part I: Ready, Set, GoLive 6!

These first chapters give you a running start with GoLive 6 by showing you how to use the key tools and letting you jump right in and use them. This part assumes very little and even guides you through some design tips. It also pops the hood on HTML and lets you know what's going on behind the scenes just in case you want to tweak some code.

Part II: Looking Good: Designs That Delight

This part brings together key elements of Web pages and GoLive 6. You find out how to enhance your Web pages and site by using key Web page elements, including forms, frames, and style sheets. In this part of the book, you find the next level of Web site authoring beyond the basics of both GoLive 6 and creating Web pages and sites.

Part III: A Site for Sore Eyes: Caring for, Feeding, and Organizing Web Sites

Part III shows you how to work both on a site level of development, design, and maintenance and how to use common components throughout a Web site. By using components, stationeries, and templates, you can create a design once and use it lots. You can not only discover ways to organize your site, but also find and incorporate some features in FTP and WebDAV that you may not have realized existed. (A *server* is the computer where you put your Web pages so that they can be accessed on the World Wide Web.)

Part IV: Swinging Pages: Tapping the Power within GoLive 6

Here's where the fun is. In this section, you'll find all those neat and crazy special effects, from bouncing buttons to team-created Web sites. Part IV introduces all the GoLive action objects, in Dynamic HTML and on plain old pages that come alive with actions. The workgroup server is a whole other application introduced in this part for working with teams at remote sites. Keep your pages looking cutting-edge with the information in these chapters and your team workings in synch. (You'll also keep yourself up way past your bedtime.)

Part V: The Part of Tens

If you want a summary of the most important things to keep in mind in designing Web pages with GoLive 6, this is the place to be. In three concise chapters, you get my ten best design tips for Web pages and sites, the ten best features of GoLive 6, and the ten worst and most common mistakes found in Web pages.

Icons Used in This Book

While writing this book, I would come to a section and think "Hey, the reader could use this tip. I use it all the time." Keep your eyes open for these helpful hints that can save you time and effort.

When a quirky little step or feature that's easy to overlook crops up, I put in a reminder. (These reminders were usually a result of my forgetting to do something and figured that you could use the same reminder.)

The technical stuff comes under the category Just Thought You Might Want to Know Why. Most of the technical stuff I mention in *Adobe GoLive 6 For Dummies* concerns code peculiarities, the different browsers, and something about the Web or the Internet. If you come across a technical note, you can take it or leave it. Whatever you do, though, don't get all tangled up in it or worried about the technical stuff. You really don't have to know this stuff to use GoLive 6. But if you're the kind who's got to know the details, some of the technical stuff might help you understand why certain features of your Web page or site work they way they do.

Warnings are just what they claim to be: They warn you that if you do certain things, you may run into unwanted consequences. For example, Internet Explorer uses marquees and Netscape Navigator does not. So you're warned of what to expect if one browser or the other views your page.

Where to Go from Here

Crank up your computer, open up *Adobe GoLive 6 For Dummies,* and start having some fun with your Web pages. Get your bookmarks, yellow marker, and all the stuff you want to make this book work for you. There's no time like the present to put together the finest Web site the world will ever see!

Part I

Ready, Set, GoLive 6!

The 5th Wave   By Rich Tennant

"You know, I've asked you a dozen times not to animate the torches on our Web page!"

In this part . . .

Get ready to jump into the turbocharged, silicon-guzzling, big, bad mother of all Web-site-building tools — GoLive 6. In no time at all, you'll be leaving those Web page tinkerers in the dust as you charge ahead with untold power and tools to crank out red-hot sites and sizzling Web pages. With more tips on design than your mother gave you on your first date, you'll quickly tap into the secrets of creating good-looking pages on budget and on time. You'll even understand enough HTML to drop the jaws of the pocket-protector crowd. What are you waiting for? Get going with GoLive 6!

This first part of this book shows you how GoLive 6 uses a system of toolbars, palettes, inspectors, menus, and windows to help you put together great sites with ease. As soon as you're familiar with the individual elements of GoLive 6, you're off and running to create your own pages and sites. Along the way, I'll let you in on the secrets of good Web site design (my own, personal bag of tricks for making your sites stand out as clear and good-looking while avoiding the most common pitfalls that come from ignoring design precepts). I'll also show you how to use the GoLive 6 visual navigation tools and palettes to ensure that visitors to your site find what you want them to find. To end things with a bang, Part I concludes with a quick and clear tour of HTML that emphasizes how to use and edit HTML tags with the GoLive Source and Outline views.

Chapter 1

Going Places with GoLive 6

*Y*ou've seen the Web, and now you want to become a part of it. No tool's better for getting you there, looking smart and looking good, than the powerful GoLive 6 program. GoLive 6 enables you to express yourself, sell your products, or get across your point with far more pizzazz than does the standard, plain-vanilla, static text and graphics you often see on the Web, set up as they usually are in a rigid, default HTML arrangement of spots and spaces. GoLive 6 makes your pages stand out and get the kind of attention you seek from Web surfers all around the globe.

You probably know what a Web page looks like on your own computer and in your favorite browser, but GoLive helps you make your Web pages look exactly the way you want on all different kinds of computers, monitors, and versions of browsers. GoLive 6 helps you develop not only a Web page but also entire Web sites of different pages that all link together, making the entire site look easy and, well, just plain *cool* to use.

GoLive 6 is smart enough to write your code, place your pictures, and even show you how your site looks on someone else's favorite monitor and computer (so that Windows users can see how it looks on a Mac and vice versa) and in any browser — whether a visitor is using Netscape Communicator or Microsoft Internet Explorer. GoLive 6 is smart, experienced (hey — this version is the fifth time out for GoLive, after all), and intuitively easy to use. It helps you avoid common mistakes in creating Web sites and has power to spare for even the most elaborate Web-slinging tasks. So whether you're making pages for the folks back in Toledo or way off in Timbuktu, GoLive 6 gets you going on the World Wide Web fast — and with plenty of class!

What's Up, Document Window?

To start using GoLive 6, just double-click the GoLive 6 icon on your desktop to launch the application or in Windows choose Start⇨Applications⇨Adobe⇨ GoLive 6. After you launch GoLive 6, the big, gray rectangle you first see on-screen is the *document window.* (Think of a document window as a canvas on which you paint your creation.) Here's where you bring together the graphics, text, movies, links, and all the other parts of your Web page. After you're inside a document window, you can use any of six different views to create (as well as keep tabs on) your ever-evolving Web site. (For the curious out there, the official names of these views are Layout, Frame Layout, Source, Outline, Preview, and Frame Preview.) Each view has its own tab sitting along the top of the document window, and you can easily toggle back and forth between views by simply selecting the appropriate tab. You get a chance to see what each view can do for you in the following sections of this chapter.

Layout view: Intuitive creations

You end up spending most of your time in *Layout view* while creating your Web pages. That's because Layout view is *the* place to go to drag graphics into position, write text, and add on all manner of goodies you simply *must* have on your Web page. Figure 1-1 shows the blank slate on which you create your masterpiece.

After you first fire up GoLive 6, the program provides a dialog box with three menu selections: New Page, New Site, and Open. Select New Page and you see a page similar to the one shown in Figure 1-1, unless you change your Preferences options to start out in some other view. (As you first start using GoLive 6, however, you're probably best off leaving the preferences in their default configurations.) Although the little icons along the top of the document window in Layout view have important functions, you don't need most of them to get going. Keep the majority of them on your mental back burner for now. You get the opportunity to become better acquainted with those features elsewhere.

One tiny box you see in Layout view, however, may prove useful now. The box in the lower-right corner displays the size value of the window in monitors of different sizes. "Big deal," you may say, and in most cases you're probably right to remain unimpressed. But if you've invested in one of those big-screen monitors and create your Web site with such a big monitor in mind, you may end up frustrating lots of folks: Those visitors with less-endowed monitors may experience difficulty viewing the length and breadth of your Web site on their tiny screens. You can plan for this situation, however, by creating your Web pages for a monitor size that those viewing your Web site are most likely to use. To change the monitor size settings, click the arrow next to the number appearing in the box to open the window-size pop-up menu, as shown in Figure 1-2. Then select the setting for the monitor size you want. A setting of 580, for example, is appropriate for a 14-inch monitor, which is the most common monitor size. For viewing on a 17-inch monitor, the menu shows you that 780 is the right choice.

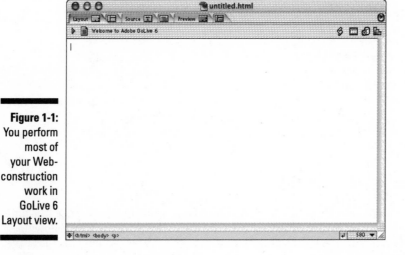

Figure 1-1:
You perform
most of
your Web-
construction
work in
GoLive 6
Layout view.

Figure 1-2:
GoLive
enables you
to create
pages for
different-
size
monitors in
the window-
size pop-up
menu.

A new feature in GoLive 6 is *Source Split view*. In this view, you can see part of your page and part of the HTML, Cascading Style Sheets (CSS — see Chapter10), and the rest of the code that makes up your page — called the *source code.* Figure 1-3 shows the split view displaying Layout view on the top and the source code on the bottom. You can use Source Split view with Layout view, Frame Layout view, Outline view, and Preview view.

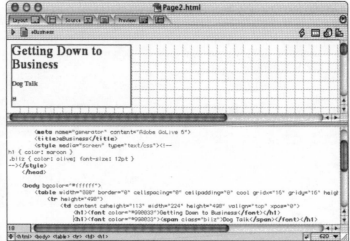

Figure 1-3: Source Split view shows both the page and the source code.

The other views

After you familiarize yourself with Layout view, you can take a quick look at the other views available to you from the document window. The following list summarizes the basics of each of these other views (which I discuss in greater detail in later chapters):

✔ **Frame Layout view:** Use *Frame Layout view* if you want to view and organize all icons of the pages in a frameset at the same time. (A *frameset* shows several Web pages on the same screen organized into sections known as *frames.*) Unlike in Layout view, you don't use Frame Layout view for editing pages — it merely shows you which pages are in a certain frameset. (Chapter 9 tells you all about frames.)

✔ **Source view:** Use *Source view* if you want to see and edit the source code for the items you add to a Web page. This view is very useful if you need to do a little code tweaking — you don't need to open a separate editor just to add a little HTML or JavaScript of your own. (Chapter 6 shows you how to use Source view to fine-tune your HTML.)

✔ **Outline view:** *Outline view* is similar in appearance to Source view except that it includes a structural view of your source code — that is, you can see the hierarchy of the blocks of HTML and JavaScript code. If you view a Web page in Outline view, you can easily insert the cool styles you create (and just as easily insert text) right into the code windows in Outline view. (Chapter 6 explains how to use this unique GoLive 6 feature.)

✔ **Preview view:** Use *Preview view* to take a peek at your page in a simulated browser. Get to know this feature because you will use it frequently.

✔ **Frame Preview view:** Use *Frame Preview view* to preview any of your Web pages in a frameset. You see all the pages in the frameset as they appear in the browser. (***Note:*** Only the Macintosh has Frame Preview view. Windows computers view both frame and nonframe pages in Preview view.)

To save some of your computer's memory, just use Preview view rather than keep a browser open to check how your page looks. Often, you need to keep several applications open as you develop a Web page — for example, a graphics program or a word processor — and these programs all take up memory. As a bonus, you can simulate in Preview view just how your page appears in different browsers on different computers, so you're not stuck knowing how it looks just in your own browser.

Le Menu du Jour

What's up with all those menus? As you do in just about every other application in Windows or on the Mac, you see plenty of menus in GoLive 6 (see Figure 1-4). Most of the work you do in the program, however, involves its various inspectors, toolbars, controllers, and palettes. The menus contain many features that are also on the support windows, bars, and palettes, and until you're comfortable using the other GoLive 6 support elements, the menus serve as a handy source for tools. As you use the support windows and bars more and more, however, you become less dependent on the menus — and accomplish your work much faster to boot.

Figure 1-4:
The GoLive 6 main menu bar, across the top of the screen, can be used in conjunction with the many GoLive palettes.

 Adobe GoLive 6.0   File   Edit   Type   Special   Site   Diagram   Movie   View   Window   Help

You also find many of the less-often-used features, gadgets, and goodies on the menus, where they don't get in the way of your work area. The Special menu, for example, contains a Select Upper Block option that's used to select the upper block of a page when using Source Split view. Usually, you just click the upper block to select it; but, just in case, you can select it from the Special menu — thankfully out of the way whenever you don't need it.

As soon as you can, you want to break the menu habit. In GoLive 6, you quickly find that using the windows, toolbars, and palettes that the program provides is much quicker than using menus. But if old habits die hard, you don't need to tangle yourself all up by *not* using the menus either — at least to get started.

The GoLive Objects Palette — at Your Fingertips

You can access several different windows from the Window menu on the GoLive 6 menu bar. The Objects palette window (or just *Objects palette*), with its 11 different tabs, is one of the more useful of these windows because it's like a toolkit from which you can choose various tools to use in creating your Web page. Each tab offers several icons you can use in creating the Web page, and you can drag each icon from the Objects palette to Layout view, which makes the task of getting exactly the tool you need for your page quite easy indeed. I suggest that you use the Basic tab of the Objects palette to start off, as shown in Figure 1-5. (To give yourself some extra room, drag the corner of a palette to stretch it out and place it at the bottom of your screen to free up space.)

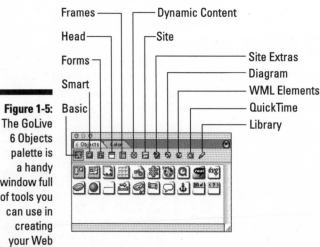

Figure 1-5: The GoLive 6 Objects palette is a handy window full of tools you can use in creating your Web page.

The general model for creating a Web page in GoLive 6 is simply to drag materials (or icons) from the Objects palette over to Layout view, just as you drag stones across a field to use in building that neighborly stone fence. The Objects palette thus provides you with a handy, intuitive tool for building your Web pages. The following list describes all the tabs of the Objects palette, from left to right, and tells you what you can do on each tab:

✔ **Basic:** Use this tab to add general icons you use on several different kinds of Web pages. The Basic tab includes familiar objects, such as tables and horizontal lines. These Basic objects also include placeholders for SWF (Shockwave) files, a grid, and floating boxes, among other objects. (Shockwave runs animated movies made with Macromedia Flash and Adobe LiveMotion.)

✔ **Smart:** The Smart tab contains a number of different kinds of objects that easily perform some of the more complex Web-design tasks. You can drag and drop a *Rollover object,* for example, to instantly set up a Rollover button. Other smart objects include Photoshop and Illustrator objects you can link and update in Adobe applications by the same name. (Chapter 14 shows how to use smart objects.)

✔ **Forms:** Forms in Web pages include different kinds of objects you use to get information from your visitors. Use this tab to access several different Web forms, such as text areas, buttons, check boxes, and menus you can add to your pages to enable users to respond to information on the page. (Chapter 8 tells you all about using forms on your Web page.)

✔ **Head:** Use the Head tab for creating special code (such as JavaScript functions) that goes in the Head section of an HTML page. (The Head section loads before the body of your page and can store important functions and information about your page.) You can put in the Head section some information about your site that helps search engines find your Web pages by using meta tags, and GoLive 6 provides a handy Meta icon for you to drag and drop in the page's head. Chapter 6 explains how. Also, your title goes in the head.

✔ **Frames:** You use the Frames tag for creating framesets. The process is very simple on this tab: Just drag and drop the frame arrangement you want from the tab to your Web page. (Chapter 9 acquaints you with this innovative and simple process for creating framesets.)

✔ **Dynamic Content:** This tab is new to the Objects palette in GoLive 6. When you're ready to link up your pages with "back end" middleware like ASP and PHP, and to databases, this tab is where you should start.

✔ **Site:** The Site tab enables you to add icons you use in the site window. (The site window enables you to see all the other Web pages, graphics files, and other media files that make up your Web site.) You can drag and drop font sets or color schemes from this tab for use throughout your entire site. You can also drag blank pages from this tab to add to the site. (Chapter 11 covers all the details for this tab.)

✔ **Site Extras:** Use this tab to retrieve your own site extras that you create in the site window. You can create and drag templates and components from this tab to your Web page. (*Components* are reusable page elements that do something for a Web page, such as an image map you want to use for navigation on different pages in your site.) After you create a cool design and devise components for it once, you can use the same design and components over and over again by simply dragging them from this page. What's more, when the original is changed, all the components in the site are automatically updated. (Chapter 12 shows how to create templates and components and then use them in your Web pages.)

✔ **Diagram:** This tab represents another new feature in GoLive 6. When working with diagrams to plan your site, you can now add to each page all the elements of the most simple or advanced site as you plan. For example, you can add a PHP element and then a database element that links to the PHP element. Your whole site, including the back end, now becomes clearly laid out before your eyes.

✔ **WML Elements:** For setting up pages for Wireless Markup Language, this new GoLive 6 feature allows you to add WML elements to any page you want. You just drag and drop the elements to the page you want. (Talk to your PDA!)

✔ **QuickTime:** Lights! Camera! Action! You can use this tab to direct your own movies in QuickTime, the video-compression software that enables you to create and view movies on the Web by using either a Windows or Mac computer. GoLive 6 enables you to edit QuickTime movies with some great special effects. (Chapter 15 shows how to put your movies in the biggest theater around — the World Wide Web.)

✔ **Library:** You can create an object on one Web page, drag the object to the Library tab, and then use it on another Web page. That process saves you from needing to reinvent the wheel every time you create a page. (Chapter 12 tells you about creating objects for the library.)

A Rainbow at Your Fingertips

You may notice that the Color palette lives in the same window as the Objects palette. The GoLive 6 *Color palette* features nine different tabs; each represents a different way to look at colors and describes the number of colors available to you for different projects, including ones you make yourself. Tab 7 (the seventh from the left) contains *Web-safe colors*, or colors that appear the same on all monitors displaying 8-bit colors — a full 216 of them. At one time, using Web-safe colors was important because so many monitors had 8-bit color processing; however, that is no longer the case, and designers no longer feel constrained by the paltry palette of the Web-safe color limits. Drag colors from the Color palette's preview pane to an object or an object's color well. Or, you can just click the many different context-sensitive color wells that appear when you select an object that can be colored. The Color palette jumps to the screen and, by selecting the color on the palette as soon as the color well fills with the desired color, the object gets colored too. Figure 1-6 shows the Web-safe (Web Color List) tab in the Color palette.

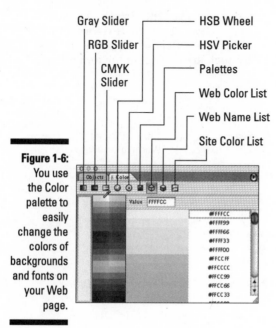

Figure 1-6: You use the Color palette to easily change the colors of backgrounds and fonts on your Web page.

Your GoLive desktop can become crowded with all the windows you open on-screen to help create Web sites and pages. By pressing Control+Tab (on the Macintosh) and Ctrl+Tab (in Windows), you can make all the palettes and toolbars disappear while you concentrate on your Web pages and site. Another press of Control+Tab or Ctrl+Tab toggles these items back to the desktop.

The Many Faces of the Toolbar

The GoLive 6 toolbar is *context sensitive,* meaning that the toolbar changes with what you're working on. (The toolbar is very smart and knows exactly what you're doing at any given moment.) The toolbar serves as a handy bar of buttons that enable you to access specific GoLive 6 features quickly. Figures 1-7, 1-8, and 1-9 in this section show three of the different GoLive 6 toolbars, all of which I describe in the following sections.

The Text toolbar

If you're placing text on your Layout page, you see the *Text toolbar* (see Figure 1-7). This toolbar provides quick access to several text-formatting tools *and* to the Link and Remove Link buttons. Believe me, using the Text toolbar is much faster than fishing through menus to find the formatting options you need.

Figure 1-7:
You use the Color palette to easily change the colors of backgrounds and fonts on your Web page.

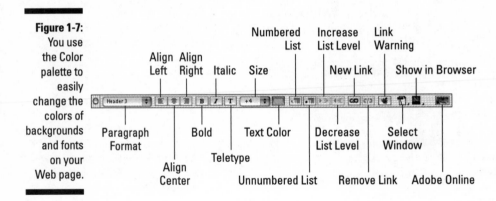

The Text toolbar with labels: Align Left, Align Right, Italic, Size, Numbered List, Increase List Level, Link Warning, New Link, Show in Browser, Paragraph Format, Bold, Text Color, Decrease List Level, Select Window, Align Center, Teletype, Unnumbered List, Remove Link, Adobe Online.

The Objects toolbar

In working with *objects* on the GoLive grid, such as graphics and text-layout boxes, you use the *Objects toolbar* (see Figure 1-8). In Chapter 3, you find out all about the grid and how it makes placing objects on the page as simple as pie — and that includes adding text-layout boxes so that you can place text anywhere you want on-screen. After you select an object, you can quickly type information about object sizes and positions in the toolbar's text boxes or click buttons on the toolbar to designate what you want the object to do without needing to fish through menus to obtain the same results. Just click the appropriate buttons on the Objects toolbar, for example, for the quick alignment of selected objects.

One browser at a time on your toolbar

The sharp-eyed among you may notice that some GoLive 6 toolbars feature a different button at the far right. In GoLive 6, you can select how many — and which — browsers launch after you click this last button. Unless you have lots and lots of memory, however (*DRAM memory*, that is — the kind your computer has only after you turn it on), launching more than one browser at a time is expensive in terms of memory use and may even result in lockups. If you have enough memory, however, and routinely examining your pages in multiple browsers is critical to you, you're likely to find this feature very handy. To make changes, just choose Edit➪Preferences from the menu bar and

click the Browsers icon in the left pane of the Preferences window that appears. In the Browser Selection window that appears on the right, select which browser you want to use as your primary one. (GoLive automatically searches your computer for browsers and then brings them into the Browser Selection window.) The checked browser's icon appears on the toolbar as a button. If you don't want either as the primary browser, remove the check mark from both browsers; a Globe button then appears with a drop-down list menu that enables you to select either one. (If you select both in the Preferences window, you also see the Globe button rather than either browser button.)

The Site toolbar

In thinking about GoLive 6, the first thing you must do is to get beyond thinking only about individual Web pages; the beauty of GoLive 6 is that it makes tying all your Web *pages* together into a true Web *site* extremely easy. And one of the tools that GoLive provides to help you do so is the *Site toolbar*.

Figure 1-8: The Objects toolbar includes text boxes you use for entering object sizes and positions along with buttons for positioning objects on the page.

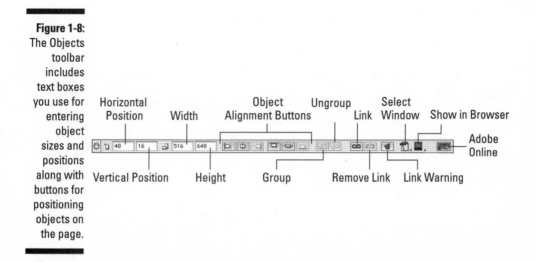

After you select the site window, the Site toolbar appears on-screen (see Figure 1-9). This toolbar provides you with easy access to the different options available in the site window and its accompanying windows and tools. Select a file in the site window and click, for example, the Page button to open it, the Trash button to delete it, or one of the other buttons on the bar to obtain information easily. The third button from the right, for example, toggles between the site window and your document window, enabling you to switch easily between Layout view of a page and one providing specific information about that page within the overall Web site — such as where it lies relative to all the other pages in the site. Click the second-to-last button on the right, and you can view any file in the site window within the browser of your choice. On the Preferences menu, you can set up your default browser to make it easier to access.

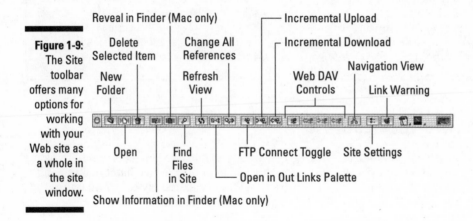

Figure 1-9: The Site toolbar offers many options for working with your Web site as a whole in the site window.

Reveal in Finder (Mac only)
Delete Selected Item
Change All References
Incremental Upload
Incremental Download
Navigation View
New Folder
Refresh View
Web DAV Controls
Link Warning
Open
Find Files in Site
FTP Connect Toggle
Site Settings
Open in Out Links Palette
Show Information in Finder (Mac only)

The Outline toolbar

As you're working in Outline view, you discover that the available toolbar buttons become pretty sparse as well — but still, the *Outline toolbar* has just what you need (see Figure 1-10). A single click of a button on this toolbar enables you to insert special code for Active Server Pages and XML, add comments to your HTML code (so that you can remember later what you want it to do), and insert text. (Chapter 6 tells all about using Outline view and its toolbar as well as HTML tags.)

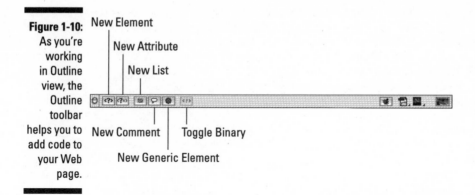

Figure 1-10:
As you're
working
in Outline
view, the
Outline
toolbar
helps you to
add code to
your Web
page.

New Element

New Attribute

New List

New Comment   Toggle Binary

New Generic Element

The Navigation and Diagram toolbars

In creating a site design, you're creating an organization and navigation system for your site. The organization of a site is how the pages are to be grouped and ordered, and the navigation considerations refer to how the groups are to be linked. Before you start making a set of Web pages, you need to get an idea of how your Web site will look. Imagine that you have little cutout cardboard squares for each page that you can lay on top of a table and organize with pieces of yarn indicating links. In the Diagram and Navigation windows, that's exactly what you do — set up a design diagram-and-navigation system to see the relationship between all your pages. Naturally, the toolbars for these windows look similar, although with some key differences (three buttons on the Diagram toolbar let you check the design for bugs and add or remove elements of the design to or from the site window), as you can see in Figure 1-11 (Navigation) and Figure 1-12 (Diagram). (Chapter 11 covers using the site diagram tools.)

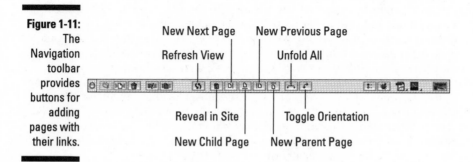

Figure 1-11:
The
Navigation
toolbar
provides
buttons for
adding
pages with
their links.

New Next Page   New Previous Page

Refresh View   Unfold All

Reveal in Site   Toggle Orientation

New Child Page   New Parent Page

Figure 1-12:
The
Diagram
toolbar is
similar
to the
Navigation
toolbar
except that
it features
a Toggle
button to
take you to
Navigation
view and
three
buttons you
can use
for turning
designs
into sites.

Submit Design

Check Design   Recall Design

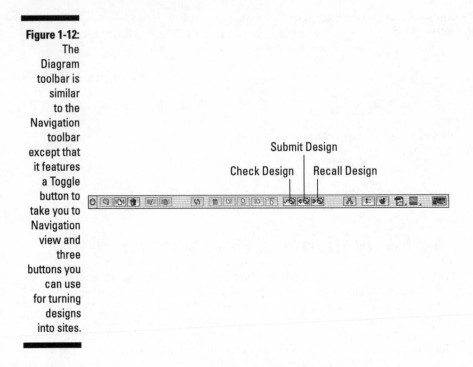

Keeping Everything in Site

Even if you plan to create only a single-page Web site, the *site window* in GoLive 6 is likely to quickly become one of your favorites. You can quickly create a site by selecting File⇨New Site from the menu bar, creating a blank site in the Site Wizard, and saving the site in a folder on your computer. You are given a new page named index.html with the site. From the Files tab in the site window, you can open that page into a document window by double-clicking the file icon. The site window shows everything you need for your site on six different tabs (or *views,* a term I use interchangeably), and it makes creating sites very easy. You can drag your files from anywhere on your computer onto the Files tab of the site window, for example, and a copy of that file goes into the root folder for the site. The Files tab shows the root folder for your site, including folders within the root folder. Figure 1-13 shows the Files tab of the site window for a typical Web site you can create in GoLive 6. All the different media appear together in a single Media folder, and you can easily see each page of the site within the window.

You can move back and forth between the Site and document windows by clicking the third button from the right on the toolbar. If you're in the site window, the button for the document window appears on the toolbar, and if

you're in the document window, the site window button appears. Pla⸏
with switching back and forth to accustom yourself to this simple switch. You
will switch back and forth frequently before you're through creating your site.

Switching between the site window and the document window makes
organizing your site much easier because you can see where everything is
and obtain a better overall sense of where your work lies in the context of the
site. So, as you're working on a page, you're likely to be looking at not only all
the pages and media you need for the current page, but also those for the
entire site.

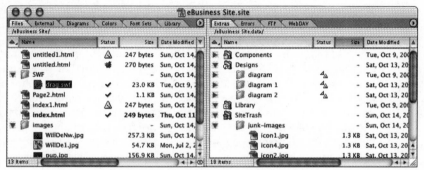

Figure 1-13:
Files view
in the site
window
shows
all files
associated
with the
site.

Files view

The first tab in the site window opens a window displaying all the files in
your site — *Files view* (refer to Figure 1-13). This handy overview enables you
to know whether all your files are in place and whether they're working right.
Different symbols in the Status column show you either that something is
wrong with a file (in which case you see a big, green bug) or that your files
are up-to-date (a check mark designating this status appears). You use the
right frame of the window for adding components, templates, designs, smart
objects, and stationeries — either those you store from previous sites or new
ones you develop for use in future sites. (*Stationeries* are pages you use as
templates, and *components* are reusable page elements — I explain both in
detail in Chapter 14.) You can also toss an unwanted file into the Site Trash
folder in the right frame.

External view

Open up External view by selecting the External tab in the site window. Ever
see a link to a Web page or an e-mail you want to put on one of your Web
pages? All you need do is to drag a *URL* (a link to an external Web address)
from a browser page to External view of the site window, and GoLive 6 stores

that link there. Then you can select text or an image and easily link it to that URL or e-mail address. The Site window's External view makes life easy because you can use your browser to surf throughout the World Wide Web, drag all kinds of links and e-mail addresses into your Site window, and then use those links and addresses whenever you need them. (Chapter 11 explains how to use External view and bring in all the e-mail and Web site addresses you want.)

Diagrams view

The Diagrams tab gives you access to Diagrams view, a new feature in GoLive 6. In Diagrams view of the site window, all you see is a list of diagrams (see Figure 1-14), but from this view you can launch your own site design windows. Think of Diagrams view as a place where you can try on all different types of diagrams and then store them. Then, after you decide that you're ready to make a design choice, you go into this view and select the one that best fits the needs of your site. Diagrams can be stored, and when submitted they become part of your Site window. You can try out several diagrams and then submit the one you like best. Part of the design-preview process includes inserting potential links between pages for a navigation overview. (Chapters 4 and 11 show how GoLive 6 handles both site design and navigation planning.)

Figure 1-14: Diagrams view is the storage shed for all the site designs you may want to use for your site.

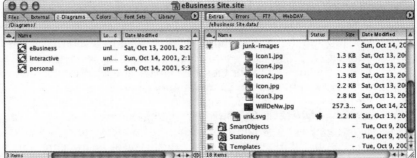

Colors view

A good Web site displays a set of colors that go well together. You can easily keep such a set of colors consistent by dragging all the colors you use on your site from the Color palette to *Colors view* of the Site window. (Access Colors view by selecting the middle tab on the left side of the Site window, as shown in Figure 1-15.) After you move a specific set of colors to the Site window's Colors view, the Color palette places those same colors together as a set on the Color palette's own Site tab (the tab farthest to the right). You can then access just the set of colors you need from either Colors view of the Site window or the Site tab of the Color palette. (Chapters 7 and 11 tell you lots more about colors and using colors in the Site window.)

Figure 1-15:
Colors view provides a way to put together a complementary set of colors and reduce the possibility of ending up with colors that clash on your site.

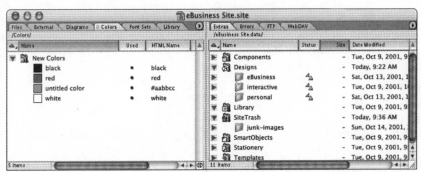

Font Sets view

Font Sets view, accessed by selecting the second tab from the right in the Site window, helps you set up the *fonts* (type styles) for your Web site (see Figure 1-16). GoLive 6 provides several different ways to put font sets on the Font Sets tab. Give the font set a name, and you can then drag it from there to text on any page in the site you want. (This process also is easier than wading through the menus to perform the same task.) As with everything else in GoLive 6, the Site window's Font Sets view makes the job of creating a great Web site that much easier. (Chapter 11 provides more details on how to get your font set and site together and the different ways to go about it.)

Figure 1-16:
Font Sets view provides easy access to the fonts you want to use in your Web site.

Library view

The final tab on the Site window is Library view (see Figure 1-17). Whenever you develop anything on a page that is so cool that you want it on several pages in the site, just drag it to Library view. You can drag everything from text to loaded Shockwave files to Library view. When you need any of the objects stashed on the Library tab on one of the other pages in your site, just drag the object from Library view to your page. (I like to think of Library view as my attic, where all sorts of odds and ends can be stored until I need them — even if I never use them.)

Figure 1-17: Library view shows the different collected objects that can be placed on other pages in the site.

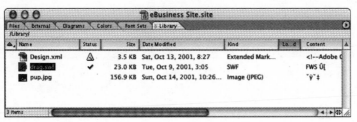

Inspector GoLive, at Your Service

As you work on different parts of your Web page or Web site, the GoLive 6 context-sensitive *Inspector* is always at your side. You soon discover that the Inspector is a bit of a chameleon, however, changing disguises as Inspector Clousseau does, as the need arises. Happily, the Inspector's changeable nature saves you from spending lots of time fumbling through menus looking for what you need, because it always pulls the context-appropriate rabbit out of its hat just at the time you need it the most.

You can summon the Inspector to your side (on-screen, of course) by choosing Window➪Inspector from the GoLive 6 menu bar. Depending on what you're doing at the time you access the Inspector, different Inspectors arrive on-screen. If you're working with text, a *Text Inspector* arrives, but if you're selecting an image, the Inspector takes on the guise of *Image Inspector* (see Figure 1-18). Using the Inspector really isn't all that complex; just remember that it changes its persona on-screen, depending on what you're doing with your Web page or site at any given time. After you entice the Inspector on-screen, you don't need to call for a different Inspector if you decide to start working with some other component of your site. The versatile Inspector changes its identity automatically as you change tasks.

Figure 1-18:
After you
select an
image, the
Image
Inspector
appears,
displaying
four tabs
you use
to work on
the image.

Watch the toolbar as the Inspector changes. Often, the toolbar changes at the same time, depending on what you're doing.

The *View* palette is the Inspector's roommate — they live in the same window. The View palette is handy for setting the appearance of your Web page in Layout view (see Figure 1-19). You can control how the page will look before you examine it in Preview view or in a browser. You can establish the type of browser and the type of computer on which you want to view your pages as you're working on them. You can set all links to appear as they do after someone visits them, for example, rather than how they look before a user clicks them. Suppose that you're working on your Mac, but you want to check to see how the page will look on a Windows computer using Internet Explorer 5. Just set your View palette, and your page appears as it will look in Windows using Internet Explorer 5, as illustrated in Figure 1-19.

Context what?

I bandy about the term *context-sensitive* throughout this chapter, so providing a little clarification here may help you to understand just what I mean by it. Something that's context-sensitive is like a really smart carpenter's assistant: If you're nailing a board, the assistant knows to hand you a hammer and nails; if you need to cut some wood, however, your assistant hands you a saw. The Inspector I describe in the accompanying section is similar to such a smart assistant in that it gives you exactly what you need when you need it. Having such a capability makes a great deal of sense if you're working on different parts of a Web page or site. If, for example, you select text that you indicate you want to use as a link (which you do by clicking the Link button on the toolbar), the Text Inspector's Link tab provides all the tools you need for finding the page to which you want to link. If you're working on a graphic, however, you need to inspect different things, so the Image Inspector provides a different set of windows and buttons you need for that purpose.

Figure 1-19:
The View
palette
provides
many
options for
changing
the
appearance
of objects.

The Rest of the Cast

The windows you use the most are the document window, the Site window, the Objects and Color palettes, and the Inspector. After you set up the View palette, you use it only occasionally. Several more windows and their palettes, however, are available for specialized tasks that I can best explain as you explore in subsequent chapters the tasks they perform. Not giving them at least some introduction here would, however, be impolite, so the following list offers a brief introduction for the rest of the windows and palettes you find in GoLive 6. (GoLive 6 groups its palettes by the windows in which they live.) The palettes are all found on the Window menu bar and in this section are grouped by the palette window in which they reside. Most of the following palettes also have a counterpart in the Inspector, who dons the appropriate face to work with the palette and object you select. (The following groupings have no intuitive or inherent combinations. They are simply grouped that way in palette pack windows. Each palette has its own tab, but they are always referenced as *palettes* in GoLive 6.)

The Transform, Align, and Tracing Image palettes

The *Transform* palette helps change an object's configuration, most notably its size.

You use the *Align* palette to arrange objects in your Document or Design windows.

You can use the *Tracing Image* palette to trace images from Photoshop in the predesign stages of your Web-page layout. You can see what the layout looks like on your page with other elements before you settle on using it.

The Floating Boxes, Table, and Actions palettes

You can use the *Floating Boxes* palette to control floating boxes in GoLive 6 on your Web page. Floating boxes can move around a page when you apply an action to them. (See Actions below and Chapter 16.)

You can set your tables and style them easily by using the new GoLive 6 features on its *Table* palette (see Chapter 5).

The *Actions* palette enables you to generate JavaScript to make your objects come alive. (These are the kinds of actions that make floating boxes fly around the page.) Just add the action you want, and GoLive 6 does the rest (see Chapter 14).

The In & Out Links, Site Navigator, Source Code, and JavaScript Shell palettes

The *In & Out Links* palette shows you the links for selected objects on your page (see Chapter 4).

The *Site Navigator* palette provides a thumbnail view of the Navigation Links or Design window icons and controls the size of the page icons in both the Navigation Links and Design windows. (Powerful little guy!) (See Chapter 4 for the details.)

Whenever you make a change in Layout view, the source code (HTML, JavaScript) appears in the *Source Code* palette. You make fine adjustments in one and view the changes in the other (see Chapter 6).

In the *JavaScript shell,* you Enter JavaScript commands and then test-drive them.

The Highlights palette

When you want to check your pages and highlight any elements or potential problems, use the *Highlights* palette. With this palette, you can check links, warnings, elements, CSS, JavaScript actions, items with URLs, text items, comments, and special items. Each feature appears in a highlight color, so it's easy to separate different elements in your page. This new feature in GoLive 6 is a nice debugging tool.

The Dynamic Bindings palette

The Dynamic Bindings palette is used for connections between middleware, like PHP and ASP and databases.

The Pending Links palette

In Site view, the *Pending Links* palette is handy for looking at the different links on the pages in the site. Just click on the page in Site view, and all the links appear in the Pending Links palette.

The Template Regions palette

When you're setting up or using a template, its different regions can be identified as objects with the new GoLive 6 *Template Regions* template. You can rename the region objects so that you can quickly individualize regions on a page.

The CSS palette

Another new GoLive 6 palette, the CSS palette, appears on the page to let you select text and apply different classes, IDs. or tags. After you start using CSS, you will want this palette handy while you're creating a dynamite site. Chapter 10 discusses using CSS, where you find out more about the CSS palette and his close cousins the CSS Definition and CSS Source palettes.

The HTML Styles palette

You will find that styles are easy to create, import, edit, copy, export, delete, and apply using the new HTML Styles palette, introduced in GoLive 6. The palette can be filled with the styles used in your site, and it makes it easy to use any style you want as well as to create new ones. The palette even has two palettes of its own — the *New Styles palette* and the *Edit Styles palette,* for creating and changing styles of your own.

The History palette

The History palette is so cool that you will use it all the time. Each time you do something in creating a page or site, GoLive 6 records that action in the

History palette. If you make an error — or several, as I do — you need a way to undo the mess. Just select the point in the palette's history list where things were going right, and the History palette discreetly removes anything that may have been added after that point.

Just Point and Shoot Me

One of my favorite features of GoLive 6 is the *Point-and-Shoot button* — the little spiral or squiggle icons you see in the context-sensitive Inspectors. By dragging a pointer line from one of these buttons to a file, a graphic, or some other object on the page, you can easily and intuitively create a link to or place that object on a Web page. Figure 1-20 shows how an image icon from the Objects palette links to a graphic in the Site window. (The buttons and their pull-lines not only are intuitive to use, but also look pretty cool.)

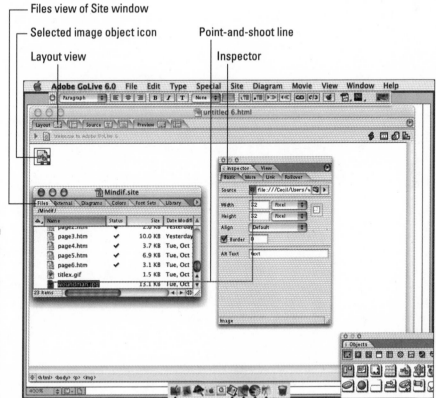

— Files view of Site window

— Selected image object icon   Point-and-shoot line

Layout view   Inspector

Figure 1-20:
The context-
sensitive
Inspector
shows a
Point-and-
Shoot
button
whenever
you need it.

Throughout this book, you find Point-and-Shoot buttons in different places besides the Inspector. If you use Point-and-Shoot buttons, all the links relate to the root (site) folder. So whenever you see the little corkscrew button, you can point, pull, and shoot your way through page design as long as you have placed your pages and media in the root folder. (You know that they're in the root folder if they are listed in Files view in the Site window.)

Chapter 2

A Running Start: Creating Your First GoLive 6 Page

In This Chapter

▶ Establishing a Web site

▶ Placing text, graphics, and links on a page

▶ Checking the view in the View palette and Preview view

▶ Saving Web pages and sites

*Y*ou can best think of GoLive 6 as both a site tool and a Web-page tool. (The site is the overall environment for the different Web pages that make up that site.) To most effectively use the program to create a user-friendly Web site, I suggest that you put yourself in the shoes (or, perhaps, the mouse) of the person who will use your site. Consider how to set up the site so that users can best navigate it while making sure that all the pages combine — or integrate — into a cohesive whole. Think of yourself as conducting an orchestra of Web pages rather than just creating single pages you get around to organizing sometime down the road.

As they were developing GoLive 6, its creators had *you* in mind as a Web-site designer and developer. So, rather than just hand you a tool for creating one page at a time, the program provides a tool you can use to create an entire Web site. GoLive 6, therefore, enables you not only to create single pages more easily than you can in other site-building programs, but also to integrate those pages into a cohesive whole. Later, after you put your Web site on a server, you can see just how well all the parts work together. Even during the development phase of your site, GoLive 6 helps you keep all your pages, media, and links working together as a unit. If you take full advantage of the site-development elements of GoLive 6, you can watch your sites bloom right before your eyes.

5-4-3-2-1: Launch Your Site!

When you first launch GoLive 6, you see a menu of opening selections: New Page, New Site, or Open (an existing page or site), as shown in Figure 2-1. This is the menu for the GoLive 6 Wizard (or The Wiz, to you). Start off by selecting New Site. A single blank page is fine if you need just one page for a Web site, but you're better off if you begin with an entire new site rather than just a new page. "Why?" you may ask. Because GoLive 6 prides itself on being a Web-*site* development tool and not just a Web-*page* development tool. (I told you so!) Most of the really neat features of GoLive 6, therefore, come into play only if you orchestrate a number of Web pages together into a true Web site. To take full advantage of such features, you want to kick off with a new site and get into a site frame of mind.

Figure 2-1:
The opening screen for GoLive 6 provides three menu selections.

To begin working on your first Web site in GoLive 6, just follow these steps:

1. **Open GoLive 6 and, when the first screen appears, choose New Site.**

   This step starts the GoLive Site Wizard, as shown in Figure 2-2.

2. **Choose the Single User button and click the Next button.**

   GoLive 6 provides the option to work with others in a group on a site or by yourself. If you work with a development team, you want a work-group using the workgroup server (see Chapter 15). Start off by learning the ropes on your own. (A single user may build the site, but there's no limit on the number of users who may view the site on the Web.)

3. **Click the Blank Site button on the page showing Options for Local Sites and click the Next button.**

   Besides opening a blank site (as shown in Figure 2-3) that will have a single index page in the site, you can import materials from an existing site you made, import from a server, or copy from a template.

4. **You see a page for naming the new site. Name it** down2Business, **as shown in Figure 2-4.**

You can name it anything you want. For this example, I use "down2Business," but you can call it MonkeyBusiness, if you want. (Before naming it anything, see the following tip.)

Later on, you may want to put your site (down2Business) on a server, and servers can get cranky about folder names. Servers don't care about upper- and lowercase letters and about spaces and special characters. So play things safe and use just a single word for your folder's name — one without any special characters, such as & or #. Figure 2-5 shows how you want the name for your new site to look.

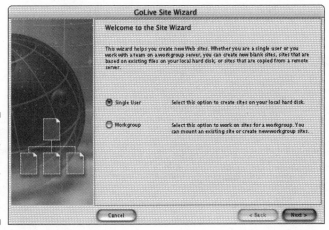

Figure 2-2: Select for a single developer or a workgroup.

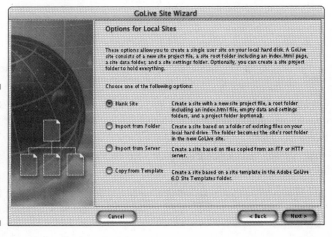

Figure 2-3: Choose a blank site to create a new site beginning with a single Web page.

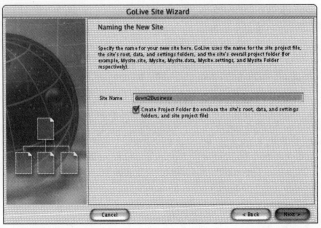

Figure 2-4:
Provide a
site name
that encom-
passes
what your
site will be.

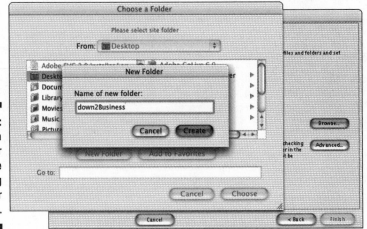

Figure 2-5:
Create a
new folder
for your site
by entering
a folder
name.

5. **Select the Desktop as your workspace by clicking the Browse button and selecting Desktop.**

   On the Mac and in Windows, you want to use your desktop area to work in and then store your Web site folder off the desktop to make room for the next project.

6. **Select a site folder or create a new one by clicking New Folder and writing in the folder's name.**

   Figure 2-5 shows the new folder name being added. When you have created the new folder, click to select it and then click the Choose button.

7. Click the Finish button to complete the process and open your new site.

You see, for example, a file with the name down2Business.site. GoLive 6 automatically generates within the site a page with the name *index.html*. Your first site window now appears, as shown in Figure 2-6. (You're looking at the site window in Files view.)

Figure 2-6:
If you create a new site, GoLive 6 automatically provides a file that it names index.html.

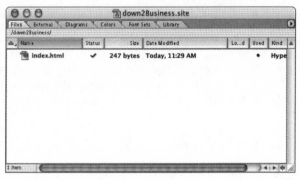

Servers usually use the name index.html as the home page in a directory (folder). The server automatically loads index.html if you provide no filename in the URL directory. If you type `www.interqualcom.com/Fred/`, for example, and the server uses index.html (or index.htm) as the default directory page, the index file for the directory Fred appears. Your server may, of course, use another default home-page name, such as welcome.html, or some other name that the server administrator dreams up. If index.html isn't an appropriate name for your own home page, however, just change it. You don't hurt GoLive 6's feelings at all by doing so. (You can change the default name by choosing Edit⇨Preferences⇨Site from the menu bar.)

To give yourself something on which to work, go ahead and open index.html by double-clicking the file icon in the site window you open at the end of the preceding steps. You see a blank page in Layout view with another `Welcome to GoLive 6` greeting next to the Page icon in the upper-left corner. The first thing you want to do is to change this "name" to reflect the page's actual title by following these steps:

1. Select the text you want to change on the new page.

In this example, you want to change `Welcome to GoLive 6` to an actual title for the page, so you select that text.

2. Type the new title for your page.

You can name your page anything you want — such as **My Home Page, Bob's House of Fun,** or (my personal favorite) **Doggie's Page.** As you type, the new title replaces the selected text.

3. Press Return (on the Mac) or Enter (in Windows).

That's it. Your index.html page now has a unique title — and maybe even one that's a bit too unique, depending on the nature of your own sense of humor!

You can, of course, start GoLive 6 by clicking the icon for an associated file from the desktop or in a file folder. You're far better off, however, if you open the site window first. (You open the site window by double-clicking the icon for a site file rather than the icon for a page file.) If you open the site window, you can immediately view all the other files associated with the site — including graphics, HTML files, and any other files you may decide to attach to a page. (Notice in Figure 2-7 the difference between the icons that GoLive 6 uses for files and sites.) Just remember that if you see the partial globe on the icon, it means that you want the whole enchilada — the site.

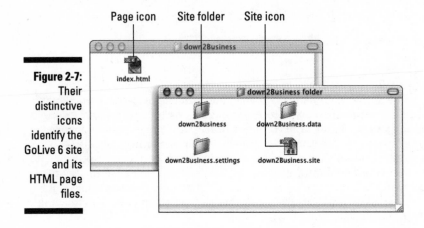

Figure 2-7:
Their distinctive icons identify the GoLive 6 site and its HTML page files.

Before getting to work on a Web page, you need not only stuff to put on your page, but also to get your stuff neatly in order (at least, relatively so). If you want to make additional pages part of the site, put them in a nicely labeled folder somewhere convenient on your computer. (I like keeping things that I need right on my desktop). Do the same to all the Flash, LiveMotion, and QuickTime movies, animated GIFs, audio files, and any other kinds of media you may want to add to your Web site. (Chapters 14 and 15 provide lots of detail on creating and embedding these files in your Web pages, but for now, just know that they have a good home.) Simply gather similar items together, just as Noah did for his ark, storing text files in one folder, audio files in another, and graphics files in another. You can use any name you want for the individual folders, but the important thing is to get everything together before going any further. Then you can simply drop any file or folder you need for your site into the site window you create by clicking and dragging those items from the desktop or folder right into the site window.

You jump back and forth between your site window and Layout page quite often in developing your Web site, which may become confusing at times. Don't forget that dragging files or folders into the site window effectively copies them into your site folder, providing you with a nice, central location where you can keep all your file and folder ducks in a row. After you get them in the site window, you can easily keep an eye on individual files, folders, and even the contents of folders.

It's All Text, Media, and Links

After you load your site window with the pages and the media you want to use on your site, you're all set to put the parts together by entering text, placing graphics, and making links. The following sections tell you how to do just that. And don't forget! Open your site first. You can use the index.html page from the site for learning how to use the page tools.

Entering text

Entering text in GoLive 6 is simply a matter of clicking the arrow at the top of the page area in Layout view and starting to write. As soon as the cursor is in position, an *I-beam cursor* replaces the arrow pointer, and you know that you're ready to start typing. The I-beam defaults to the upper and left of the page relative to whatever else is on your page. After you enter the text, you can perform most basic formatting and all coloring tasks by using the toolbar or the Color palette. More elaborate formatting, however, requires the use of the GoLive 6 menus and other guises of the Inspector, as I discuss in Chapter 1.

Make sure that you use only Layout view for entering text; if you try to type text in Preview view, for example, nothing appears on-screen. (For more information on the various views at your disposal, refer to Chapter 1.)

Using the toolbar to format text

What kinds of makeovers can you achieve by using the toolbar? Take a close look at Figures 2-8 and 2-9 and see what a little magic can do. By employing that same bit of magic, you too can now transform any mousy bit of text by changing its font size, paragraph alignment, and font style. Look closely at Figure 2-9, and you can see the technical tricks behind this formatting magic: The buttons for Center alignment, Bold typeface, and Size 6 fonts (*not* six points or pixels) are selected on the toolbar.

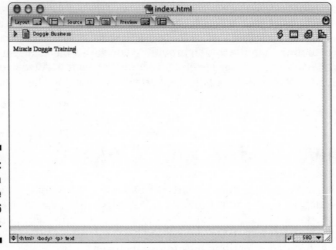

Figure 2-8:
Plain-vanilla
text in the
GoLive 6
Layout view.

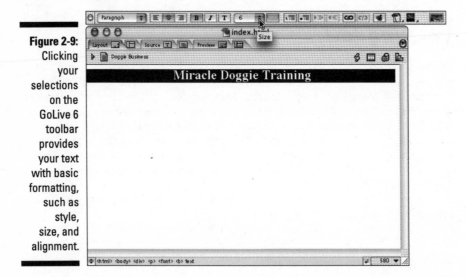

Figure 2-9:
Clicking
your
selections
on the
GoLive 6
toolbar
provides
your text
with basic
formatting,
such as
style,
size, and
alignment.

Your toolbar offers the following format selections, from left to right:

- **Paragraph Format:** Use this set of six drop-down heading selections to change the font sizes for page and section titles. Header 1 is the largest, and Header 6 is the smallest.

- **Alignment (Left, Center, and Right):** The three alignment buttons place text where you need it relative to the page margins. You generally center page headings and left-align most text; anything you need to put off to the side, you right-align — for example, numbers, dates, and mothers-in-law.

- **Bold, Italic,** or **Monospace (T) font styles:** You can use these buttons to set type styles to your liking. Be careful about using italics, however, because italicized type can prove hard to read in smaller sizes. (By the way, the *T* on the monospace button stands for *Teletype* — use that wisdom the next time you're stuck for something to offer the conversation.)

- **Font size:** You set font sizes to one of the seven standard HTML sizes and not in standard point measures. The 7 selection represents the largest, and 1 represents the smallest — just the opposite of the HTML heading sizes. You can use the font size selections to create large caps to kick off a paragraph or just to adjust the overall font size to enable easier reading of your messages.

- **Text Color well:** The Text Color well is a handy device for adding color to your text. When this option is selected (clicked *once*), it automatically brings up the Color palette and transforms any selected text to the color you click on the Color palette.

- **Numbered list:** You can order your sequences by using a numbered list. After you click this button and create the initial paragraph, the numbered-list function automatically numbers sequential paragraphs and indents them. This feature comes in handy, for example, in explaining a sequence of steps you use in dancing the rumba.

- **Bulleted list:** If list elements fall in no specific order, you can use a bulleted list (like this one). Bullets are good for listing major points you want to emphasize on a page.

- **Increase or Decrease List level:** You can use these handy tools for indenting lists further to provide different levels — as you find in an outline. You can also use the same tools for indenting even blocks of text displaying no list properties. Indented blocks of text serve to break up long streams of text and make the page more interesting.

Coloring text

You can brighten things up a bit by adding color to the text you add to your page. First, select the text by clicking and dragging across it with your mouse. Then click the Text Color well on the toolbar or choose Window⇨Color from the GoLive 6 menu bar. The Color palette dialog box appears, offering a rainbow's worth of colors from which to choose. You select from nine different collections of colors and different ways to bring up a color. With the Text Color well selected, all you need to do is to click any color on the Color palette, and as soon as you see the color in the Text Color well, your text has been transformed to that color. If you want to take things a little slower and first view the color in the preview pane of the Color palette, don't click the Text Color well on the toolbar. Just click any color on the Color palette to bring it into the preview pane, and then take a good, long look at it. If that color satisfies you, click and drag it from the preview pane to the selected text. Presto, change-o — your text becomes the selected color.

You must *first* select a block of text before trying to add color. (Don't try to select a color first and then the text — it doesn't work.)

Formatting from the menu bar

Because you want to spend most of your time on the desktop and not riffling through menus, you use the toolbar for the bulk of your formatting. Some formatting items on the menus, however, aren't available on the toolbar, so you need to know how to use the menus for formatting too. You can perform a task as basic as selecting a font for your text, for example, only from the menu bar. If you want to use Underline, Superscript, Subscript, or the ever-annoying Blink format, you must use the Type menu to access these features.

To prevent user madness, try to avoid using the Blink style. (This style makes text continuously blink on and off with the effect of distracting viewers from whatever message you may have on your page.) Early amateur designers of Web pages often used this odious style because it was a style not available on paper. If you simply *must* use it, do so on a site you design specifically to annoy your enemies. (Of course, you're certain to try it out now just to see what's so annoying about Blink.)

Choosing a font is easy. Just follow these steps:

1. **Select the text you want to style by pressing and holding the mouse button while dragging the pointer over the text.**

2. **Choose Type⇨Font from the menu bar and then, on the Font submenu that appears, drag the mouse pointer over the font you want and release the mouse button.**

   Each font name is highlighted as you drag the mouse over it, so make sure that the font style you want is highlighted before you release the mouse button. (The first time you select a font, you see only a limited list of fonts available.)

If you don't see the font you want on the Font submenu, GoLive 6 enables you to add fonts and font sets of your own liking. To do so, follow these steps:

1. **Select the text you want to style, as I describe in Step 1 of the preceding steps.**

   You can too easily go through all the work to set up a special font style and then realize that you didn't select the text you want to style. D'oh!

2. **Choose Type⇨Font⇨Edit Font Sets from the menu bar.**

   The Font Set Editor appears, displaying the existing font sets and the names of the fonts in each set.

3. **From the drop-down list in the Font Set Editor's lower-right corner, select the font you want.**

   The name of the font appears in the window to the left of the drop-down menu. At this point, you can either add a new font name to an existing set or create a new font set. You will create a new font set.

4. **With the font selected, click the Create New Font Set button, just above the drop-down menu list of fonts. It's the little button to the right of the Cross (+) button.**

   You now see the font listed separately as a new font set with the name of the font you selected. Select any font you want from the drop-down list, but remember that an unusual font may not appear on someone else's computer. Palatino, for example, is a fairly common serif font. If George, in Wallaby Gulch, Australia, doesn't have Palatino on his computer, however, you have no way of telling what George will see. In GoLive 6, fortunately, all you need to do is to select another font from the list that then appears in place of the primary font if the primary font isn't on a computer that someone uses to view your Web page. Times, for example, is a common serif font on virtually every computer. To add Times to the Palatino font set, just click the font drop-down list again and select Times. This time, press the Add New Font Name button (it's to the left of the Trash button, right above the fonts list menu.)

5. **Click OK and you're done.**

After you create a new font set, it appears in the initial set of fonts on the Fonts submenu of the Type menu, and you don't need to go through the process again.

Here's a way to get a desired font without going through the font menus every time you want to use a certain font in your text. After you have all the fonts you plan to use on a page, you can copy and paste a font from any of the text on the page. Select a piece of text with the desired font from the page. Choose Edit⇨Copy from the menu bar and then choose Edit⇨Paste. After you paste the text, backspace over the existing text and start typing in the font style of the text you just backspaced over. By using this method, you can save the time of going through the menu sequence. You can change the size too, if you want, without losing the font settings.

Adding a graphic

As is true of everything else in GoLive 6, adding a graphic is intuitive and simple. The following steps describe how to add graphics to your page:

1. **Choose Window⇨Objects from the menu bar.**

   The Objects palette appears.

2. **Click the Basic tab (the first tab on the left), if necessary.**

   The Basic tab is the default tab, so it's probably already selected — but if you've been experimenting with the Objects palette, just make sure that it's set on the Basic tab of the Objects palette.

3. **From the Basic tab of the Objects palette, drag the Image icon (the one with the geometric shapes) on the page, as shown in Figure 2-10.**

   The graphic jumps toward the upper-left part of the screen. To control where your graphics go, see how to use the grid in Chapter 3.

4. **Select the Image icon on the page by clicking it and then choose Window⇨Inspector from the menu bar to open the Inspector window (if it's not open already).**

   The Inspector window opens as (or changes into) the Image Inspector.

5. **Click the Select Window button on the toolbar (the third button from the right) to toggle the Site window to the front, and then move the Site window so that you can view both the Site window and Layout view.**

   Aligning the two windows just right so that one doesn't cover up crucial parts of the other can prove a little tricky. You may need to change the window sizes so that you can see everything. (Scooting around windows is a talent you acquire after working with them for a while.)

6. **On the Basic tab of the Image Inspector palette, place the pointer on the Point-and-Shoot button (the one to the far left of the Browse button) and drag the point-and-shoot line to the image in the site window that you want to appear on your page, as shown in Figure 2-11.**

   The image you indicate in the Site window replaces the Image icon placeholder on your page. (Notice the arrangement of the windows for this point-and-shoot operation.) As a further reminder, be sure that the image is in the site window and is one of the Web-supported formats (JPEG, PNG, or GIF.)

After you click the Point-and-Shoot button on the Image Inspector, you can switch between the Site window and the document window by pulling the point-and-shoot line from the Point-and-Shoot button to the Select Window button on the toolbar (the third button from the right). This action brings the Site window to the front so that you can select a file or link without needing to stop and rearrange your windows. Remember to keep holding the mouse button until after you select the image you want from the Site window. After you finish placing your graphic, just click anywhere on the Layout page to bring it to the front. The Site window then sits hidden behind the Layout page until you need it again.

Figure 2-10:
A place-
holder icon
you drag
from the
Objects
palette sets
the initial
placement
of images
on your
Web page.

Figure 2-11:
Using point-
and-shoot to
connect an
image file to
the image
placeholder.

Drag and drop till you drop

You can also drag and drop a graphic directly from its source onto a page. In
fact, you don't even need to use the graphic placeholder (the Image icon)
from the Objects palette in most cases. All you do is select the graphic from
the Site window — or even from any other folder containing graphics — and
drag and drop it where you want it to go. As you do in all drag-and-drop
operations, you simply select the graphic file and then, holding the mouse

button, move the pointer to the position you want on the page. Finally, just release the mouse button, and your graphic is in place. By using this method, however, you don't get to use the Point-and-Shoot button; nor is the Browse folder available in the Inspector to help you find a graphic you didn't place in your site's root folder.

You can save a step by dragging a graphic directly from your Site window to your Web page, but you need to be careful. If you nicely organize all your graphics in the Site window, dragging them onto the page directly without using the Image-icon placeholder doesn't present a problem. If you just start dragging media files from all your computer's folders and disks directly onto your Web page, however, you're likely to end up with bad links between the page and some of the graphics. So, if you decide to use the drag-and-drop method with media files, limit it to only those that reside in the Site window.

Although arranging everything neatly in Files view of your Site window before you start cranking out Web pages is a good idea, GoLive 6 has a heart for those of you who post signs proclaiming "Neatness is a sign of insanity." Chapter 11 shows how to use the Clean Up Site command, which collects the stray files you place in pages residing in your root site. For the time being, however, to quote Mom, "Clean up your site!"

Arranging text around your graphic

After you place a graphic on the page, you must decide where to place the text relative to the image. In GoLive 6, you handle such image/text issues by using a drop-down list in the Image Inspector. You need to select the image first and then open the Inspector by choosing Window⇨Inspector from the menu bar. (Remember that the Inspector is context-sensitive and changes to the Image Inspector after you select an image or image icon.) Click the Alignment drop-down list box and select the alignment you want from the list that appears, as shown in Figure 2-12. A check mark appears next to the alignment you select after you choose it.

Image formats the Web likes

In creating pages for the Web, your choice of formats for graphics files is a bit limited, at least at the time this chapter was written. (You can always hope for rapid advances soon, I suppose). The formats you can now use on a Web page are

- *GIF* (Graphics Interchange Format), including GIF89a for transparent images and animated GIFs
- *JPEG* (Joint Photographic Experts Group), including progressive JPEG
- *PNG* (Portable Network Graphics)

Figure 2-12:
The
Alignment
list in the
Image
Inspector
aligns the
selected
image.

GIFs support transparency and animation, but are not good choices for gradients, blends, or continuous tone (photos). JPG gives excellent blends, gradients, and continuous tone, but no animation or transparency. PNG was created to be the best of both: continuous tone quality plus animation and transparency, but it creates large files and requires a plug-in.

If your favorite graphic isn't in one of these formats, you can transform it easily enough by using any of several graphics programs. Adobe Photoshop is a great one to use to get your graphics ready for the Web. Similarly, you can use Fireworks, Illustrator, and FreeHand to load your graphic file and then save it as a GIF, JPEG, or PNG file.

Making a link

Links (or *hyperlinks*) connect your Web page to the following different elements:

 ✔ Another Web page

 ✔ A resource (a file you can download)

 ✔ An e-mail address

 ✔ An anchor (a link to a target on the page)

For the sake of convenience, I refer to links to pages on your site (those you view in the Site window) as *internal links* and links to other sites as *external links*. To set the stage for either an internal or external link, you first need to add a *destination page* to the site. Then you need to add some more text to your main page and format it so that it can act as the link to your destination page. You don't need to add much text; in fact, a single word or short phrase can act as the link. The following sections explain the process in greater detail.

Adding a page to your site

You use both the Site window and the Objects palette to add a page to your site. To do so, follow these steps:

1. **Open your Site window by clicking the Site button on the toolbar or by choosing File⇨Open⇨*Sitename* from the menu bar or by pressing Ctrl+O (in Windows) or ⌘+O (on the Mac).**

   The Site window appears, showing you the pages, files, and folders associated with your site.

2. **Choose Window⇨Objects from the menu bar to open the Objects palette if it is not already open, and then click the Site tab (the seventh tab from the left on the Objects palette).**

   The Site tab of the Objects palette displays a number of icons associated with different site tasks.

3. **Select the Generic Page icon (the first icon from the left in the top row) and drag it to your Site window, as shown in Figure 2-13.**

   This action adds to your site a Page icon with the name untitled.html.

Figure 2-13:
Drag the
Generic
Page icon
from the
Site tab on
the Objects
palette to
the Site
window to
add a new,
blank page
to your site.

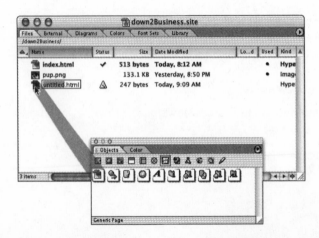

4. **Rename the new page by first selecting the page icon's title ... window and then typing a new name to replace the existing name**

I suggest that you choose a name that's both short and informative. Doing so helps you further down the road because the page name then gives you a clear idea of what's on the page. Take a look at the Status column next to the list of files, folders, and pages in your Site window. A yellow triangle in the Status column means that you haven't done any work on the page yet. (It's a blank page.) As soon as you do some work on the page and save it, the triangle changes to a check mark.

Hooking up to your site pages

After you have a page in your site to which you want to link, you can make the actual link in several ways. I recommend that you use the point-and-shoot technique — the same one I show you how to use in the section "Adding a graphic," earlier in this chapter, to select an image for the site. To make a link by using this method, follow these steps:

1. **Select the text for the link in the document window's Layout view.**

   If your document window is behind the Site window, just click the third button from the right on the toolbar to toggle it to the front and select Layout view (see the first step in Figure 2-14).

2. **Click the Link button on the toolbar (the sixth button from the right — the one displaying two chain links), as shown in Step 2 in Figure 2-14.**

3. **In the Site View window, click the file you want to link, as pointed out in Step 3 in Figure 2-14.**

   Remember: If you can't see the Site window, just click the site button on the toolbar or choose the button from the pull-down menu.

The selected text now appears on the page underlined and in the correct link color. The GoLive 6 default link color is blue, but you can change the default color by clicking the Page icon in the upper-left corner of the Layout page, right under the text reading Layout (on the Layout tab). Use the Color palette (which you access by choosing Windows⇔Color from the menu bar) to choose a new link color, and then drag that color to the Link, Visited Link, and Active Link Color windows that appear in the Page Inspector. (Surprise! After you click the Page icon, the Inspector opens to its Page tab, becoming — ta-da! — the Page Inspector.)

The Unlink button on the toolbar (fifth from the left) and the Inspector is very useful, too. If you accidentally set up the wrong link or you want to change a link, just select the text of the link and click the Unlink button. If you don't unlink a link before you change it to unlinked text, the correct Inspector may not appear.

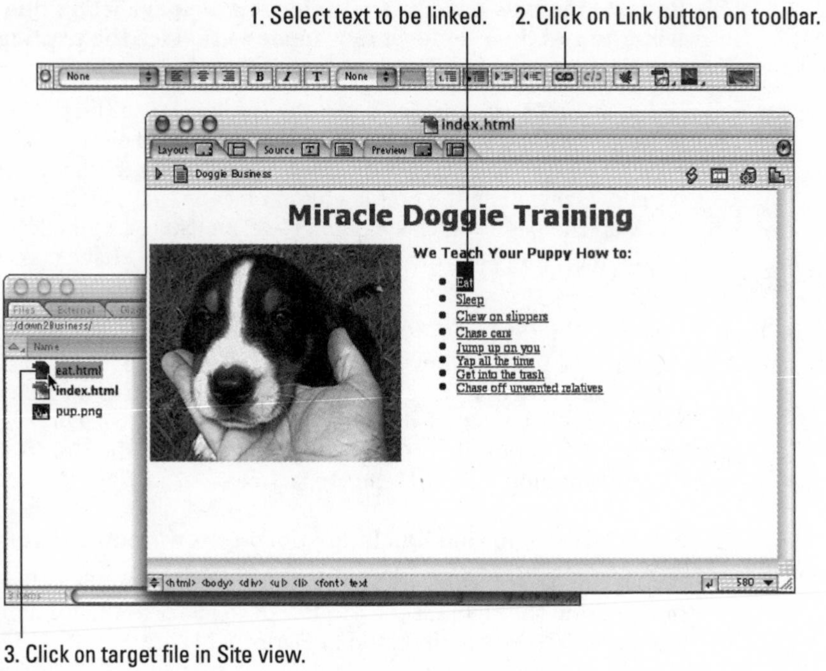
1. Select text to be linked.
2. Click on Link button on toolbar.
index.html
Layout
Source
Preview
Doggie Business
Miracle Doggie Training
We Teach Your Puppy How to:
Eat
Sleep
Chew on slippers
Chase cars
Jump up on you
Yap all the time
Get into the trash
Chase off unwanted relatives
eat.html
index.html
pup.png
<html> <body> <div> <ul> <li> <font> text
3. Click on target file in Site view.

Figure 2-14: Use the Link button on the toolbar to convert selected text to a link.

Making connections to the whole wide world

If you want to link your page to an external file, you need to know the *URL* (Uniform Resource Locator — the Web address) of the file. The steps you take are similar to those for linking to a file on your own site, but you must add the step of typing in the URL. Follow these steps:

1. **Choose Window⇨Inspector from the menu bar.**

   The Inspector appears on-screen.

2. **Select the text for the link.**

   After you select text, the Inspector automatically becomes the Text Inspector.

3. **Click the Link button on the toolbar.**

4. **In the Text Inspector, type the entire URL in the URL text box.**

   In the Text Inspector's text window, you see the phrase `(Empty Reference!)`. You type your URL over `Empty Reference!`. Make sure that you start off the address with `http://` or whatever the correct protocol is (for example, `https://`). The browser doesn't need to think as much if you include `http://`, and GoLive thinks that it's a bug if the `http://` part is missing on an external link.

Use Ctrl+Alt in Windows or Option+⌘ on your Mac when you click the Browse button, and a much larger window opens in which to place your URL. It's also a good idea to copy and paste a URL into the URL window so that you make sure you have the address just right.

Controlling the View: Looking Before You Leap

If Web page designers had a Web fairy godmother, they would all wish for the same thing: page consistency in different browsers and computer platforms. The next best thing to pixie dust, however, is the GoLive 6 View palette and Preview view.

Using the View palette

After you finish creating a Web page, you're all set to look at it. It looks fine in the GoLive 6 Layout view, but before you do anything else, you need to look at it from different perspectives. You want to make sure that what you create on a Macintosh looks good on a Windows PC and vice versa. In addition, you may want to see how the page looks in different browsers. GoLive 6 offers you a designer's dream in the View palette. It enables you to view a page as it appears on different computers using different browsers and even different versions of browsers. (The View palette is the Inspector's roommate — they live in the same window.) To use the View palette to look at your pages from many perspectives, follow these steps:

1. **In Layout view, choose Window⇨View.**

   The View palette appears on-screen. (Of course, if you're already using the Inspector, you can just click the View tab to bring the View palette to the forefront.)

2. **In the area where you see** `Profile`, **open the drop-down list and select the type of computer or phone on which you want to view the page and the type and version of browser for that computer.**

   After you set the View palette for the type of computer and browser through which you want to view the page, both Layout view and Preview view provide images of how the page looks on that respective computer and browser. Figure 2-15 shows a page displayed on a Mac that shows what the page looks like on a Windows PC, in Version 4 of Internet Explorer. Compare that to Figure 2-16 showing what the viewer will see on a Nokia cell phone.

Figure 2-15:
The page
set to
Explorer for
Windows
on a
Macintosh.

Figure 2-16:
The page
set to the
view on a
Nokia
phone.

You may face serious design consequences for your creations on different platforms. What may look great on a Macintosh can look simply awful on a Windows PC. The fonts look big and bulky, and the alignment is different. Similarly, if you do your designing on a Windows PC, the guy looking at your page with an iMac may see itty-bitty fonts and poor alignment. Hence, try out your page on more than one platform and browser preview before you declare it a done deal. Also, the gamma (brightness of display) is different on the Mac and in Windows. To avoid pages looking too dark on Windows PCs, look at a design layout on a PC and set up your color template accordingly. (If your site is for cell phones, you *really* need to consider one of the phone views for checking out your site.)

Using Preview view

Besides looking at your page in Layout view from the perspective of different computers and browsers, you also want to use Preview view to look at your pages before saving final versions. Some of the work you do in Layout view uses tools, such as the grid, that don't appear on-screen if you view the page in a browser. (I discuss the grid in Chapter 3.) You should use Preview view, therefore, to examine these pages to see how they look after they're on the Web.

As I note in Chapter 1, the Windows and Mac versions of GoLive 6 are different in that the Macintosh version offers two Preview views and the Windows version only one. The only difference is that after you begin working with frames in Chapter 9, Mac users need to select the Frames Preview view, and Windows users can view both frame and nonframe pages by using the same Preview view.

To preview your page, follow these steps:

1. **Select File⇨New or Ctrl+N in Windows or ⌘+N on a Mac to create a new page in Layout view of the document window.**

   A new page appears. Go ahead and write text on it or put an image on it just so that you have something to look at.

2. **Select the Preview tab in the document window.**

   Your page now appears as it does in a browser. (Try some different views by using the View palette, which I describe in the preceding section.)

Saving Your Page

Saving your page isn't exactly rocket science, but you must do it right. As is the case with everything else on computers, until you save your page, it exists in an electronic silicon dream. As soon you turn off your computer, the dream is gone unless you save it first — and so is all your work. Save often and save backups of your pages. After you save your pages and create folders for them, you need to remain aware of some important guidelines. Because you're building a Web site and not just a Web page, you need to save *both* the site and the page. To do so, follow these steps:

1. **In the document window, choose File⇨Save or press Ctrl+S (in Windows) or ⌘+S (on the Mac).**

   While in the document window, you save only the page on which you're working. If you have other pages open, you need to save them separately.

2. **Switch to the Site window by either selecting the Select Window button on the toolbar (third from the right) or choosing it from the pull-down menu.**

   You are switched to the Site window. If a piece of the Site window is in view while you're in the document window, you can switch by clicking on the visible portion of the Site window.

3. **In the Site window, choose File⇨Save or press Ctrl+S (in Windows) or ⌘+S (on the Mac).**

   Changes you make in the Site window may include saving several different Web pages. If you save a new page to the site, that action changes the site, and so you must save these changes as well.

As I said, it's not rocket science, but you do need to remember to save your pages. Fortunately, GoLive 6 helps you remember by presenting a dialog box that asks whether you want to save your pages or site before you quit the program — just in case you forget.

In the past, you faced severe limits on what you could name your files and folders. Guess what? Remembering some of those old habits is probably still a good idea. Unlike personal computers, some servers are fussy about names. (Remember that Web pages eventually go onto servers.) Follow a few guidelines in naming your files and folders:

- ✔ Keep filenames relatively short. Some servers limit the number of characters they accept in a filename.

- ✔ Don't put spaces between words. Puppy Dog isn't a good name for a file or folder that's going on a server, but pup or PuppyDog is fine.

- ✔ Be as descriptive as possible in creating filenames. PupTraining.html is clearer than PuTrn.html.

- ✔ Don't use these characters: @ # $ % ^ & *. Invariably, they have special meanings to the server.

- ✔ If you rename a file, make sure that GoLive 6 updates any links involving that file. If you make a name change to a file with a link, a number of dialog boxes appear and ask whether you want to update the links. Always say "You're darn tootin' I do." (Either that or click OK.)

Chapter 3

Looking Good

- -

In This Chapter

▶ Creating clear pages that make your point

▶ Using the GoLive 6 grid to make design easy

▶ Constructing pages with balance and alignment

- -

*N*oticing what's wrong with something is often easier than pointing out what's right. That's because, if something's wrong, the parts are incongruent — like a traffic accident or a sliver in your finger. If nothing's wrong, nothing's there to notice. Often, *beautiful is invisible* because nothing's jarring the senses. Everything flows as it does in nature. At other times, the designer wants to jar the senses, but he does so in a way that engages and intrigues rather than annoys or repels the viewer. After viewing good Web design, the viewer wants to see more but perhaps can't explain exactly why. ("I think it's cool.")

A good-looking Web page, however, doesn't happen by accident or chance but rather because the Web-page designer knows what she's doing. In some part, this ability to create such a page comes from an artistic talent on the part of the designer, but more often it's simply the result of lots of hard work and an understanding of certain principles of design. Most of these design principles are common to both paper and Web pages, but some are unique to designing Web pages. This chapter covers the principles of good Web-page development and then shows you how using the GoLive 6 grid feature makes applying such principles simple.

Talent borrows; genius steals!

In working to make a page look good, the best place to start is with good-looking pages. That's how professional graphic artists start. Design is a skill and talent you develop over years of study and practice, and most people who want to create a Web page don't have that kind of background. To find out a great deal about what makes a good-looking Web page, however, you can explore the Web for award-winning designs — or just for designs that appeal to you. Study the way the various parts go together and why the pages and sites appeal to you as they do. Then adopt for your own Web pages those elements you find most attractive. A good place to start such a search online is at www. killersites.com. David Siegel provides a wealth of tips and examples of well-designed sites. Click the Design Tip link on his core page to see what the pros consider in making a Web site. If you want some fundamental guides, see Yale University's guide, at info.med.yale. edu/caim/manual/. Yale's online guide focuses on the most fundamental Web design elements that you should know. For other links to good designers and cool sites, check out www.adobe.com — the hometown of GoLive 6.

Design Tips to Get the Right Kind of Attention

Design is half (some would say 90 percent!) *not doing the wrong thing* and half *doing the right thing.* This section provides tips on doing a little of both. Certain design tenets you can follow by way of a set of rules can prove extremely useful for novice designers. The guidelines of mature design reflect a corpus of knowledge developed over centuries of design development in everything from architecture to book design. The rules have been extrapolated and modified from examples and design theory. Experienced designers not only know these rules, but they also know how and when to bend and break them and still come up with a good design. Even the most experienced and creative designers, however, consider a number of guidelines before plunging ahead. Furthermore, although typography and graphic design enjoy rich histories, Web design is a little different from other types of design, so a good deal of experimentation and innovation often is in order — while you still keep older design guides in mind.

Communication

A Web page is a means of communication. As is true in all communication, you have *senders* and *receivers.* Even if the Web page includes feedback forms for Web viewers to fill in, to take advantage of the forms those viewers must first understand the message you're sending that tells them to fill in the form. This point is important to remember because you must always consider the people who are meant to understand any message you send.

Audience: To whom exactly are you talking in that manner?

Whenever I visit Mexico or Spain, I try to speak Spanish. Now, my Spanish may bring tears to the eyes of native speakers, but I'm communicating my respect for the culture and customs. Sending a message is easy, but for the person on the other end to understand or even read the message may prove more difficult. Because Web pages are messages, your first consideration is to find out everything you can about your audience. If your audience consists of members of your flower club or business organization, you probably know a good deal about their interests already. If, however, you're trying to create a Web page for a new audience about whom you know little, you need to take some time to find out something about them. If you want people to understand you, consider the following tips:

✔ Avoid (as you would the plague and taxes) anything your audience dislikes. Young, adolescent audiences don't want you to preach to them, and hobby groups don't like people making their hobbies the butt of jokes. (Seriously, folks, the teddy bear collectors take umbrage with anyone who thinks that collecting teddy bears is silly — and the same goes for the Barbie doll enthusiasts.)

✔ Provide the audience with an incentive for looking at your page. Among the most common incentives you see on the Web are free downloads. (Adobe, at www.adobe.com, for example, provides free trial downloads of its software.) Other incentives include daily information about a topic (as at www.weather.com); something fun, such as a daily fortune (check out www.excite.com); or interesting graphics and photos (as you find at www.eyewire.com). Ask yourself the following question: "What incentives attract me?" The chances are good that those same incentives attract others who have the same area of interest.

✔ Take a look at some books on the topics of marketing and advertising. Web sites hardly represent the dawn of the concept of attracting people to an idea, service, or product. Many classic books on marketing and advertising offer great information. (You may not believe how corny some of that advice on advertising and promotion seems today — but it still applies.) So head for your library, bookstore, or online sources and see what you can find.

✔ Look at trade publications for your target audience. You can't perhaps launch a full-scale marketing survey, but you can find plenty of information about every conceivable audience you can imagine in both online and paper publications. Many trade publications also conduct marketing surveys for their readers that can give you just the information you need.

✔ Talk to people in your target audience and then, listen, listen, and listen. If you have a client who wants you to sell her product or service, listen to what she tells you. Sit in on chat rooms online that discuss a particular hobby, service, or product. Sign up for an online discussion group with a focus on your target audience's interests. You can ask questions and get the information you need. Good designers are good listeners.

You may even consider creating different Web pages for the same message. Suppose that you receive an e-mail list for readers of an adventurer's magazine, the audience of which is mostly male. At the same time, you obtain another e-mail list of readers of a women's magazine. Your job, by the way, is to sell travel packages to Timbuktu — not an easy task. (At least you didn't get Afghanistan or Burbank.) Women designers need to ask men what could possibly interest them in a trip to Timbuktu, and men need to ask women the same question. You're dealing with two different audiences here — one's from Mars and the other's from Venus — so your work is cut out for you.

Figure 3-1 shows a Web site design for the readers of the men's adventure magazine. A Web page that wants to attract male adventure-magazine readers considers what such readers may do or want to do. The page in Figure 3-1 combines text, graphics, and color to kindle in the mind a trip that's risky but worth it. In the text, words such as *adventurous* and *dare* are prominent, implying the conquering of a challenge. The graphic shows a skyline with many openings for exploration but without a known inner side. It also displays a fortress-like appearance — shades of the French Foreign Legion. I use the GoLive 6 color palette to select FireBrick (a terra cotta red) as a color — not only to complement the image, but also to characterize the desert setting of Timbuktu.

A female audience may have different interests. Selling a place such as Timbuktu can prove a challenge at best, even to a gung-ho bunch of men looking for new adventure. Women's interest, however, may lie in different types of challenges and desires. A Web page you want to appeal to women, therefore, may take an entirely different approach. Figure 3-2 shows what may seem to appear as an entirely different location, but it's still just Timbuktu. First, I change the spelling to *Tombouctou* — the French spelling and the one you find on most contemporary maps. The art nouveau graphic font elicits a feminine style (see the accompanying sidebar). Finally, the exotic Islamic architecture unique to the city provides an invitation for women travelers in that it's less forbidding than the fortress-like image I use for the men. The many windows create more of a bazaar atmosphere, where shopping is a distinct possibility. Even the French spelling of the city makes it appear, quite by design, less a remote rat hole than an inviting destination.

Figure 3-1:
The type of
Web page
you may
design
particularly
for men.

Figure 3-2:
This Web
page offers
a more
feminine
invitation to
Timbuktu.

Note: You can find good information at Spook Central. For a good source of basic information and maps of just about any place on earth, check out the CIA's home page, at www.cia.gov. Major demographic information is extensive there, and the simple maps provide a good overview of a country and its neighbors. Because this site represents the taxpayer's dollars at work, the graphic maps are public domain, so you can freely use them on your own Web site. Just go to the site and, from the CIA home page, click The World Fact Book link listed under Library and Reference. Then click the link for the country you want from the country listing. When the country appears, so too does the map.

Funny fonts for effective results

In Figure 3-2, I use the Harrington font to spell *Tombouctou;* this font isn't likely to reside on all the computers that may view this page. Rather than use a text font, therefore, I create the header by using a graphic font (or just *graphic* because that's what it really is in GoLive) and then insert it in the page by using GoLive 6. Graphic fonts take up more memory, but if you require a certain look and feel to communicate the spirit of a page, this type of font is worth the extra memory you use. (While you're thinking about it, look also at the art-deco font I use in Figure 3-13, later in this chapter. It too is a graphic font.)

Inserting graphic fonts uses exactly the same steps I describe in Chapter 2 for placing graphic images on your Web pages. You need a graphic program such as Photoshop, CorelDraw, Fireworks, or some other graphic application that includes a text-writing module. Save the graphic text as either a GIF or JPG file and then put it where you want it on your Web page. Using the GoLive 6 grid that I describe in the section "Put Your Objects on the GoLive 6 Grid," later in this chapter, makes placement simple and precise.

On a clear day, you can see my Web page

Another key design consideration for Web pages is *clarity*. Whenever people visit your Web page, you want them to see clearly what your page is all about and how to get more information. After all, how can a muddled page that's difficult to understand attract people? The KISS (Keep It Short and Simple) advice *generally* applies to Web pages — and almost always to the first page. Figure 3-3, for example, shows a very clear, simple, and complete message for its viewers. The page may be a bit minimalist for some, but the page you see in the GoLive 6 Preview view in this figure clearly shows *and* distinguishes these choices for the viewer. The page announces its options, presents a picture of each one, and provides a message telling the viewer what to do. Even if the viewer arrives at the page by mistake, what he sees on-screen is clear enough to suggest to him that he needs to click the Back key on his browser and browse elsewhere.

Simple and clear, however, doesn't need to mean *uninteresting*. After all, to a person who wants information about either predators or prey, what this page offers is clearly interesting. If a page is unclear because it's attempting to appear interesting and clever, a visitor is more likely to skip it than to view it. The design here is clean, however, offering no distracting elements, and so the viewer knows exactly what's what.

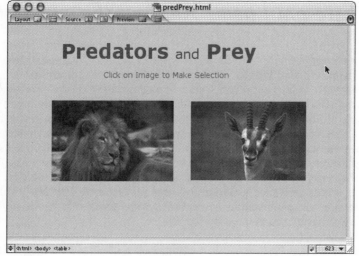

Figure 3-3:
Web pages
need to
provide the
viewer with
a clear
choice and
directions
on what
to do.

In using graphic images on a Web page, you need to remain aware that a few large images work better than several small ones. Two tricks can help you make your page look better if you're using a pair of images as clickable links: Make sure that both images share at least one common dimension, and then place both images within the same grid on your page. (The second part of this chapter explains using the GoLive 6 grid.) In Figure 3-3, for example, I make sure that the vertical heights of the two images are identical. You can make them pixel-identical by matching the image size in Adobe Photoshop. You don't need to give all your images identical dimensions on all sides, however, because doing so requires too much cropping or distortion of the images. If, however, the vertical sizes (or the horizontal sizes, depending on placement) are the same, this similarity helps reinforce the clarity of your message.

A more complex page than that shown in Figure 3-3 can also be clear. Clarity in design relates more to the viewer's ability to understand what's on a page than to how much information is on that page. The clearer a page is, the more quickly a viewer knows how to access more information or use the information on the page. Well-organized images and text can be clear — even if they're relatively small and abundant in number. You can find good examples of clear but fairly complex pages at the Web sites of most online retailers. Dell computer, at www.dell.com, for example, uses a clear home page containing a great deal of information. The main categories have graphic and textual links to the offerings. Along the top of the page on the right side and across the bottom are links that make getting lost difficult. Each main category is clear so that the viewer has a clear idea of what sort of items the category describes. Excellent organization keeps the entire page clear and functional, however, despite all the information you find on it.

Where am I now? Am I on the same planet?

Ever since the great Ralph Waldo Emerson penned the lines "A foolish consistency is the hobgoblin of little minds, adored by little statesmen and philosophers and divines," many have believed that something is inherently wrong with consistency. Well, plenty's wrong with *foolish* consistency because it's blind to change and misuse — a common problem of many Web pages. An *intuitive* consistency, however, is an elegant thing and a delight to the viewer. Good Web page design incorporates intuitive consistency in laying out a common theme that pulls together all the pages in a Web site. At all times, the Web surfer is in a familiar place, knows where she is, where she has been, and what to do next. As the viewer explores the site, she's never lost because a consistent look and feel tells her that she's still in the same site, and a consistent navigation system enables her to easily know where she wants to go next on the site.

Your navigation system needs a common and familiar look and feel. The viewer also needs to know at all times where she is and where she can go. One navigation scheme is to set up a central or core page that shows where everything is, along with a set of icons as a common set of tools to point the viewer in the right direction. Figure 3-4, for example, shows a *core page* with links to the main subcategories. The user immediately sees where she can go from this perspective. Figure 3-5 shows another page from the same site — notice that the same navigation system lets the viewer know that she's in the same site and can use the same navigation bar along the top to get where she wants to go. By using a common navigation system throughout your site, you provide a consistent guide to the viewer and thus ensure that a viewer can navigate through your site with confidence. Don't forget that the more at home a viewer feels in your site, the more likely she is to return to check out your Web site again.

Intuitively clear

Steve Krug summed up good navigation in the title of his book *Don't Make Me Think* (Que, 2000). The book's subtitle, *A Common Sense Approach to Web Usability* (Sybex, 1998) further stated what the viewer wants — an intuitively clear navigation system. Some designers have different navigation systems for different pages or, for the more creative sorts, a navigation system so abstract that the viewer has to play "link tag" to both find the links and determine where they lead. Vincent Flanders, the co-author of *Web Pages That Suck,* calls the overly abstract navigation systems "mystery meat navigation." (See his Web site, www.webpagesthatsuck.com, for a collection of Web design disasters — even by some very good artists and designers. Figures 3-4 and 3-5 show a simple, clear, and consistent navigation system from the main page to one of the subpages in a site.

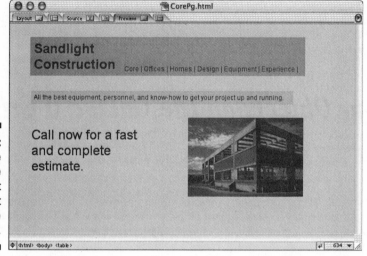

Figure 3-4:
A core page
shows the
viewer what
to expect
at the
Web site.

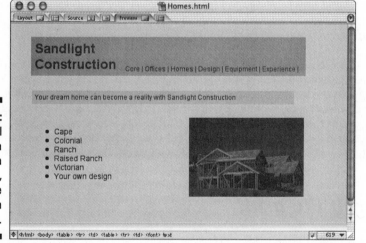

Figure 3-5:
Internal
pages in a
site offer a
common,
intuitive
navigation
system.

The best test of success for a good navigation system is whether the user can intuitively *sense* what to do next to get anywhere on your site. Getting someone else to try out your navigation system before you post it to your Web site is always a good idea. Don't tell your tester what to do; just ask him to look at your site and tell you what he thinks. Watch to see whether he navigates the site the way you expect. A *consistent* navigation system means that a visitor needs to figure out the system only once. An *inconsistent* system requires a visitor to figure out each different navigation system you set up on a site.

Recruit someone to test-drive your Web site *before* you post it. If you do, you can ask questions and make adjustments while you still have time. If you wait until your site is up on the server, strangers using your site don't ask you how to navigate. They just give up and go somewhere else.

Put Your Objects on the GoLive 6 Grid

In Chapter 1 (where I describe the Objects toolbar), I make a reference to the GoLive 6 *grid* and do so again in Chapter 2, while discussing Preview view. This section shows you how to use this great tool in setting up your pages.

Having all the best design principles down pat doesn't help much if you don't have a way to cleanly and efficiently carry out what you want to do. Transforming a great idea into something that actually runs on a Web browser isn't always easy. One of the major challenges for anyone putting a Web page together, for example, involves making the text and graphics behave on the page itself. Getting the different parts of the page to go right where she wants in HTML is often a nightmare for the designer. Fortunately, an easy way to lay out your page is available: Simply use a piece of graph paper and clippings of graphics and text and links. (Links? You know — *hyperlinks.*)

I highly recommend such a low-tech beginning to the Web-layout process: Get hold of a nice piece of graph paper (or regular paper, if you haven't kept graph paper in the house since high school) and sketch out a rough plan showing exactly where you want to place the text, graphics, and links on your Web page. After you get a pretty good idea of where you want things to lie on the page, you can go ahead and transplant your design from low-tech paper to high-tech electronic format. The following section shows you how to do so.

Grab the grid!

The *grid* feature of GoLive 6 puts a nice set of horizontal and vertical lines on your computer screen, enabling you to easily line up the elements of your Web page just right. As you place an object, such as a graphic, on the grid, it snaps into place right where you place it. Accessing the grid in Layout view is as simple as using the grid to create your Web page. Just follow these steps:

1. **Open GoLive 6 (if it's not already open), and open a new site and new page by double-clicking the Index page in the Site window.**

   A new, blank page appears in Layout view. (Chapter 2 provides more details on how to open a site and a page if you need to review the page- and site-opening process.)

2. From Layout view, choose Window⇨Objects from the main menu bar.

The Objects palette appears, displaying its 12 handy tabs. The default view shows the contents of the first tab, known as the *Basic tab*.

If you aren't doing so already, keep the Objects palette and the Inspector open and nearby. If you have a number of palettes open at the same time, the screen can get pretty crowded, but keeping these key windows open is easier than running back to the Window menus every time you need one of them.

3. Click the Layout Grid icon (the first icon on the left in the first row of the Basic tab of the palette) to select it, and then drag it onto your blank page.

A square grid pattern appears in the upper-left corner of the page.

4. Use your mouse to pull one of the corners or sides of the grid to resize the grid until it covers the entire page.

The grid expands to cover your entire page. The grid pattern changes to show the number of horizontal and vertical lines you specify.

5. Open the Inspector by choosing Window⇨Inspector or undock it by clicking the Inspector tab at the side of the screen.

The Inspector shows the dimensions of the grid. For a 14-inch monitor setting, the grid is about 580-by-330 — that's 580 pixels wide and 330 pixels high. You can change the size by changing the values directly in the Width and Height text boxes of the Inspector.

Figure 3-6 shows an example of what the Inspector looks like after dragging the grid to fill the screen. Notice that other options in the Inspector enable you to specify the size of the grid boxes or add a background color. Such fancy features aren't necessarily important for someone just wanting a few simple lines as an aid to keeping Web page elements nicely in line on the page.

Figure 3-6:
The Inspector helps you set up a grid in Layout view on your Web page.

After you set up the grid, you can drag and drop text and graphics right on the page where you want them to go — and they snap right into place. The following sections show exactly how to accomplish these tasks.

Getting your words down pat

Entering text into a Web page by using the grid involves more than just inserting your cursor somewhere on the page and then typing away. You first must set up a special area (known as a *layout text box* in GoLive 6) on your Web page and then type text into it. The layout text box is a great help for Web-page designers because it enables you to determine exactly where to place text on the page. To add a layout text box to your page, follow these steps:

1. **Choose Window⇨Objects to open the Objects palette (if it's not open and selected already).**

   The (by now familiar) Objects palette appears, displaying the contents of the Basic tab.

2. **Click to select the Layout Text Box icon (the second icon from the left on the first row of the Objects palette's Basic tab) and drag and drop it onto the grid where you want it to go on your Web page.**

   A layout text box now appears on your Web page. Notice too that the toolbar changes to the Objects toolbar.

3. **After adding a layout text box to the Layout page on the grid, type any text you want into the layout text box and then resize the text box and its text by dragging the corners and sides, as shown in Figure 3-7.**

   A made-to-order text box, complete with scintillating prose, now graces your Web page. Resizing the layout text box simply tidies up the page and gives you more room to add new objects. If you want to add new text to the box later, the layout text box automatically grows to accommodate the new text.

4. **Select the text in the layout text box as you would any other text on the page and apply the desired format.**

   There is no special formatting technique for text in a layout text box. Use the text-formatting techniques shown in Chapter 2.

GoLive 6 treats layout text boxes as objects and not as text. If you have several layout text boxes on the same page, select two or more of them and use the Objects toolbar to help arrange them. If you select the text within a layout text box, however, notice that both the Inspector and the toolbar change to text mode. In text mode, you can use all the text-formatting tools in GoLive 6. (No, you're not schizophrenic — but GoLive 6 may be.)

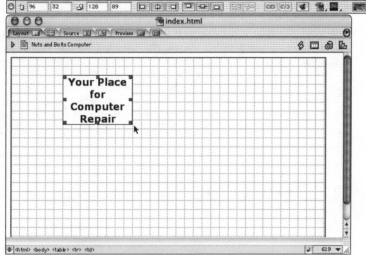

Figure 3-7:
Layout text
boxes hold
text you
place in a
grid on your
Web page.

Placing your image anywhere

Adding a graphic to your page is just as easy as adding a layout text box. If you place a graphic on your page without using a grid, the graphic automatically gravitates to the upper-left area of your page. If you're using a grid, however, you just drag and drop the graphic exactly where you want it to go. Before you start, make sure that the Site window is open and your graphic file is in the site root folder. (Remember that if you see the file in the Site window, the file is in the root folder.) Follow these steps:

1. **Choose Window⇨Objects to open the Objects palette (if it's not open and selected already).**

   The Objects palette appears, displaying the contents of the Basic tab.

2. **Open the Inspector by choosing Window⇨Inspector.**

   Sometimes, I forget that the Inspector lies in the same window as the View palette. Remember that if the View palette is on-screen, all you need to do to change it to the Inspector is to click the Inspector tab. Just think of them as roommates.

3. **Click to select the Image icon (the fifth icon from the left in the first row on the Objects palette's Basic tab) and drag and drop it on the grid where you want it to go on your Web page.**

   An Image icon now appears on your Web page right where you put it. The Inspector (now in its Image Inspector guise) shows the Point-and-Shoot button and is providing image information.

4. **Pull the point-and shoot-line from the Image Inspector to the Select Window button on the toolbar to bring up the Site window. After you bring up the Site window, pull the point-and shoot-line from the Image Inspector to your graphic image file located on the Files tab of the Site window.**

The graphic image now replaces the Image icon and stays put where you had it on the grid. (Alternatively, you can drag the graphic directly from the Files tab of the Site window onto the grid.) Figure 3-8 shows how a point-and-shoot line selects the graphic, with the grid in Layout view in the background.

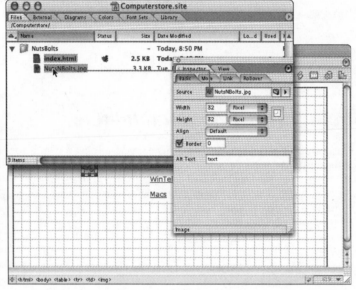

Figure 3-8:
Just point-and-shoot objects onto your page and place them where you want on the grid.

Placing links in the design

Links are just as much a part of a basic Web page design as text and graphics are — mainly because links are just text and graphics with a twist: You can make them act as springboards to enable people to jump to other pages, either on your own site or elsewhere on the World Wide Web. Placing a word, phrase, or image you want to act as a link, therefore, is no different from placing a standard word or phrase of text or a graphic image. The twist comes if you want to make a particular word, phrase, or image "hot" so that it can act as a hyperlink to another page.

To place phrases or words, just choose Window➪Objects to open the Objects palette and then click the Basic tab (if it's not already selected). Select the Layout Text Box icon (the second icon from the left on the first row of the

Objects palette's Basic tab), drag the icon onto your page where you want it to go, and then type into the text box the word or phrase you want to use as a link. (See the section "Getting your words down pat," earlier in this chapter, for details on how to place text.) To place images, grab from the Site window the icon for the graphics file you want on your page and drag it onto the page. (The preceding section, "Placing your image anywhere," shows how to do just that.)

Now you need to transform your run-of-the-mill word, phrase, or image into a link. To do so, follow these steps:

1. **For words or phrases, go to the layout text box on your Web page and select the word or phrase you want to change into a link; if you want an image to act as a link, select the image.**

   The word, phrase, or image you select doesn't matter. You can turn almost anything into a link.

2. **Open the Inspector by choosing Window⇨Inspector.**

3. **Click the Link button (the one showing the two links of a chain joined together) on the Inspector or the toolbar.**

   On the Link tab of the Inspector you see a window with an (Empty Reference!) message in the URL text box, a Point-and-Shoot button, and a Browse button (showing a folder icon). (*Note:* You see the same link information in the Inspector whether you select text or an image.)

4. **Type in the URL text box of the Inspector the name of the file you want to serve as the target of the link.**

   Figure 3-9 shows how this setup looks on the grid and on the Link tab in the Inspector. Leave the Target text box blank for now. In Chapter 9, where I discuss frames, you find out how to use targets.

5. **In the Title text box, type a short, descriptive name for the link's target.**

   As a viewer passes the mouse pointer over the link word or image, a little message appears on-screen in your browser and displays that title. You can leave this text box blank if you want, but adding a title gives the user more information and looks sort of cool. (How'd that designer *do* that?)

   Although typing the name of the file is sometimes just as quick as using the point-and-shoot method, the Point-and-Shoot tool doesn't make typos that end up linking your page to a nonexistent URL or file. Dragging the mouse from the Point-and-Shoot button to the file on the Files tab of the Site window is all you need to do. (Refer to the section "Placing your image anywhere," earlier in this chapter. Point-and-shoot works the same if you're placing an image as it does if you're selecting a link to a page.)

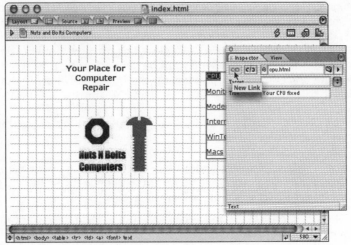

Figure 3-9:
Create a link
from text
in a layout
text box by
using the
Inspector's
Link tab.

Forgetting to click the Link button on the Inspector or the toolbar whenever you want to make a link is all too easy. One way to remind yourself to do so is to look at the URL text box in the Inspector. If you *don't* see (Empty Reference!) in the Inspector's URL text box, it means that you *didn't* click the Link icon. This feature works the same whether you're linking text or images, so you just need to remember the same thing for two different operations. (Well, it helps a little.)

Adding the finishing touches

To finish the text chores in your Web page, you can color the text. You select the text in the layout text boxes and color text by first clicking the Text Color well on the toolbar and then selecting the color you want from the Color palette, as I describe in Chapter 2. To color the text links, just select the Page icon in the upper-left corner of Layout view and then fill in the Color wells in the Inspector, as I also describe in Chapter 2 (in the section about hooking up to your site pages). In attempting to color text, make sure that you're selecting the *text* and *not* the boxes.

Just in case you have any interest in looking at the source code for a page you create by using the grid (either by choosing Window⇔Source Code to open the Source Code palette *or* selecting Source view in the document window *or* clicking Split view in Layout view), prepare yourself for a surprise. GoLive 6 uses HTML tables and table cells to create a page that puts everything where the designer (that's you) wants it. (For more information about tables, see Chapter 5.) You see lots of <TR> and <TD> tags, but don't let them bother you. Those tags are just keeping things where they belong on your page. The tables

I show you how to create in Chapter 5 are for the same purpose, but function in a much simpler way. GoLive 6 can put tables on a regular layout or on a grid. It does all the work so that you can design your Web pages with fewer limitations, more creativity, and less pain.

Line 'Em Up and Move 'Em Out

Alignment and balance are two elements that are crucial to a good-looking Web page. If you use the grid, aligning the page components becomes quite easy. To show you how to align objects on the grid, I designed a page that incorporates nothing but graphics. (Skip ahead to Figure 3-13 if you want to see the finished version of this page.) Even the text with the fancy shadowed backgrounds, I created by using graphic images. The real problem to solve isn't the placement of elements on the page — that's relatively easy. The hard part (and it's not really all that hard) involves getting everything to line up just right.

Selecting and aligning graphics

The first step for any Web designer is to situate everything on your page in the general arrangement you want. Grab stuff from your site window, as I explain in Chapter 2, enter text by using text boxes, and format that text to your heart's content by using the Text toolbar. Figure 3-10 shows what I initially came up with for my page, before I had a chance to fix the alignment.

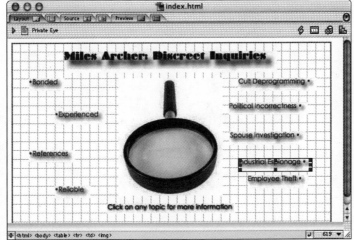

Figure 3-10:
Scattered
objects
need
alignment
on your
Web page.

To get that neat shadowed effect, by the way, you need to use a tool such as Photoshop, ImageStyler, Fireworks, CorelDRAW, Illustrator, FreeHand, or some other graphics program that offers an option for creating a shadow on JPEG, GIF, or PNG files. Creating the effect isn't hard if you have the right tool. Remember, too, that by putting graphics on your page, both the size of the file and the load time for the page in a Web browser are greater than if you were just using regular text. (If you're very resourceful, you can create drop shadows by using Cascading Style Sheets, or CSS, as I discuss in Chapter 10, without needing to use graphics at all.)

The first thing you should do is line up the three central components (heading, magnifying-glass image, and informational banner at the bottom) down the center of the page. To align such elements, follow these steps:

1. **Shift+click the graphics you want to select.**

   On my Web page, I Shift+click the magnifying-glass image, the heading, and the informational banner. By holding the Shift key as you select objects, each object remains selected even as you click another object. After you select it, a frame with little blocks at each corner and on each side appears around the image. (Figure 3-11 shows these three objects selected.)

2. **Choose Window➪Align from the menu bar.**

   The Align palette appears on your page (see Figure 3-11). The Align palette's two roommates are Transform and Tracing Image. If either one of those palettes is on the page, click the Align tab to bring up the Align palette.

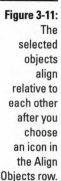

Figure 3-11:
The selected objects align relative to each other after you choose an icon in the Align Objects row.

3. **Click the second icon from the left in the Align Objects row of the Align palette.**

   You see the three figures align themselves relative to each other's center. If you want to align the three objects to the center of the page, you select instead the second icon from the left in the Align to Parent row of the Align palette. You can also align the objects to a common horizontal center, to the left or right, or to a top and bottom point relative to each other by selecting one of the other icons. The vertical or horizontal line on the various Align icons indicates the orientation and placement of the alignment.

Automating your distribution

Lining up the big guns down the center of your page is one thing, but how do you distribute any smaller elements evenly along the right and left sides of your page? Follow these steps:

1. **Shift+click each object on the left side to align and distribute all the objects.**

   You can tell that each is selected if a rectangle with little blue boxes on the lines surrounds each selected object.

2. **Click the first icon in the Align Objects row of the Align palette.**

   The selected graphic text objects left-align. (Don't deselect the objects just yet.)

3. **With the same objects still selected, click the rightmost icon in the Distribute Objects row of the Align palette.**

   The Distribute Objects icons evenly distribute selected objects horizontally (the first three buttons in the Distribute Objects row) or vertically (the second three buttons.) If you have several objects in a column or row, make sure that you select all the objects to ensure even distribution. Otherwise, GoLive 6 distributes only the selected objects and leaves the others alone.

4. **Follow steps 1–3 for the objects on the right side to align and distribute all these objects, except in Step 2, click the *third* icon in the Align Objects row of the Align palette.**

   Figure 3-12 shows both the left and right sets of graphic text images aligned and evenly distributed.

Figure 3-12:
The rightmost icon in the Distribute Objects row on the Align palette distributes selected objects vertically so that even spaces appear between each object.

If you want objects on your pages distributed evenly on a diagonal, you must place them initially on the page in rough diagonal order. Then you select all the objects on the diagonal and use the Distribute Spacing row on the Align palette to space them evenly horizontally and vertically by using both icons in the row. (You usually must click both icons until the diagonal straightens out and the objects are evenly distributed.)

The page is now ready, but to really see what you created, you first should view it in Preview view to examine the results. Just open the page you want to preview and click the Preview tab in the document window (see Figure 3-13). As you can see in the preview of the page I just created, the grid is invisible (probably the result of magic), and if you view the page itself in a browser, it looks clean, clear, and professional. Many more options for placing text or images by using the grid are available to you, by the way, than simply placing them all on the left side, all in the center, or all on the right side. But what you now see on this Web page is the design you want with all the parts sitting in the right places. Compare Figures 3-10 and 3-13 to see the difference that good alignment and distribution make.

Figure 3-13:
The Web
page is
centered,
aligned, and
balanced,
thanks to
effective
use of the
Align
palette.

Resize Up the Situation

In the process of getting everything lined up and squared away, you may
resize an image. "Resize" occurs when you adjust the size of an image after
you have loaded it by changing the image's height and width in the Image
Inspector or by dragging a corner or side of an image to make it larger or
smaller. The image may not look bad if the proportions are maintained, but if
the image looks like an elephant stepped on it, you can easily restore it to its
original dimensions. This task probably calls for realignment of the objects,
but with *GoLive,* that's easy using the grid. Here's how to fix an image that
has been resized:

1. **Begin in Layout view of the document window.**

2. **Undock the Inspector or choose Window⇨Inspector from the menu
   bar to open the Inspector.**

3. **Click to select the resized image.**

   Resized images are identified by a Resize Warning icon in the lower-right
   quadrant of the image. The Inspector becomes the Image Inspector. Also,
   the Inspector's Resize button becomes active when an image is resized.

4. **Click to select the Basic tab of the Image Inspector.**

5. **Click the Resize Restore button in the Image Inspector.**

   The Resize Restore button (see Figure 3-14) resides in the right portion of the Image Inspector window and resembles the Resize Warning icon. As soon as you click the button, the image is restored to its original size.

Resize icon   Resize Restore button

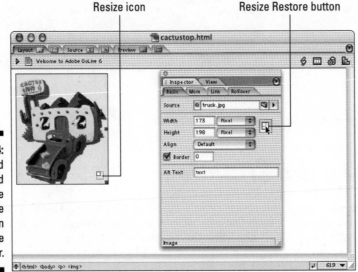

Figure 3-14:
A resized
image and
the Resize
Restore
button in
the Image
Inspector.

You should always make your images the size you want them in your graphic-editing program — not in Layout view of GoLive. If you have a big image and you resize it to a small one, the big image is still loaded into memory. You just waste bandwidth that way. If you load a small image and resize it, often it looks bad, and it may be distorted. (Adobe Photoshop does a good job of changing the image size.)

Use Adobe ImageReady or Macromedia Fireworks to optimize the size of your graphic images for the Web. They do it automatically, saving time and guesswork. Also, smart objects allow you to resize the object, and GoLive goes back to the original PSD, TIFF, or EPS file to remake the JPG file.

Tracing

What if you could get a preview of all the images on your page before you put them on the page? And what if you could crop your images to just the right size *without* resizing them? With GoLive 6, you can do that and more using the Tracing Image palette (with a little help from the Transform palette).

The process works by importing an image file (including both Web and non-Web images). You can import Photoshop 8-bit RGB images as well as JPG, GIF, PNG, BMP, TARGA, PCX, PICT, PIXAR, and Amiga IFF. After you import the images for tracing, the entire image or parts of it can then be cropped and saved as Web-safe files to then be placed on your Web page. Here's how you do it:

1. **Begin in Layout view of the document window.**

2. **Select the Inspector by choosing Window⇨Inspector from the menu bar.**

   A generic Inspector appears on the screen.

3. **Choose Window⇨Tracing Image from the menu bar.**

   The Tracing Image palette appears with its roommates, Align and Transform. You may need to use Transform with the Tracing Image palette.

4. **Click the Source check box of the Tracing Image palette and select the file you want to import by clicking the Browse button (the one with the image of a folder) and selecting your file from the list in the directory window that opens.**

   If you drag the file to the page from the Files tab of the Site window, the page treats the file as a regular file and you can't trace it; so you have to use the Browse or point-and-shoot method of transfer. You see a dimmed image on the page if the link is successful.

5. **Drag the Opacity slide tool to the left (less) or right (more) to adjust the opacity of the image on the page.**

   I find that setting the opacity around the middle works fine. If an image is too opaque, you cannot distinguish it from any other images you have on the page. If an image doesn't have enough opacity, you can't see it at all.

6. **Click the Move Image Tool button (the little hand icon).**

   Now you can drag the image around the page to position it where you want it to go. Find a good place for the image and release the mouse button.

7. **Click the Cut Out tool located between the Move Image tool and the Cut Out button.**

   A crosshair-icon mouse pointer appears. Drag around the image until you see a cropping window with pull tabs.

8. **Adjust the cropping window with the mouse by dragging the pull tabs until you have selected the part of the image you want on your page, or until the cropping window surrounds the entire image, and click the Cut Out button.**

   The Save For Web dialog box opens, as shown in Figure 3-15. Even if you are using a Web-safe image, you are given four tabs, each with a different rendering of the image you just cropped. You may adjust the settings in the dialog box or just click the image you like the best if you select a tab with multiple images. (If you don't see four images, click on the 4-Up tab.)

9. **Click the OK button after making your selections.**

   You are first shown a directory Save window and a name with an extension (PNG, GIF, or JPG); select the directory you want and rename the file if you want to change the default one generated by GoLive.

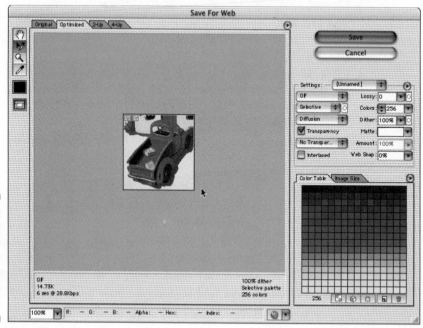

Figure 3-15:
A cropped image appears in the Save for Web dialog box.

10. **Click the Save button after your directory and name selections are made.**

    The image you just cropped and saved appears on your page in a floating box, as shown in Figure 3-16. (Chapter 16 fully explains floating boxes.) If you pass the mouse pointer over the sides of the floating box, the hand pointer changes from a vertically pointing hand to a horizontal one. When the hand is in the horizontal position, you can move the box. Move the box with the image in it until it resides where you want it.

When you find that you need to use more than one palette or Site window view at the same time, GoLive 6 provides a handy function. If you drag the tab of the palette or view away from the window it is in, it separates the tab from the window. You don't have to go back and forth clicking tabs because both are open simultaneously. When you want to put the tabs back, just drag a tab back into the home window. (If you really want to have some fun, drag a tab from one window and back into another.)

This process gets everything ready for your page. As each image is cropped and saved, you accumulate the images you need. The preview positioning is accomplished by dragging the cropped images in the floating boxes anywhere you want on the page. After you have everything where you want it, you remove all the items from the page, place a grid to cover the page, and then bring in all the images you have saved and position them using floating boxes where you had them before. Figure 3-16 shows a traced image and the cropped image (the pickup truck) in the floating box. Only the cropped image is saved to a Web-usable format.

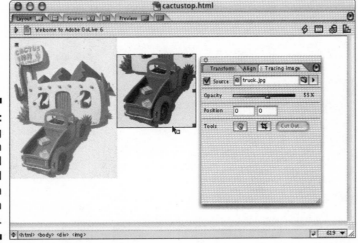

Figure 3-16:
Tracing images can be cropped and placed to assist in the design of a page.

Design with Templates

Another neat feature for designing Web pages with GoLive 6 involves using the template. For inexperienced designers, a template offers a professionally designed Web site *as a starting point.* Basically, a template in GoLive 6 is a designed page with all its components. Images and text that serve only design purposes are *placeholders* for actual images and text you provide. Essentially, templates are designs without content. You provide the content and don't have to worry about the design. Here's how to get one up and running:

1. **Launch GoLive 6 by double-clicking the GoLive 6 icon and select New Site.**

   The GoLive Site Wizard opens.

2. **In the GoLive Site Wizard, select Single User and click Next.**

   The Copy a Site Template page comes up.

3. **Select one of the templates that appears on the right side of the window.**

   You see a thumbnail image and an outline of the site structure. Figure 3-17 shows a selected site template.

4. **Select the design you want, type the name you want for your new site in the Name New Site text window, and click the OK button.**

   Note: When you first select your design, the default name for that design appears in the New Site Name text box. Be sure to type over the default name in the New Site Name text box with the site name you want to use. Otherwise, you get the generic template name that may be hard to find if you have seven other sites with the same name.

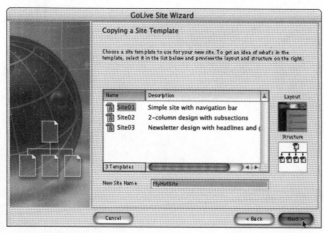

Figure 3-17:
Select a
template
from the
dialog box.

Web page design can be one of the most satisfying endeavors you can undertake. The more you study good design technique, the better your designs, and although templates are the last GoLive 6 feature covered in this chapter, it may well be one of the first you want to try out. With the Web, remember that the whole world can see your work, and that means that you can look good to a pretty big audience.

Chapter 4

Navigating the Reefs of the Web

. . . .

In This Chapter

▶ Using the Site window to organize files

▶ Creating anchors and setting up links to them

▶ Organizing the site by using the Navigation and Link windows

▶ Making links out of images

▶ Creating image maps and using them to make links

▶ Using the In & Out Links palette

. . . .

*T*hink globally and act locally. That piece of political populism applies to your Web site. You need to think of your Web site as something that people all across the World Wide Web are viewing and using, from What Cheer, Iowa, to Katmandu, Nepal. That's what thinking globally means. But to get your Web site working correctly, you need to think *locally,* and in GoLive 6, that means that you must gather your pages together in your *site folder* — otherwise known as your *site window.* The site folder is the *root folder* for your entire site, and all links are relative to the root folder. If you square away your root folder, you find that, as you place your pages on the Web, all the pages perform just as you expect.

Getting Your Site Together

I dedicate this chapter to dealing with the link issues for a Web site and the tools available in GoLive 6 that help you create links. GoLive 6 provides a really great way of organizing all your pages and page elements in its site windows. It helps you organize everything on your Web site, and it makes doing so easy.

You find the basics of linking text to internal and external pages in Chapter 2. This chapter shows you how to put the pieces of a Web-site-to-be in the Site window by using the Navigation and Link windows. In addition, you see how to place page navigation links, called *anchors,* on a Web page.

Adding text links

Figure 4-1 shows the starting page of a Web site that's under construction. You can see the handy grid lines that all smart Web designers use to line up elements on a page cleanly and efficiently. (For more information on using grids, see Chapter 3.) You also see some graphics on the page and a few blocks of text. Hovering over the starting page is an open Site window containing a number of graphics files ready for you to link to this starting page.

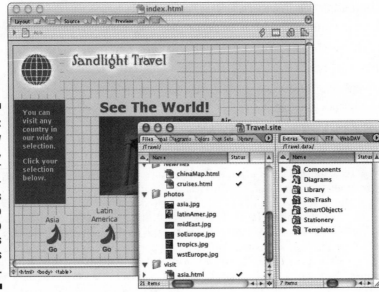

Figure 4-1: This new Web site, still under construction, needs links to other files to increase its usefulness to visitors.

To get things going, the text block on one Web page is used to link to another Web page. The following steps show how to establish that link:

1. **Access your site by choosing File⇨Open from the main menu bar or by pressing Ctrl+O (in Windows) or ⌘+O (on the Mac). Select the site you want from the list in the Open dialog box that appears and click the Open button.**

   The Site window for the site you choose appears. The name of the site appears at the top of the site window. In my example, my site's name is Travel.site. In GoLive 6, all sites use the extension SITE. The extension helps to distinguish them from Web pages in the site with similar names.

2. **Find the filename of the page you want to open on the Name list of the Site window's Files view and double-click that file's icon.**

   Your starting page now appears in Layout view. (The name of my starting page is `index.html` — the default home page name.)

3. **Open the Inspector by choosing Window⇨Inspector from the menu bar.**

   The Inspector appears on top of the document window.

4. **Select on the page the word that you want to act as the hot spot for the link and click the Link button (the one displaying two intertwining links of a chain) on the Inspector.**

   I'm selecting the word Air from the list to the right of the photo. (I use the term *hot spot* to refer to any text or graphic that acts as a link or initiates an action.) After you click the Link button, the button becomes pale, indicating that your hot spot is ready to accept a link. The Inspector now shows (Empty Reference!) in the URL text box for you to replace with the name of your link file or a URL.

5. **If you know the name of the file to which you want to link, type the filename into the URL text box of the Inspector and press Enter in Windows or Return on the Mac.**

   This action establishes the link — and you're done! If you don't know the name of the file to which you want to link, please continue on with Step 6. Figure 4-2 shows the selected hot spot highlighted and the Inspector standing by for a URL to be selected using the Browse icon button.

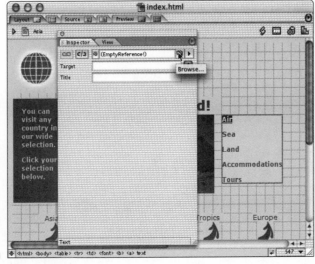

Figure 4-2: The Inspector provides several ways to help find the files for your links.

6. **If you're not sure of the name of the file to which you want to link, click the Browse button at the right side of the Text Inspector.**

   An Open dialog box appears, as shown in Figure 4-3. By using this dialog box, you can navigate through your directories to find the file you want. The name of the Air travel page file in the folder is airAccom.html in my example. Figure 4-3 shows a page's icon and the page you want selected.

7. Navigate to the file to which you want to link, select its name from the list, and then click Open to establish the link.

The dialog box disappears after establishing the link. Now, whenever you click the hot spot Air on your first Web page, you instantly jump to a page displaying the contents of your linked file in a browser or in Preview mode.

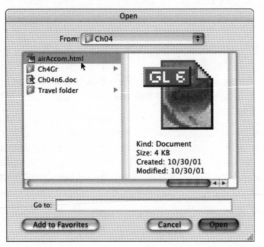

Figure 4-3: The Open dialog box enables you to navigate to the file to which you want to create a link.

Establishing a link is simple enough in GoLive 6, but the real power of the program lies in its capability to gather in all the internal links. You need to round up and corral all the stray Web pages in the Site window. (Ride 'em, cowboy!)

Corralling all your links

You should keep any and all internal links for your Web site in your Site folder. Web sites are dynamic, so you need to update and change your links as time passes. With all your files in the same Site folder and visible in the Site window, keeping track of even complex Web sites becomes as easy as pie. If you can't see an internal link in your Site window, you should move it there. Keep in mind that the files you see in your Site window represent the root folder of your site. Just follow these steps to round up the strays:

1. Establish a link, as I outline in the steps in the preceding section, and then click the Select Window button on the toolbar (the third button from the right).

The Site window appears in all its glory.

2. **Click anywhere in the Site window to select it and then choose File⇨Import⇨Files to Site from the menu bar.**

   The Add to Site dialog box appears, as shown in Figure 4-4.

3. **Use the top pane of the dialog box to navigate through your directories to the file you want by clicking the scroll arrows to scroll up or down the list or by selecting and opening folders or directories by using the pull-down list.**

   You see file and folder icons.

4. **Select the desired file or folder and click the Add or Add Folder (or Add All, if you want everything in the window) button to include the file in the Select Items to Add pane at the bottom of the Add dialog box. Repeat this process for every file and folder you want to include in the Add pane.**

   After you add a file or folder to the bottom pane, it disappears from the top pane. Don't worry. GoLive 6 isn't deleting your file or folder from the directory or drive. Removing items from the top pane is just the GoLive 6 way of helping you keep track of what you want to copy into the Site folder. (If you grab the wrong ones, you click the Remove button to send them back to the top window.)

5. **After all the files and folders you want appear in the Select Items to Add pane, click the Done button next to the bottom pane.**

   GoLive 6 copies the selected files to your Site window.

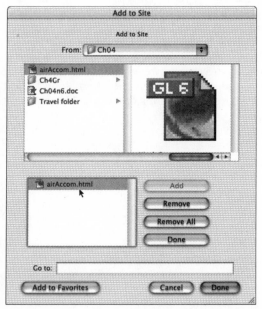

Figure 4-4:
Use the Add to Site dialog box to add files to your Site window. GoLive 6 sends to the bottom pane any files you want to add to your site.

After you copy any file from its original folder to your Site folder, GoLive asks whether you want to update your file. Yes! Of course, you want to update your file! After all the work you go through to get it into your Site window, you're darn tootin' you want to update it. (GoLive 6 doesn't assume that your brain is addled, by the way; it's just reminding you that after you change a file's location, the link information also changes.)

GoLive 6 is a Web-*site* development tool. The more you think in terms of creating a site and not just a single page, the more sense all these instructions will make. GoLive 6 is a powerful Web-page tool as well, but good Web pages that appear disorganized aren't a pretty sight (or site!). Just imagine writing a book and working on a single page without any thought to the page's relationship to all the others in the book. What a mess you can end up with if you don't know where you're storing the link's target! By helping you to think about the site as a whole rather than just about individual pages, GoLive 6 helps you avoid that kind of mess.

Anchor Your Page, Matey

To understand anchors, you need to know what they do. Some Web pages scroll beyond the limitations of your screen, so you need links to jump to anywhere on the page that lies beyond the screen's limits. *Anchors* are targets on a page that can serve as links to various page locations.

As a general rule, you don't want your pages to scroll beyond two vertical screens, but sometimes you need more than two screens of information on a single page. This situation becomes the case especially if your page is a long index, menu, or text list. The following text layout, for example, shows a long list that scrolls directly off-screen as soon as you put it on a Web page. You can get a hint of how anchors work, however, because the page consists of a main page, with a list of countries vertically arranged along the left side. In the lower part of the page, several options (cities) within the countries are listed for the Asia page:

Japan

China

Vietnam

Korea

Taiwan

....

Below that, out of the viewer's sight, are the countries listed with a number of cities the tourist may want to visit:

Japan

>Tokyo
>
>Yokohama
>
>Kyoto
>
>Sendai
>
>Osaka
>
>Kobe

China

>Beijing
>
>Guanzhou
>
>Shanghai
>
>Lanzhou
>
>Chendu

Vietnam

>Can Tho
>
>Nha Trang
>
>Qui Nhon
>
>Long Xuyen

Korea

>Seoul
>
>Pusan
>
>Mokpo
>
>P'ohang

>....

Anchors provide some much-needed help for this page. Whenever you place text in Layout view (the default view for any new Web page), the page is just about ready for adding anchors. One thing, however, is still missing: a way to get back to the top of the page after jumping to a lower level. That situation is easy to remedy by inserting an anchor link word (Top) that returns you to the top of the page after you click the word.

When you have a long page with anchor links way, way, way down the page, getting your link all the way back up to the top can be awkward. All you have to do is to drag the top anchor icon down the page with you, make all the links you want, and when you're finished just drag the Top anchor icon back to the top. In that way, you don't have to waste your time trying to scroll to a point-and-shoot position. When you follow the steps in the following section, remember this tip.

Placing anchors and anchor link words

To place anchors and anchor link words on your page, follow these steps:

1. **With your page open, access the Objects palette by choosing Window⇨Objects from the menu bar.**

   The ever-helpful Objects palette appears on-screen, displaying the contents of its Basic tab.

2. **Drag the Anchor icon (the third icon from the end on the Basic tab — the one that looks like an anchor, of course) to the location on the page where you want the page to jump, as shown in Figure 4-5.**

   The Anchor icons appear on the page wherever you place them. In my example, I want to jump from the top of the section for each succeeding Asian country, so I place an anchor next to each country. The heading of each section serves as a good positioning point for the anchors. The word Top is placed at the bottom of each country group and becomes a hot spot when it is linked to an anchor at the top of the page. (All the Top links are connected to a single anchor at the top of the page.)

3. **Repeat the process that Step 2 describes for any other anchors you want to place.**

4. **Close the Objects palette after you finish placing your anchors.**

   Nothing more is required of the Objects palette for now, and it's a good idea to move it aside to make more room for other palettes you may need.

Sometimes, an anchor doesn't take you to the place on the page that you expect. Depending on where the Anchor icon and its information appear on the page, relative to the size of your screen, the screen either shows you what you want after you arrive at the target location of the anchor . . . or it doesn't. You may need to experiment with placing anchors to get them set so that the page goes exactly where you want it, especially in different browsers your visitors may use. (Remember to view the page in different configurations in Preview view so that you can see what the other guy will see!)

Figure 4-5:
Use the Anchor icon on the Basic tab of the Objects palette to place anchor links on your page.

Naming anchors

After you place an anchor, you still must name it so that GoLive 6 can keep track of it for you. Fortunately, naming anchors is as easy as 1-2-3-4. Just follow these steps:

1. **With your page open, choose Window⇨Inspector from the menu bar.**

   The Inspector appears.

2. **Select an anchor on the page in Layout view by clicking it.**

   After you select an anchor, the Inspector displays a text box for you to use in naming the anchor.

3. **In the Name text box of the Inspector, type a name for the anchor you select.**

   Use a name that is descriptive and that relates to the anchor on the page, as shown in Figure 4-6. For the different countries, use the country name. The anchor at the top got the name Top. Now all those Top labels at the bottom of each level have an easy name to link to.

4. Repeat Steps 2 and 3 for each anchor on the page, but make sure that you give each anchor a unique name.

You can use the same name for anchors on *different pages,* but for any single page, make sure that you give each of your anchors a unique name Figure 4-6 shows that I'm giving the anchor for China the startlingly original name China. By the way, you *never* see the anchor's name on the Web page. It's just a target name so that a hot spot has something to hook up with.

Use intuitively clear names for anchors. Names such as Top, Middle, and Bottom help you remember the placement of the anchor. Using esoteric names is fine, but remember who must recall what they mean six months from now as you're updating the pages. (Pachyderm? Why did I use *that* anchor name?) With the use of Top, both the anchor name *and* the hot spot name are the same. That's really hard to forget!

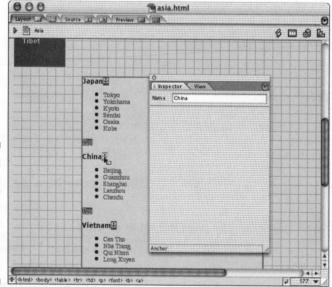

Figure 4-6:
Use the
Inspector to
give each
anchor on
a page a
unique
name.

Linking to anchors

After you place and name all the anchors on a page, you need to create the actual links so that all these carefully named anchors can *do* something for you. The process of linking anchors is virtually identical to that of making any other kind of link. Just follow these steps:

1. **On your page, where you placed the anchors, type the text you want to use for your hot spots — the text you want to use to link to the anchors.**

   In my example, I already have the names of the countries to visit on a menu bar along the left side of the page, as shown in Figure 4-5.

2. **Select the text you want to use for a hot spot for a particular anchor and click the Link button on the toolbar or Inspector — the one showing the two chain links.**

   Make sure that you pair up your hot-spot text names and anchors correctly. Linking up the wrong pair is easy if you're not careful. After you click the Link button on the toolbar or Inspector, it goes pale and the Inspector displays a text window for the anchor (the URL window) along with a Point-and-Shoot button (the button with the corkscrew icon) and a Browse button (the one showing a folder).

3. **Drag the point-and-shoot line from the Point-and-Shoot button to the anchor to which you want the hot spot to link and then release the mouse button, as shown in Figure 4-7.**

   If you can't see the target anchor from the hot spot text, drag the point-and-shoot line down or up, and the Layout page scrolls until the target anchor becomes visible. The point-and-shoot operation automatically puts in the name of the anchor along with the pound (#) sign in the URL window. So you see `asia.html#Japan` in the URL window if you select the Japan anchor with the point-and-shoot line.

Figure 4-7: Creating a link from a hot spot to an anchor by using the point-and-shoot line.

After you establish your link by releasing the mouse button, you can see the anchor name in the Text Inspector window whenever you select the hot spot text. A link to an anchor automatically includes a pound sign (#) in the link name, even though you don't use that symbol in naming the anchor. During the point-and-shoot operation, the name of the Web page appears along with the anchor name, as you can see in Figure 4-7. Don't worry, however. As soon as you release the mouse button, the Web-page name disappears and you get the anchor name with the pound sign only.

This Tool Is Outta Site!

One of the handiest site tools for working with your links is the Site window's *navigation window*. By using this window, you can add to your site some pages you can actually see, providing you with a better sense of your overall site. Figure 4-8 shows my travel site from the navigation window. I don't have much there yet, but as I build it, I can easily keep track of the pages in the site by using this window.

Figure 4-8:
The navigation window provides a graphical picture of your site as you develop it.

Adding pages for link targets

At this stage of the site development, I need to add another page to handle information about the airline flights (and flights of fancy). Rather than choose File⇨New from the menu bar to start a new page, however, I can simply develop the new page directly in the Site window, and GoLive 6 automatically places the page in the site's root folder. To start and develop a new page in the Site window, follow these steps:

1. **Choose File⇨Open from the main menu bar or press Ctrl+O (in Windows) or ⌘+O (on the Mac). Select the name of the site you want from the list in the Open dialog box that appears and click the Open button.**

   The Site window for the site you select appears on-screen.

2. **Choose Diagram⇨Navigation window from the menu bar.**

   The navigation window appears. You see some of the pages in your site with lines indicating navigation links (refer to Figure 4-8). Notice that the toolbar changes from the Site toolbar to the navigation window toolbar.

   When you open the navigation window, you see only a couple of pages initially. If you want to see all your site pages, choose Diagram⇨Resolve Hierarchy from the menu bar. However, if you look in the Link window (the navigation window's roommate), you find that all links, including links to graphics and other media, are automatically updated. If you want to look at what you have done in other views using the navigation window, remember to use the Resolve Hierarchy trick.

3. **Select in the navigation window the page icon *from* which you want to link a new page.**

   In my example, index.html is the file from which I want to link, as shown in Figure 4-9. The selected page darkens so that you know which page you're selecting.

4. **Click the ninth icon from the left on the toolbar (the one that displays the label New Child Page after you rest the mouse pointer over it — the one with the line under it).**

   A new, untitled page appears in the window (see the lower-right side of Figure 4-9).

5. **Choose the Select Window button on the toolbar to bring the Site window to the forefront and click the Files tab in the Site window.**

   In Files view, you can now see that GoLive automatically creates a folder by the name NewFiles along with a file, untitled.html, that goes in the folder. Put differently, the file is placed in the Site folder and given the filename untitled.html (see Figure 4-10).

6. **Change the name of the file to one you want to use by selecting the filename in the Name column of the Site window's Files view and then typing the new name to replace the existing one.**

   You haven't yet started working with the page at this time, so a yellow triangle appears in the status column, next to the new file.

In addition to adding a new child page, you can add a parent or sibling page. A *child* page enters the hierarchy below the selected page, and a *parent* page enters the hierarchy above the selected page. The New Next Page and New Previous Page are sibling pages — on the same level as the selected page. (No surprise there.)

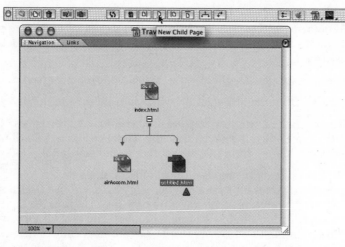

Figure 4-9:
Adding a
new page
in the
navigation
window.

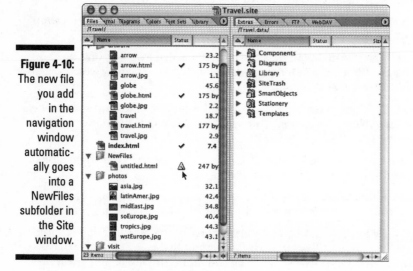

Figure 4-10:
The new file
you add
in the
navigation
window
automatic-
ally goes
into a
NewFiles
subfolder in
the Site
window.

The next thing you need to do is to create a link from your index page to the new page. Just follow these steps to create a link:

1. **With the navigation window open, double-click the page from which you want to create a link.**

   The page you select appears in Layout view. Because I want to open index.html, I double-click it in the navigation window.

2. **Select the text on the page from which you want to establish a link and press the Ctrl key (in Windows) or the ⌘ key (on the Macintosh) to insert a Point-and-Shoot button.**

   The Point-and-Shoot button is pretty easy to recognize, by the way; it combines a pointer arrow with a distinctive spiral figure. In my example, I want to establish a link between the index page and my page that shows available sea cruises, so I select the Sea label from my menu on the right side of the graphic, as shown in Figure 4-11.

3. **Continuing to press the Ctrl key (in Windows) or the Command key (on the Mac), drag the resulting point-and-shoot line to the target page icon in the navigation window.**

   Your link is now established between the source and target page. Creating links in this manner by using the Point-and-Shoot button helps you see the pages in the context of a Web site and not just as one Web page linking to another.

Keep a steady hand while pulling the point-and-shoot line from Layout view over to the navigation window. If the navigation window is behind the document window, it appears after you drag the point-and-shoot line to any part of the navigation window. If you find the point-and-shoot method awkward, you can always use the Browse feature of the Inspector. Using the point-and-shoot technique, however, guarantees that the connection you make is in your root folder.

Figure 4-11:
You pull the point-and-shoot line from Layout view in the navigation window to establish a link and provide a visual picture of how the site is developing.

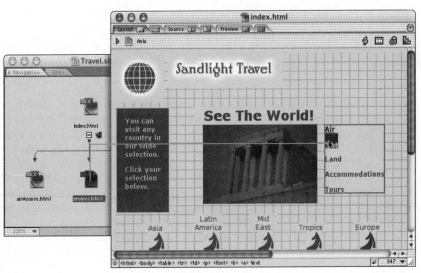

Improving the view

Establishing a link doesn't even raise a sweat. The perspiration may come, however, if you start adding more and more pages to your site with more and more links joining them. How's a person to keep everything straight?

A closer look at Figure 4-11 shows that GoLive 6 already offers a solution to that problem. The navigation window provides a graphical representation of pages in your site. You can change the information you see in Navigation view. In Figure 4-12, you can see the links between the pages and along with a thumbnail view of the graphics and text on the page. The one page without any materials on it yet simply shows up as an icon.

Figure 4-12:
The naviga-
tion window
and the
View palette
work
together to
provide
a clear
picture of
your links.

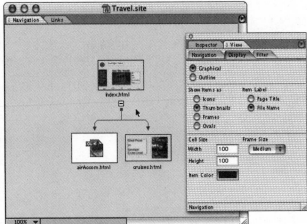

In selecting a style for displaying items on your page, you get your choice of four options from the Display tab of the View palette. (To access the View palette, just select Window⇨View from the menu bar. Also, remember that the View palette's roommate is the Inspector, so if you have the Inspector on your page, just click the View tab.) You can choose icons, thumbnails, frames, or ovals. In Figure 4-12, I'm selecting to show the items as thumbnails, but you can see in the figure that an icon still represents one of the pages (airAccom.html). I added that page, but I have yet to work on it. Nothing is on it, so it has nothing to show other than an icon. You can also select frames or ovals. Select the one that works best for you. Remember that the goal is to clarify the links in your site. To use the Links window, follow these steps:

1. **If your site isn't already open, choose File⇨Open from the main menu bar or press Ctrl+O (in Windows) or ⌘+O (on the Mac). Select the name of the site you want to open from the list in the Open dialog box that appears and then click the Open button.**

The Site window for the site you select appears, open to its Files view.

2. **Choose Diagram⇨Navigation from the menu bar.**

   The navigation window now appears on-screen.

3. **Choose Window⇨View from the menu bar or click the View tab if the Inspector is already on-screen.**

   The View appears on-screen, ready to use.

4. **Click the Display tab of the View palette to open it.**

   The Display tab of the View palette displays options for showing the files in graphical or outline format.

5. **Select from the View palette the options you want for your display by clicking the appropriate radio buttons, filling in the text boxes, and choosing from the drop-down list.**

   Outline format looks pretty much like the display of Files view in the Site window, so I generally select the Graphical option in the Show area. Displaying the images as thumbnails helps you to visualize the pages you're building in relationship to the other pages in the site. The selections available in the Cell Size area enable you to make the images larger or smaller depending on how many pages you're viewing. If you have lots of pages, you want to use the smaller size. You can even color them if you want by selecting a color from the Item Color well.

Making Graphic Links

In addition to linking to text hot spots, you can also use graphics to create links. For the most part, little difference exists between the processes of linking a text or graphic hot spot in GoLive 6. These *little differences,* however, are most important.

To start, imagine that you've already added a consistent graphical linking image to the starting page of your Web site. Now you want to use these images as links to the different travel locations — Asia, Latin America, the Mid East, the Tropics, and Europe, for example. (Figure 4-13 shows that I used an arrow graphic with the word *Go* built into the graphic. The labels above the graphics are text.) You must now transform your images into link hot spots and then add five new pages to your site to act as the new hot spots' targets. "That's a tall order," you may think, but the following sections show that it's not that tall an order after all. (Check Chapter 2 to see how to add graphic images.)

In using graphics as links, you want to avoid being overly clever and creating abstract graphics the user may not understand. The Go arrow graphic is the same for all the destinations that are clearly labeled above each graphic so that the user knows what to expect by clicking any of the Go arrows. (Remember that your Web page should not be a multiple-choice quiz. The answers are right up front.)

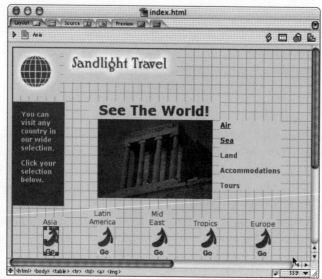

Figure 4-13:
Using
consistent
images
rather than
text to link
pages.

Hooking Up Graphic Links

After you place your graphic image where you want it on your page, you link
it to a page in your Site window by using the Point-and-Shoot button and line
in *almost* the same way as you do with text. And, as you also do with text, you
need to put your graphics into the Site folder. Follow these steps to create a
link to an image:

1. **If your site isn't already open, choose File⇨Open from the main menu
   bar or press Ctrl+O (in Windows) or ⌘+O (on the Mac). Select the
   name of the site you want from the list in the Open dialog box that
   appears and then click the Open button.**

   The site appears on-screen in Files view of the site window.

2. **Find the filename of the page you want in the Name column of Files
   view and double-click the file's icon.**

   Your page now appears on-screen in Layout view.

3. **Find and select the image you want to use as a hot spot.**

4. **Open the Inspector by choosing Window⇨Inspector from the menu bar.**

   Because you're selecting an image, the Inspector appears in its Image
   mode.

5. **Click the Link tab of the Inspector.**

   You see the Link button and the URL text box appear in the Inspector.

6. **Click the Link button (the one displaying two links of a chain) in the Inspector *or* click the one on the toolbar.**

   Both the Link buttons do the same thing, so which one you use is strictly a matter of your preference.

7. **Click and hold the Point-and-Shoot button on the Link tab of the Image Inspector and drag the resulting point-and-shoot line into the Site window and to the file to which you want to establish the link, as shown in Figure 4-14.**

   Holding the mouse button down while pointing and shooting allows you to scroll through the Site window and open folders.

Figure 4-14: Making a link to a file by using a graphic: The Inspector's Link tab provides the correct Point-and-Shoot button to use in hitting the HTML file in the Site window.

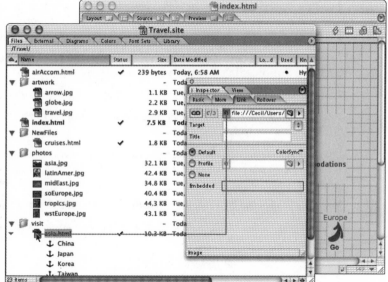

Be very careful that you click the *Link tab* in the Image inspector. The Basic tab also contains a Point-and-Shoot button, but you use that button for placing graphics and not for creating links. So, watch it!

A new feature in GoLive 6 is the fly-out menu on the Link tab of the Inspector. Click the little arrow next to the Browse folder and the menu appears, showing you pages available in the Site window. With your link graphic selected, you just select the target page from the menu. Try it out, and if you like it better than the Point-and-Shoot method, use it instead. (It's not as cool as pointing and shooting, but if you've got lots of work to get done, it helps move your project right along.)

Creating and Using Image-Map Links

If you divide a single image into different *zones,* or *hot spots,* you call that image an *image map.* Image maps are great tools because you can have a single image with many different hot spots. Rather than divide an integrated image into several little images and attempt to align them, however, you can easily set up a whole image in GoLive 6 so that you can click it in various spots for different links. Just follow these steps:

1. **As always, access your site by choosing File⇨Open from the main menu bar and selecting from the list in the Open dialog box that appears the name of the site to which you want to add an image map.**

   The site appears on-screen in Files view of the site window. If you have not done so, drag a graphic from one of your computer's directories (folders) to File view of the Site window to secure it in the site's root folder.

2. **Find in the Name column of Files view the filename of the page you want and double-click the file's icon.**

   Your page now appears on-screen in the document window's Layout view.

3. **Drag the image you want to use as an image map from the Files tab of the Site window to Layout view.**

   If you don't use a grid, the image defaults to the upper-left open space on the page. Where you place it doesn't matter for you to use it as an image map.

4. **Open the Inspector by choosing Window⇨Inspector from the menu bar.**

   Because you're selecting an image, the Inspector appears in its Image mode.

5. **In the Inspector, click the More tab.**

   The More tab of the Inspector comes to the front. In the middle of the More tab, you see a Use Map check box.

6. **Select on the page in Layout view the image you plan to use as an image map and click the Use Map check box on the More tab of the Inspector.**

   In the Name text box next to the check box, GoLive automatically enters the image map name `value`. Rename it to any name you want.

7. **If the toolbar is not on the screen, choose Window⇨Toolbar from the menu bar or press Ctrl+0 (Windows) or ⌘+0 (Mac). (That's a zero and not a capital letter O.)**

   You see the different region tools for drawing image-map link areas on the toolbar.

8. **Click one of the buttons for the Region tools (Rectangle, Circle, or Polygon) on the toolbar.**

   You can use whatever tool you select to drag an area around the part of the image you want to use to create a hot spot — an area of the image you can then use as a link, as shown in Figure 4-15. (Notice in Figure 4-15 that a rectangle outlines the city of Beijing.)

9. **Select the pointer button (the arrow) from the far-left side of the toolbar and select one of the outlined areas on the graphic.**

   After you select an image map hot spot, you see the little boxes appear on the perimeter of the hot spot, as is the case with the city of Beijing in Figure 4-15. The Inspector becomes the Map Area Inspector. To edit the map, you can double-click it with the pointer tool and move the handles around.

10. **Type the URL for the target of the link in the URL text box of the Map Area Inspector.**

    In the example shown in Figure 4-15, I type the URL because the target is external and doesn't appear in the Site window. (Chapter 11 describes how to place external URLs in External view of the Site window.) If you have external URLs stashed away there, you can use the Browse option or the point-and-shoot tool to make the link rather than type the URL.

As you see, you generate links for image-map hot spots just as you generate links for text or graphic hot spots. Image mapping is efficient because you can use a single graphic for as many hot spots as you can fit into the graphic. Image maps also offer viewers an intuitive way to navigate through your site. Map your hometown and put hot spots on all the hot spots! In that way, you can even create an online Chamber of Commerce.

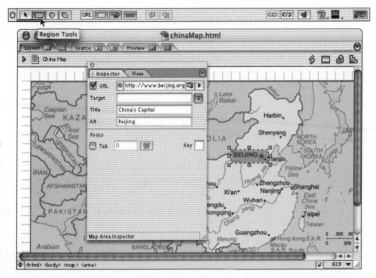

Figure 4-15:
You can turn selected areas of the image map (hot spots) into links.

Make sure that you add some text to alert viewers to click the areas you're using for hot spots. Otherwise, all they see is a graphic image with no discernable clue that the graphic is an image map. Although the hot spots are visible during development in Layout view, they're invisible in a browser window.

Up Close and Personal with the In & Out Links Palette

The navigation window used with the Site window gives you a nice graphical representation of your site as a whole, offering the Big Picture perspective on all the pages and links in your site. At times, however, you want to narrow your focus and zoom in for a closer look at a particular page. The In & Out Links palette is the perfect tool for providing such an ant's-eye perspective on a particular page. Think of the In & Out Links palette as a magnifying glass for your Site window, except that, rather than see all the pages and links in a site, you see the details of a single page. To use the In & Out Links palette, follow these steps:

1. **Choose Window➪In & Out Links from the menu bar.**

   The In & Out Links palette appears on-screen.

2. **Access your site by choosing File➪Open from the menu bar or pressing Ctrl+O (in Windows) or ⌘+O (on the Mac). Then, from the list in the dialog box that appears, select the name of the site you want to inspect and click the Open button after you find your site.**

   The Site window appears on-screen in Files view, displaying your site.

3. **Select any file in the Name column of Files view by clicking its name.**

   The In & Out Links palette provides a graphical representation of all the links to and from the page you select. On the left side of the window, you see all the files with links *to* the selected page, and on the right side of the window, you can see the files with links *from* the selected page (see Figure 4-16).

4. **Click the mouse pointer on any file in the In & Out Links palette that displays a link to or from your selected page.**

   The file you select now replaces the current file as the central file in the In & Out Links palette and displays all the links to and from the file.

Use the In & Out Links palette to get a quick look at any page's links to other pages, graphics, or other media. The In & Out Links palette also indicates any broken links. In Figure 4-16, for example, the link to latinAm.html is broken, indicated by a question mark in the page icon. If you have only a few pages in your site, the In & Out Links palette probably isn't a great help. After your sites start getting large and you need a way to inspect the links on each page quickly, however, you're going to be glad that you have the In & Out Links palette to check out what's connecting to any given page.

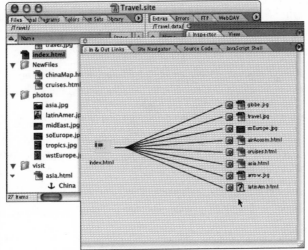

Figure 4-16: The In & Out Links palette at work.

Substituting site links by using the In & Out Links palette

Getting the inside dope on all the links to a page is a great help, but the usefulness of the In & Out Links palette doesn't end there. After you finish inspecting the pages of your site, you can use the In & Out Links palette for some major rearranging as well.

Take another look at Figure 4-16. Notice the Point-and-Shoot buttons right next to the center page as well as those next to all the linked files on the right. Using your steady hand, you can point-and-shoot your way into swapping a new file for one already on your site. Just follow these steps:

1. **Click the Files tab in the site window (if it's not already open in Files view) or open it by following Step 2 of the steps in the preceding section if it's not open.**

   Files view appears, displaying in the Name column the various files in your site.

2. **Choose Window⇨In & Out Links from the menu bar to open the In & Out Links palette.**

3. **Select the file for the page you want to rearrange in the In & Out Links Palette by clicking its name or icon in Files view of the site window.**

   The file appears in the In & Out Links palette window, showing links to and from the file. Web pages, graphic files, and other media files, such as QuickTime movies or SWF (Shockwave) files, all qualify for selection on the In & Out Links palette. (It's a very democratic palette.)

4. **Locate the replacement file in the Name column of the Site window's Files view.**

   If the replacement file you want is in a folder, you first need to open the folder so that you can see the file in the Name column of Files view. You may need to move your In & Out Links palette window slightly to the side to see all the files that Files view lists in the Site window.

5. **Pull the point-and-shoot line from the file or object on the In & Out Links palette you want to replace to the one in Files view with which you want to replace it.**

   The file you select by using the point-and-shoot line now replaces the file you chose to replace.

After you complete the point-and-shoot operation, the next time you open the page in the navigation window, the new link file shows up in the window's graphical representation of your site. Figure 4-17 shows that I'm swapping the file I call arrow.jpg for a file with the name newarrow.jpg. If you then view the page index.html in Layout view, you see that the file newarrow.jpg is now replacing arrow.jpg in *all* instances where arrow.jpg was previously used.

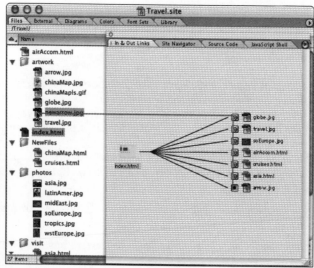

Figure 4-17:
You can use the In & Out Links palette to change links to any kind of file.

At first, you may think that the In & Out Links palette is a nice little extra but not something you're likely to use often. If you're maintaining a big Web site and you want to update your pages regularly without needing to open each page in the document window, select a current link, click the Unlink button on the toolbar, select the Link button again, and put in the new link, you will treasure this nifty little tool. All you need to do is to create the updated page, pop it on the Files tab of the Site window, and then point-and-shoot it to replace the old page.

If you swap image files by using the In & Out Links palette, GoLive 6 maintains the parameters (height and width) for the original file. If you make such a swap, therefore, you need to make sure that the files are of the identical size, or else you need to change the parameters. You get a visual clue that an exact fit doesn't exist between the two images you want to swap if the Resize Warning icon (a dotted rectangle with a solid rectangle within the dotted one) appears. More dramatically, the new graphic file looks warped as you view it on your Web page. If the image is selected, the Image Inspector's Resize Warning icon comes alive. If you click the icon, it remolds the selected image to its original size. See Figure 4-18 for the location of the Resize Warning icon on both the images and in the Image Inspector.

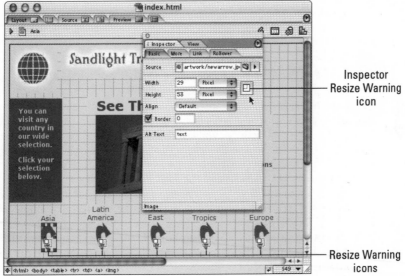

Figure 4-18: The Resize Warning icon appears on the replacement images as well as in the Image Inspector.

Viewing external links in the In & Out Links palette

If the links don't appear in the navigation window or they reside on an entirely different site, the In & Out Links palette uses a different icon.

The In & Out Links palette is a good tool to use if you're changing a page's links or you're trying to figure out what connects to a given page. In looking at wider connections, you can use the navigation window and then zero in on a page by using the In & Out Links palette to examine and make the necessary adjustments for links to Web pages and media. Figure 4-19 shows how the off-site icons appear. The links from the page travel.html are from image maps, and GoLive 6 shows them as it shows any other link to an external site.

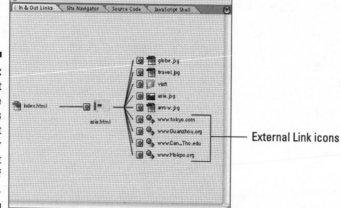

Figure 4-19:
The In & Out Links palette displays different icons for different types of links.

External Link icons

All the Links All the Time

The navigation window is handy for quickly designing your site because it shows the key important links between Web pages in your site. Likewise, the In and Out Links palette shows you the close-up-and-personal view of any single page's links. To see the wider (or taller!) organization of your site, you use the Links window (the roommate of the navigation window.) This next set of steps shows you how to use the Links window to see your site's links in all their glory. Figure 4-20 shows what the sample site looks like — even in its incomplete state, it takes up more than can be viewed in a single window!

1. **Access your site by choosing File⇨Open from the menu bar or pressing Ctrl+O (in Windows) or ⌘+O (on the Mac). Then, from the list in the dialog box that appears, select the name of the site you want to inspect and click the Open button after you find your site.**

   Files view appears, displaying in the Name column the various files in your site.

2. **Choose Diagram⇨Navigation from the menu bar.**

   The Navigation and Link windows live in the same window.

3. Click on the Link tab in the navigation window.

All the pages in your site and all the links appear with lines showing where the link begins and ends. Even small sites have so many links that the entire site with all the links showing will not fit in a single window, as shown in Figure 4-20.

The Links window, like the In and Out Links palette, shows both the good and bad links. Note in Figure 4-20 that the link to the file, latinAm.html is still bad, indicated by both a question mark and a stop sign icon. Also note that the toolbar provides a button for changing the orientation from horizontal to vertical in case a different angle would better display all the links. Using the View palette, you can change the icons, just as was shown with the navigation window.

In most cases, you cannot see all the links in a Web site — there are too many of them to display in your screen's area. You can collapse any of the pages or folders to give you a better perspective and more room to inspect your site's links. However, for the most part, you will probably use the In & Out Links palette to view your links.

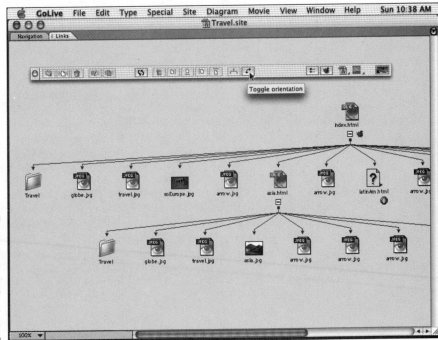

Figure 4-20: All the links are displayed in a hierarchy in the Links window.

Chapter 5

Table Manners

*U*sing tables is a great way to organize and present text, numbers, and graphics. You can place any object from a Web page into a table; each cell in a table can have its own background color or graphic, different-size borders, and placement of objects relative to the margins and sides of the cell. Sometimes, I like to think of a table as a photo album, too. Each page of the album is like a Web page, and the arrangement of the photos and captions in the album make up the various cells in a table. The table gives you a great deal of flexibility and control for creating a page that looks just as you want it to look. And, if you use the new GoLive 6 Table palette, making your page a masterpiece is even easier than before.

This chapter covers all the tools GoLive 6 has to make your tables look great. I include examples and explanations on how to format, color, configure, and reconfigure tables to meet your needs.

Setting the Table

You can place tables directly on your page in Layout view, or you can place tables on a grid. (I introduce GoLive 6 grids in Chapter 3.) Tables act the same as other objects you place on your Web page in Layout view. If you lay them on a grid, tables pretty much stay where you place them, but if you place them directly on the page without using the grid, they migrate to the upper-left corner relative to other objects on the page. So, in many ways, tables act the same as any other object you put on a page in Layout view.

To start using tables on your Web pages, follow these steps:

1. **Launch GoLive 6 by double-clicking the GoLive 6 icon on your computer's desktop and click the New Page icon from the menu that initially appears.**

   A new page appears on-screen in Layout view with its Welcome to GoLive 6 message in the upper-left corner of the document window.

2. **Choose Window⇨Table from the menu bar.**

   The Table palette appears on-screen. It's blank because you haven't yet placed and selected a table on your page. Notice that the Table palette contains two tabs: Select and Style. Click the Select tab to bring it to the front.

3. **Choose Window⇨Inspector from the menu bar.**

   The Text Inspector appears on-screen.

4. **Choose Window⇨Objects from the menu bar.**

   The Objects palette appears on-screen.

5. **Click the Basic tab if it's not already open as the palette appears.**

   Note that the fourth icon from the left in the top row is the Table icon.

6. **From the Basic tab of the Objects palette, drag the Table icon to the new page in the document window.**

   After you drag the icon to the page, a table replaces the icon on the page displaying three rows and three columns with big, fat bars for cells. The Table Inspector comes alive, and the Table tab of the Table palette displays the rows and columns of your table.

Now you're all set to do some serious table design. The ever-useful Inspector is on hand again to help out, but now the Table palette stands alongside it as its companion to make controlling tables even easier than with the Inspector alone.

The Table palette and the Inspector are here to serve your table

The Table Inspector provides a host of adjustments for your table. The three tabs in the Table Inspector offer you plenty of control over on-screen details for working with tables in Layout view, as shown in Figure 5-1. The Table tab sets the general parameters for your table, so look at it first. It's easy to use, and for such a handy little window, it sure packs a great deal of power. You need to keep in mind, however, that the Inspector remains in its Table mode only as long as you're working on a table — while some portion of the table remains selected. (If you deselect the table, the Inspector changes to another mode depending on what you next select.)

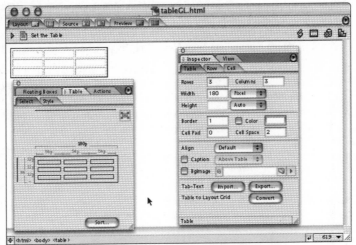

Figure 5-1: The Table palette, with its Select tab open, and the Table Inspector, with its Table tab open, show you the default settings of a new table.

The Table palette works together with the Inspector in helping you work with tables. Its job is to provide sorting and design assistance. If the Select tab is open on the Table palette, whatever cells you select on the Table palette, you also simultaneously select in the table — and vice versa. Just click any cell in one or the other, and you see that you're selecting the same cells in both. If the Style tab of the Table palette is open, you can add designs to a table with a simple click of the mouse. Styles range from serious Budget styles for laying out facts and figures to the colors of the 1970s that you can use as a photo album for the Days of Disco. With GoLive 6, you can create and save your own design.

Too many palettes to see everything? Press Ctrl+Tab to remove *all* your palettes and toolbar from the screen. When you want them back, just press Ctrl+Tab again. (I wish it were that easy to clean my room!)

Setting the table properties

To start working on your table, you need to make a number of decisions about how you want it to look. Step through the options in the Table Inspector and the Table palette to see what's available. After creating your table by following the steps in the section "Setting the Table," earlier in this chapter, you can set the basic dimensions of your table by following these steps:

1. **On the Table tab of the Table Inspector, enter in the Rows and Columns text boxes the number of rows and columns you want in your table.**

   The default dimensions provide three rows and columns. Nothing is magical or even particularly useful about the default number of rows and columns, so don't hesitate to make a change. After you set the number of rows and columns for your table, the Table palette changes to reflect the new version of your table, showing the number of rows and columns you specify in these text boxes.

2. **Set the width and height of the table in terms of one of three units of measure — Pixel, Percent, or Auto — by entering values in the Width and Height text boxes and selecting the appropriate unit of measure from the drop-down list box to the right of each text box.**

   The kind of measurement you use affects how your table reacts on other computers. The following paragraphs further discuss how to decide which unit of measurement to use and the consequences of using each type. (To continue setting up your table, continue with the set of steps that appear in the following section.)

Selecting the whole table or parts of it can be tricky. When you move the cursor along the left side of the table or one of its corners, look for the arrow-box icon. When you see the box appear next to the pointer, give the mouse a click to select the whole table. The I-beam cursor means that you're in a cell so that you can write text in it or place media in the cell. When you see the small arrow pointing leftward or downward on the side of the table, it means that you can select the row or column. Clicking the lower-right corner of a cell selects the cell.

After you decide on the number of rows and columns you need for your table, you need to decide what units of measure to use. Often, the other elements on your page determine the unit of measurement your table can use. If you have two graphics that take up exactly 300 pixels horizontally together, for example, you may want to select Pixel so that you can limit your table width to that number of pixels (plus a few more for margins). If you have lots of different graphics to insert into the table's cells of different sizes, however, you probably want to select Auto so that the table automatically adjusts itself to the widest row or column that the graphics occupy. Designers often use the Percent selection so that, no matter what screen size the viewer is using, the table's width takes up only a given percentage of the viewing window. Such a setting preserves the page's design proportions.

In other circumstances, you may want the design to preserve a certain size that you measure in pixels. You may choose the Pixel setting, therefore, to maintain sufficient room for a text layout or some other design element. What's really important, however, is that you use the measurement *that works best for your design* and that you don't just assume that the default values are the best ones. As Groucho Marx once remarked, "Who you going to believe? Me or your eyes?" Believe your eyes!

Don't forget to look at your table from the view of different browsers and types of computers. Click the View Controller tab in the Inspector (they're still roommates) and look at your tables from different perspectives. Chapter 2 gives you techniques for mastering different views with the View Controller. (This becomes especially crucial if your page is being designed for a cell phone!)

Looking after your table's appearance

After you set your table's basic dimensions, you're ready to go to work on how your table will look. The Appearance area (in the bottom half) of the Table Inspector provides these options. The basics I describe in the following steps give you the control you need over how your table will look.

Watch where you click the table in Layout view. If you click a single cell, the Inspector jumps from the Table tab to the Cell tab. You may find yourself filling in values that work for only the selected cell when you actually want those values to apply to the whole table. D'oh! To select the entire table, move the cursor along the left side of the table and look for the arrow-box icon. When you see the box appear next to the pointer arrow, give the mouse a click to select the whole table. (Oddly, if you select a row by clicking those itty-bitty horizontal arrows that crop up around tables, the Inspector *doesn't* jump to the Row tab. It jumps to the Cell tab.)

Follow these steps to set the appearance of your table:

1. **Making sure that you first select the entire table in Layout view, enter a value in the Border text box of the Inspector's Table tab.**

   As a rule, less is better. On the great majority of my tables, I set the border to 0 or 1. If it's too thick, a border can sometimes get in the way of the overall message of your design, with the viewer paying more attention to the border than to the text and graphics in the table. Creating a really ugly table that detracts from the message is all too easy if you're not careful. See the Tip at the beginning of this chapter for finding out how to grab the whole table and individual cells.

2. **Enter values in the Cell Space and Cell Pad text boxes.**

   The distance between cells (the *cell space*) refers to the distance between the cell's borders. *Cell padding* consists of the distances between the materials inside the cell and the cell border. If things look too crowded or spaced apart in your cells, just change the cell padding and spacing values until they look right. (In the example shown in Figure 5-2, the padding is set to 2 and the spacing to 1.)

3. **If you want a table color, click the Color well on the Table Inspector's Table tab.**

   The Color palette appears, and you color the table by clicking the colors on the Color palette. (Fuchsia? The board will *love* that.)

4. **Select a table alignment from the Table Inspector's Alignment drop-down list if you don't want to use the default alignment setting.**

   You can use the Inspector to align your table to the left or right of the page. I recommend, however, that you initially leave the table in default mode unless your design definitely calls for it to align to the left or right. (See the Tip that follows these steps for the lowdown on why you should keep the default setting for now.)

5. **Click the Caption check box to put a check mark in it and then select from the drop-down list box whether you want the caption to appear on your page above (the default) or below the table.**

If you prefer no caption, leave the check box blank. Although the Caption text box is part of the table, it's not a table cell, row, or column and has no borders. Figure 5-2 shows how a table looks after you select the Caption check box and then select Above Table from the list box. (To continue setting up your table, follow the steps in the section "Stuffing the Table," later in this chapter.)

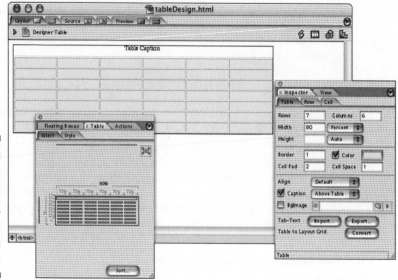

Figure 5-2:
A table on a page in Layout view, all set for you to add text and images.

At this point, you have your basic table. Other than the background color, your table consists of just an empty set of cells.

If you leave your table's alignment in default mode, you can align your table on the page by using the text-alignment buttons of the toolbar. Just place the cursor to the left of the table and click the alignment button you want (Left, Right, or Center) on the Text toolbar. (Of course, you can also use the Grid feature, which I discuss in Chapter 3, to place your table exactly where you want it on your page.) Figure 5-2 shows a sample table I created by using the Inspector and the Text toolbar's Center alignment button.

Easy styler

The Style tab of the Table palette provides some ready-made styles you can just plunk onto your table. This section describes how to use the Table palette to give your table a quick, new style that looks good without a great deal of work. Follow the six steps in the section "Setting the Table," at the beginning of this chapter, to place your table (along with your Table palette) on the page and then follow these steps:

1. **Select the entire table in Layout view by moving the cursor along the left side of the table and clicking when you see the arrow-box pointer.**

   On the Select tab of the Table palette, you should see a blue line across the top and left side of the thumbnail of the table on the Style tab.

2. **Click the Style tab of the Table palette.**

   You see a pattern of colored cells appear on the palette. (The style you selected the last time you used the Table palette determines which style you see now. You may see, for example, an orange layout with the name Orange appearing in the Style tab's drop-down list.)

3. **Open the Style tab's drop-down list by clicking the list located directly under the Style tab's actual tab and to the left of the Apply button.**

   The style you select now appears on the Style tab of the Table palette. Go through several different styles to find one you like. Some styles, like Budget and Just the Facts, don't tell you much about their colors, but others, like Rainbow and Green, give you a better idea. (Watch out for Yellow Press — its color scheme is black and red, but Yellow/White are — well, I'll let it be a surprise.)

4. **Click the Apply button next to the drop-down list.**

   Quick as a wink, your table transforms in color pattern and possibly in size to that of the style you select. (A certain style may affect only the colors in the table, but some styles may also change the cell padding, borders, and cell space.)

To be sure, setting the color scheme and layout of the table can be done by using the Table Inspector to select colors for the table, row, columns, or individual cells. However, using the Style tab of the Table palette, you can do everything at one time.

Create, save, and apply your own design

Why do you have to accept one of the canned designs GoLive 6 makes available? You don't. You can change and save the set of designs that is supplied, and you can add your own table patterns to the existing set. Here's how:

1. **Follow Steps 1 and 2 from the preceding section.**

2. **Choose Window⇨Color from the menu bar.**

   The Color palette appears on-screen.

3. **Click the New Table Style button at the bottom of the Table palette. (It's the button right next to the trash can button.)**

   A New Table Style dialog box appears.

4. **Type the name for the new style you will create.**

   I used the name of the colors of my old high school, Green 'N Gold, which, coincidentally, was the color scheme I decided on. (Go, Santa Barbara High Dons! (*Snuffle* — I miss the good old detention room there.)

5. **Select the top row (below the caption row) by moving the cursor along the left side of the table and clicking the mouse button when the tiny row-selection arrow appears.**

   The top row shows the selection marks outlining each of the cells in the row.

6. **Select a color from the Color palette and drag the color from the selected color pane to the Color well on the Inspector palette.**

   Because you selected a row, the Inspector automatically has changed tabs to the Cell tab. You have just placed the color into the Cell tab color well, and you see your row colored in the selected color because all the cells in the row are selected.

7. **Repeat Step 6 with the other rows (or columns or even individual cells) until you have completed the color pattern you want.**

   You should now see the whole table in the desired color pattern.

8. **Click the Capture Table Style button at the bottom of the Table palette. (It's the button with the camera icon right next to the button with the pencil icon.)**

   You now see your pattern appear on the Style tab of the Table palette. The next time you open up the Style tab, you see your style listed with the others. Figure 5-3 shows a new style being created.

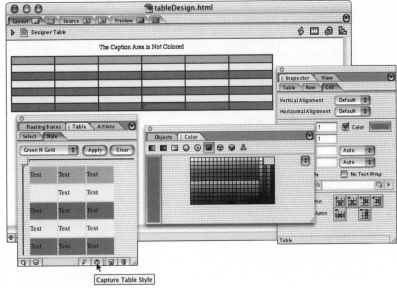

Figure 5-3:
Adding a new style to the Style tab of the Table palette.

Stuffing the Table

After completing the basic table setup (and perhaps some additional styling) as I describe in the preceding sections, you still need to add text and graphics to the table. By placing the cursor in the different cells and in the Caption area of your table, you can easily see where everything goes. Just follow these steps to fill in your table:

1. **Select the table by moving the cursor along the left side of the table and clicking when you see the arrow-box icon, and then place the cursor anywhere in the Caption area above (or below) the table on the page in the document window.**

   You now see an I-beam cursor centered in the Caption area, and the Text Inspector appears. You can change the alignment to left or right using the Text toolbar's alignment buttons. Type the caption for the table.

2. **Select the new text in the Caption area and change it to the style and color you want.**

   No difference exists between changing the text style and color in a table and changing it on the page directly. Just select the text and apply the style and color by using the Text toolbar. (See Chapter 2 for more on using the Text toolbar.)

3. **Place the cursor in the different cells in the top row and type column headings in each cell (assuming that you want column headings).**

   For example, you may have a price list with the cost, shipping, and tax labels in the column headings and items and prices below that.

4. **Choose Window⇨Inspector from the menu bar to open the Inspector.**

   The Inspector appears.

5. **Reselect the table.**

   The Inspector becomes the Table Inspector.

6. **Choose Window⇨Table from the menu bar to open the Table palette.**

   The Table palette appears.

7. **Click the Select tab of the Table palette (if it's not already open), place the pointer to the left of the top row of icons in the tab, and click the mouse button to select the entire row.**

   The row appears darkened on the Table palette, indicating that you have successfully selected the entire row. (If you experience any eye/hand-coordination problem in placing the pointer correctly to select the entire row, just press and hold the Shift key and click all the cells in the row one at a time.)

8. **Click the Row tab of the Table Inspector.**

   Notice the Color well and check box that appear as this tab opens.

9. **Click the Color well on the Table Inspector's Row tab.**

   If the Color palette isn't already open, it now appears on-screen.

10. **Click any of the colors on the Color palette and drag the color from the Color pane (the big column of color on the left side of the Color palette) to the Row tab's color well.**

    The selected row changes to the color on the Color pane (see Figure 5-4).

    If you put a style on your page by using the Style tab of the Table palette, it locks the colors for that style on your page and you can't use the Color palette to color your cells. You can easily change these set colors, however: Just select the table, click the Style tab of the Table palette, and click the Clear button on the Style tab. The set colors for that style disappear, and you can now use the Color palette to color your cells.

11. **Open the Horizontal Alignment drop-down list on the Row tab of the Table Inspector and select Right to make the text align to the right side of each cell.**

    You often use the Right alignment selection for text in tables that consist mainly of numbers. That way, it's easier to line up the decimal points.

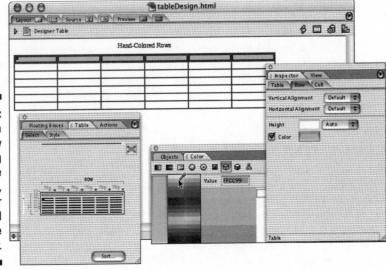

Figure 5-4:
Coloring a
table row
by using
the Table
palette,
Color
palette, and
Table
Inspector.

12. **Open the Site window by choosing Window⇨Site from the menu bar and drag from the Site window into the appropriate cells any media files you want to place in your table, as shown in Figure 5-5.**

Drag media files from Site window to table cell.

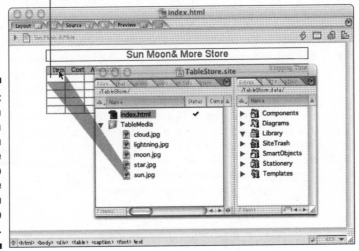

Figure 5-5:
You can
drag media
files from
the Site
window into
a cell of the
table on
your Web
page.

Remember that you can also toggle between the document window and the Site window (if it's already open) by clicking the Select Window button on the toolbar (the third one from the right). You place image files in the cell of a table the very same way you place them on the grid, as I describe in Chapter 3, or on a blank page. You can also place more than a single media file in a cell, just as you can place more than one on a Web page. (See Chapter 2 for information about placing images on a page.)

Adjusting the Table

The table makes automatic adjustments to graphics and text you place in the table cells. After you place everything you want in the table, however, you may want to make your own adjustments. You may, for example, want to change a font in the table. You change fonts in table cells the same way as you change fonts outside of a table, as I describe in Chapter 2. After you put your text and images into a table, however, you may need to make adjustments to the table because the materials you add may distort its appearance.

You may face the temptation to resize the graphics in the cells so that they better fit the size you want or conform to the size of the other images. Resizing is very easy to do in GoLive 6, but by resizing such graphics in tables, you can slow down the load time of your page. Smaller graphics do take less time to load, but graphics you resize to make them smaller still take the same amount of time to load as full-size graphics. For an important page — one that you want to load as quickly as possible — take the time to change the image size of your graphics rather than merely resize them. Changing the size of images is very easy to do in programs such as Adobe Photoshop.

The difference between resizing an image and changing an image's size lies in two different processes: one for Web pages and the other for graphic editing. The size change in Web pages distorts the image because it shrinks or stretches the actual graphic file to fit in a table cell. In graphic editing, unnecessary pixels are removed when a file is made smaller and pixels are added to make it larger. So if you resize an object to make it larger, it doesn't have enough pixels to make it look good; if you make the object smaller, you don't get rid of the extra pixels, but you still carry the weight of the file. (See the end of Chapter 4 for information about recognizing the Resize Warning icon on both the graphic and the Image Inspector.)

Adjusting table sizes

The first thing you may want to adjust is the dimension of the table itself. Table dimensions are originally set to 75 percent of the page and remain at that size until you change the table's dimensions. To change a table's dimensions, follow these steps:

1. **Choose Window⇨Inspector from the menu bar to open the Inspector.**

   The Inspector appears on-screen.

2. **Select the table on your page by moving the cursor along the left side of the table and clicking when you see the arrow-box icon.**

   The Inspector becomes the Table Inspector.

3. **In the Table Inspector, change the setting for both the Width and Height drop-down lists to Pixel.**

4. **Change the values in the Width and Height text boxes by entering new values until the proportions of your table look better.**

   Notice in Figure 5-6 that the table is 300 x 400 pixels.

Figure 5-6:
If you
change the
dimensions
of your
table, text
may stack
in a cell.

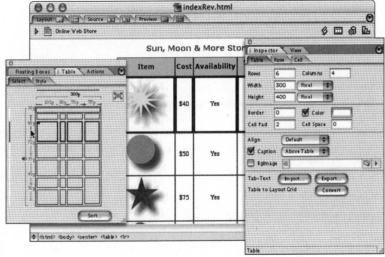

Adjusting cell sizes

After your table is adjusted to the dimensions you want, you can make adjustments to the individual cells:

1. **Choose Window⇨Inspector from the menu bar to open the Inspector.**

   The Inspector appears on-screen.

2. **Choose Window⇨Table from the menu bar to open the Table palette.**

3. **After the Table palette appears on-screen, click its Select tab if that tab isn't already open.**

4. **Select any cell by clicking the cell on the Table palette.**

   You can select a cell for editing on either the Table palette or the table itself. Sometimes, I find it easier to use the Table palette because I know that I won't accidentally select the cell for entering text or media (the I-beam cursor shows) when I want to select the cell for editing (the arrowhead cursor appears).

5. **On the Cell tab of the Table Inspector, change the setting for both the width and height of the selected cell drop-down lists to Pixel.**

   Using pixel units to measure a cell provides closer matches between the size of the media in the cell and the cell size than does a percentage unit of measure.

6. **Change the values in the Width and Height text boxes by entering new values until the proportions of your table look better.**

   If the table width is set, sometimes when a single cell's width is changed, it affects the width of other cells. For example, in Figure 5-6, you can see that the column label Shipping Time is stacked because the cell width was reduced because of a cell in another column being expanded.

The tricky part of changing a single cell is its effect on the rest of the table. Suppose that you have a table set to 400 pixels wide. If you have four cells in each row, and each is 100 pixels wide, when you change any one of those cells, it ripples through the entire row. For example, if you change one cell to 160 pixels width, the other three cells automatically change to 80 pixels to maintain the table width of 400.

Adjusting color and alignment

After you make the necessary adjustments so that the size looks better, as I describe in the preceding sections, you may find that the rows of your table also look better if you make each row a different color and align the text in the center of each cell so that it better lines up with the column headings. To do so, follow these steps:

1. **Choose Window⇨Inspector from the menu bar to open the Inspector.**

   The Inspector appears on-screen.

2. **Choose Window⇨Table from the menu bar to open the Table palette.**

3. **After the Table palette appears on-screen, click the Select tab if that tab is not already open.**

4. **Select all the rows in your table by dragging your mouse pointer down the left margin of the table on the Select tab of the Table palette.**

   All the rows on the Table palette are highlighted with a thicker border. Why not select the entire table? If you select the whole table, the Row tab alignment pull-down menus are inactive. (Hold down the Shift key to select multiple rows in this manner.)

5. **Click the Row tab of the Table Inspector (if that tab is not already open) and use the Vertical and Horizontal drop-down list boxes on the Row tab to change the vertical and horizontal alignment of the text to Center and Middle, respectively.**

   By selecting all the rows at one time, you adjust the horizontal and vertical alignment of the rows in a single operation.

6. **Select an individual row by clicking to the left of the row on the Select tab of the Table palette.**

   Note that when you select a row, the arrowhead mouse pointer changes orientation to the right and changes to a little arrow. When it makes the orientation change, you're ready to click yourself a row.

7. **On the Row tab of the Table Inspector, click the Color well.**

   The Color palette appears on-screen (if it's not already there). The selected color appears in the Preview pane on the Color palette, and the selected row takes on the color you select. Repeat Steps 6 and 7 for all the rows in the table you want to color.

8. **Select the entire table by moving the cursor along the left side of the table and clicking when you see the arrow-box icon. On the Table tab of the Inspector, change the value in the Border text box to 0 to remove all the borders from around your table.**

   Now, different colors, rather than borders, separate the rows of your table, as shown in Figure 5-7.

To color columns, you just select the column you want to color on the Select tab of the Table palette by placing the mouse pointer at the top of that column and clicking it after the pointer turns downward. Then, on the Cell tab of the Table Inspector (click that tab to open it), click the Color well. Doing so opens the Color palette; from there, just click the color you want for the column. Repeat this procedure for every column you want to make a different color.

You can probably see the design problem with the page shown in Figure 5-7. Transparent GIF graphics, which display white backgrounds to pick up any drop shadows, cause a big block of white space to appear around the shadow. You can fix that problem by using one of two methods: You can either get rid of the drop shadows or change the background of the column to white. To use GoLive 6 to fix this problem, simply press Shift, click all the cells you want to change, and then drop in a white background by using the Cell tab of the Table palette. Click the Color well and choose white from the Color palette. This procedure doesn't affect the rest of the cells in the row. Figure 5-8 shows how the table looks after you change the background color of the cells this way. Compare Figures 5-7 and 5-8 to see the difference.

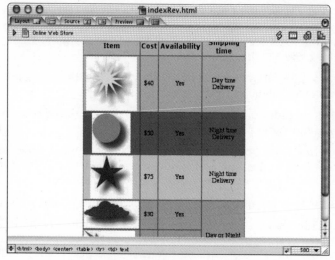

Figure 5-7: You can use colors to separate rows (or columns) in your table.

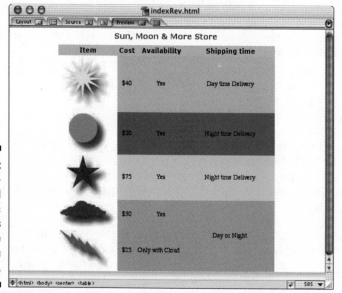

Figure 5-8: Cell backgrounds and graphic backgrounds match in the first column of this table.

Span the Rows and Columns!

Sometimes, you need a row or a column to consist of more than one cell. When you expand a cell to cover more than a single row or column, it's known as a *span*. (You can add a span to either rows or columns.) In the sample table shown in Figure 5-9, you can combine the Lightning and Clouds rows into a single row. That example serves to show you first how to add a row span and then how to add a column span.

The selected row increases downward the indicated number of rows in the Row Span window.

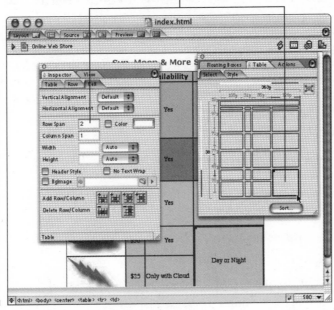

Figure 5-9: The Row Span value you enter on the Cell tab of the Table Inspector expands the cell into the next row by the entered value minus one.

Adding a row span

To add a row span, you use the Cell tab of the Inspector. (***Note:*** Although the expression *row span* uses the term *row,* you're expanding only a single cell at a time.) To add a row span, follow these steps:

1. **Choose Window⇨Inspector from the menu bar to open the Inspector.**

   The Inspector appears on-screen.

2. **Select the table on your page by clicking its left side.**

   The Inspector goes into its Table mode.

3. Choose Window⇨Table from the menu bar to open the Table palette.

4. After the Table palette appears on-screen, click the Select tab if that tab is not already open.

5. Select the Cell tab in the Table Inspector.

6. On the Select tab of the Table palette, click the cell to which you want to add a row span.

   Row spans create an additional row downward from the selected cell. After you complete a row span, the color and text from the selected cell extend into the span.

7. In the Row Span text box of the Table Inspector's Cell tab, enter the number of rows you want to add to the selected cell to create the span.

   If you enter a **2** in the Row Span text box, for example, the cell then takes up two rows — it doesn't *add* two more rows to the existing row. Figure 5-9 shows how to create such a row span from the original selected cell on the Table palette by using the Cell tab of the Table Inspector. As soon as you click the newly expanded cell, the Table Inspector shows a miniature representation of the expanded cell in your table at the bottom of its Select tab.

Adding a column span

Besides adding another row to a cell, you can span a column. Columns all *span to the right*. To add a column span, follow these steps:

1. Choose Window⇨Inspector from the menu bar to open the Inspector.

   The Inspector appears on-screen.

2. Select the table on your page by clicking its left side.

   The Inspector becomes the Table Inspector.

3. Choose Window⇨Table from the menu bar to open the Table palette.

4. After the Table palette appears, click the Select tab if that tab is not already open.

5. Click the Cell tab in the Inspector.

6. On the Select tab of the Table palette, click the cell to which you want to add a column span.

   Column spans merge the selected cell with the cells in the next chosen columns. The color and text from the selected cell extend into the new span.

7. **In the Column Span text box on the Cell tab of the Inspector, enter the number of columns you want to add to the selected cell.**

   The number you enter includes the cell itself plus the number of spans you're adding to the right. A value of **3**, for example, creates two spans to the right.

The table shown in Figure 5-10 now shows a column span in the row with the lightning bolt (in addition to the row span that is already there). The only other difference between this figure and the preceding one is that a value now appears in the Column Span text box on the Cell tab of the Table Inspector and a different cell is selected on the Table palette.

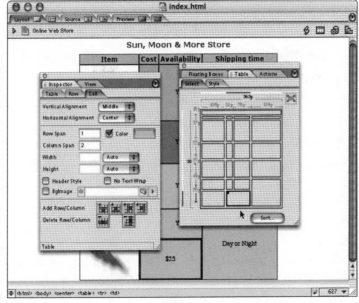

Figure 5-10:
Column spans expand to the right of a selected cell, as is the case of the middle cell in the last row containing any information.

To remove a span, just select the cell and enter **1** in the Row or Column Span text boxes in the Table Inspector. The sample table for this chapter really doesn't need the column span, so I'm deleting it by placing **1** in the Column Span text box. After you remove a span that way, you also delete all the text you add to the span, including that of the original cell. If you add a span that you don't really want and realize it immediately, use the Edit➪Undo command from the menu bar or Ctrl+Z (in Windows) or ⌘+Z (on the Mac). You can also use the History palette to more precisely undo materials. Select from a list on the History palette the point you want to undo back to. (It's like a time machine: Just select the part you want to restart at, and everything goes back to that point.) By undoing a span, you get back your original cell and its contents.

Deleting and Adding Rows and Columns

In developing a Web site, you often find that you need to pare down or expand a table. New information comes in, you add a new product or service or delete an old one, or some other kind of change requires you to change the table. In GoLive 6, you don't need to rebuild the entire table — just cut and paste your rows and columns as necessary.

Making row and column deletions

If you refer to Figures 5-9 and 5-10, you may notice at the bottom of the table an extra row that contains nothing in its cells. I put it there as a sacrificial lamb to show you how to remove a row. Just follow these steps:

1. **Choose Window⊃Inspector from the menu bar to open the Inspector.**

   The Inspector appears on-screen.

2. **Select the table on your page by clicking its left side.**

   The Inspector goes into its Table mode.

3. **Choose Window⊃Table from the menu bar to open the Table palette.**

4. **After the Table palette appears, click the Select tab if that tab is not already open.**

5. **Click the Cell tab in the Table Inspector.**

6. **On the Table palette, select any cell in the row or column you want to delete.**

   You need to select only a single cell in the column or row awaiting deportation into silicon vapor (and *any* cell works); you don't need to select the entire row or column.

7. **Click the appropriate Delete Row/Column icon (red) on the Cell tab of the Table Inspector (the first icon to delete a row and the second to delete a column).**

   The left icon is for rows, and the right icon is for columns. Make sure that you click the left one to delete the row. Otherwise, you lose a column instead. Notice, too, that the delete icons are red and the add icons are green. (You can't tell in this book if you're looking at the Inspector in a figure, but the colors on-screen are quite apparent.)

Because the little Delete Row/Column icons are right next to each other, be very careful not to click the wrong one! If you do, immediately use the Undo command to retrieve the lost element: Ctrl+Z (in Windows) or ⌘+Z (on the Mac). *Do not* try to get a row or column back from row/column heaven by immediately clicking the Add Row/Column icon. If you do, you get a row or column back, but you still lose all the text and media in the cells of the deleted row or column. So practice using Ctrl+Z or ⌘+Z (or choosing Edit⇨Undo from the menu bar if you prefer doing things the hard way). As Ms. Sternum used to say back in the third grade, "*Pay attention!*" (especially if you're deleting rows or columns).

Creating new rows and columns

Deleting rows and columns is pretty straight forward, but adding them is a little trickier — although not much. Follow these steps to add a column or row:

1. **Choose Window⇨Inspector from the menu bar to open the Inspector.**

   The Inspector appears on-screen.

2. **Select the table on your page by clicking its left side.**

   The Inspector becomes the Table Inspector.

3. **Choose Window⇨Table from the menu bar to open the Table palette.**

4. **After the Table palette appears on-screen, click the Select tab if that tab is not already open.**

5. **Select the Cell tab in the Inspector.**

   Notice the four green icons near the bottom of the Inspector.

6. **On the Table palette, select the cell next to the column or row you want to add.**

   New columns are inserted to the left or right of the cell and new rows are inserted above or below the cell.

7. **Click the button with the green icon with the bar relative to where you want your new column or row to be inserted.**

   Note the position of the green line on the icon buttons, select the one you want, and give it a click. See the following Tip.

GoLive 6 employs a handy method of showing you exactly where you can expect to see your new row or column appear in your table. A green bar appears above or below or to the right or left of a green box in the appropriate icon at the bottom of the Table Inspector. The green box represents the selected cell, and the bar shows you where in the table you can expect to see your new row or column appear.

Ta-da! The completed table

Before going any further in this book, take a look at the completed table I'm using as an example in Figure 5-11. It doesn't even look like a table, but rather like a clearly organized set of information. The purpose of a table is to help organize information in text and image forms. The borders are optional, and in this example, rather than use borders to delineate rows, I'm using background colors. Color on Web pages costs the same as black and white, so use color generously to communicate and clarify data in a table.

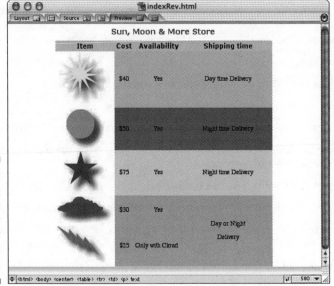

Figure 5-11:
A table on
your Web
page may
not actually
look like
a table.

Before you start making a serious table for yourself or a client, play around some with the GoLive 6 table tools. Experiment with row and column spans, background colors, or border sizes, and try adding and deleting rows and columns. You find that these tasks become quite easy after you play with the program for a while, and you build up the intuitive skills that the GoLive 6 design encourages by doing so.

Chapter 6

Inspecting HTML in Your Web Pages

*U*sing GoLive 6 relieves you of needing to write HTML (HyperText Markup Language) code into your Web pages. GoLive writes HTML code automatically as you drag and drop graphics, enter text, and format your pages. Knowing something about how HTML works, however, can come in handy. You may, for example, see features on someone else's Web page that you want to incorporate into your own. By looking at the page's source code, you can find out how to create those features. HTML code can reveal anything from a simple background color to more advanced features, like a rollover graphic.

HTML is the universal code for the Web, so code written in Palo Alto, El Paso, Cambridge, or New Delhi is all from the same source. Sometimes, either by Web page designer error or because of a glitch in the way a Web page is put together, little problems can crop up. Knowing something about the way HTML works will help you identify and correct some of the little problems. For the most part, though, GoLive 6 takes care of such problems for you.

Looking at HTML

GoLive gives you three tools to enter and edit HTML code: Source view, Source palette, and Outline view. A new GoLive 6 split view shows both Source view (in a bottom window) and Layout, Outline, or Preview view. The most direct way to edit code is by using either Source view or the Source palette. Source view turns your document window into a view where you see nothing but source code made up of HTML and generally some JavaScript or Cascading Style Sheet code. You cannot see the elements on your pages, as you can from Layout view. The GoLive Source palette enables you to look at a page in Layout view and see at the same time the code that generates the page. (Using both the Source and Outline views requires you to close one to see the other.) I focus on the Source palette to explain the basics of HTML and how to create and edit HTML in GoLive 6.

If you're familiar with HTML and want to tweak your pages, the built-in HTML editor in GoLive 6 serves as a simple and helpful code editor and debugger.

More experienced HTML and JavaScript users (as well as those who use ASP, PHP, XML, FileMaker, or Cold Fusion) are sure to be happy that GoLive 6 uses 360Code. Essentially, *360Code* means that GoLive 6 accepts coded scripts from these other languages and any HTML editor.

Switching from a view to a source code

The easiest way to familiarize yourself with HTML is to begin with a Web page created in GoLive 6 and then to look at the code in Source view. Figure 6-1 shows a page that contains basic elements: text, a graphic, and a link.

Figure 6-1:
A basic
Web page
containing
text,
a graphic,
and a link.

Keep in mind that a Web page is really made up of HTML instructions that your browser interprets, so the underlying code is really a description of how you place different elements on the page. Think of the code as a set of commands that tell the text, graphics, and links what to do. Follow these steps to look at HTML code for a page:

1. **Choose File⇨Open⇨filename.html to load a page into the GoLive 6 document window.**

   If you're already working on a page, you don't need to open another one. Save any page you're working on in the document window before you go to Source view. Choose File⇨Save from the menu bar or press Ctrl+S in Windows or ⌘-S on the Macintosh.

2. **Click the Source view tab of the document window.**

   All the text, media, and links disappear and you see a sea of code.

Voilà! You just entered the realm of HTML code. Not as exciting as a bungee jump, but you can now see the inner workings of a Web page. Figure 6-2 shows the code for the Beauty page.

Figure 6-2:
An example
of source
code for a
Web page.

If you want to take a peek at the source code of some recently completed pages or site, take advantage of the GoLive 6 ability to quickly grab a recent page or site. Choose File⇨Open Recent Files to see a list of recently opened pages and sites created in GoLive 6.

Both Netscape Navigator and Internet Explorer enable you to look at HTML code. To see a page's code in Netscape Navigator, choose View⇨Page Source. In Internet Explorer, choose View⇨Source. Sometimes a page's code is hidden, but most of the time, if you can see the page, you can see the code.

Viewing the page and the source code

The GoLive 6 new Source palette lets you look at the source code *and* the page in Layout view, but in different windows at the same time. If you make a change in the Source palette, you see those changes immediately in Layout view. Figure 6-3 shows the page and its source code together on-screen. To open the Source palette on the screen, simply choose Window⇨Source Code. The Source palette appears on-screen with its Source Code tab selected.

Figure 6-3:
You can view the source code on the Source palette and the page in Layout view simultaneously.

Using Split view

Another way to inspect your HTML along with another view is by using the new Split view. All you have to do is to click the little dual-arrow toggle button in the lower-left corner of the document window. You can drag the split bar up and down to show either more source code or more of the page objects or outline elements. Figure 6-4 shows how Split view appears when activated. (It's perfect for designers with split personalities.)

Figure 6-4:
Using Split
view, you
can see
parts of the
source code
and parts of
either the
Layout,
Outline, or
Preview
page.

Stating Your Preferences

Preference settings affect what you see in Source view of the document
window. You may not need to change preferences, but seeing how they affect
what you see in Source view is a good idea. Follow these steps to look at or
set preferences for Source view:

1. **Choose Edit⇨Preferences.**

   The Preferences window appears.

2. **Click the Source icon in the left pane of the Preferences window.**

   Settings for Source view appear on the right side of the Preferences
   window, as shown in Figure 6-5. If a check mark appears in the check box
   for the options in the right pane of the Preferences window, that option
   is selected and active.

You're ready to set preferences. All changes can be reversed, so don't be shy
because you are changing the way *you want* your source code to appear.

GoLive 6 gives you the following five preference settings from which to
choose (see also Figure 6-5):

✔ **Enable Dragging of Marked Text:** This option is a good one to keep
   unless you want to minimize the possibility of dragging text or code to
   the wrong place.

✔ **Bold for Tags:** Checking your source code is easier only if the tags
   appear in bold. Leave this option selected to make debugging easier.

✔ **Auto Indent:** Usually, this option is a good one to leave selected because you can better distinguish whether your coding is correct if it's indented — see the section "Containers and nests," later in this chapter. Spotting a bug or editing is also simpler with indents. The amount of indent for each level is the "tab size" of the indent. Generally, I like 4 or 5 for my tab size. It's enough to clearly indent, but not so much as to cause word wrap with too many of the indents.

✔ **Line Numbers:** Line numbers can clutter a page, but if you know that you have a bug on line 572, these numbers make that line easier to find. (You can leave the Line Numbers option unselected here, however, and then toggle it on and off from the Source toolbar or context menu.)

✔ **Word Wrap:** Selecting this option enables you to see all the code in a horizontal window: If you don't select this option, code listings can extend beyond the right side of your screen, requiring you to scroll left and right to see it all. The soft wrap doesn't include a carriage return at the end of each line, but you can see and edit code in a single eyespan. Selecting the Word Wrap option in the Preferences is the only way to wrap code listings on the Source palette. (Source view has its own Wrap icon that you can toggle on and off, as does the context menu.)

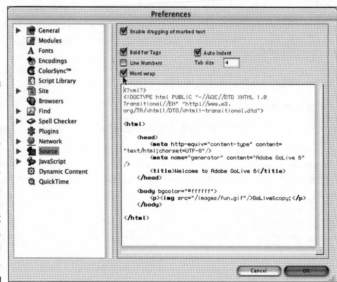

Figure 6-5:
The Preferences window enables you to set your preferences for the document window's Source view.

You can set other options by clicking additional items on the left side of the Preferences window; click the arrow next to the Source icon and open its drop-down list. Select which parameters you want to change and make the changes you want, including those I describe in the following list:

✔ **Browser sets:** Prepare code that works for both the major browsers and in different versions of those browsers. Versions before Version 3 are archaic and don't support Dynamic HTML and other nifty features of Web pages. I usually prepare my code for both browsers from Version 3 onward. This decision is important because excluding earlier versions of a browser means that certain features of a Web page don't work if a viewer sees them in an older browser. (Yeah, I know. Browsers are free, and why would someone refuse to upgrade a browser?) With all the new features that Version 6 browsers have (new JavaScript Document Object Models (DOMs), for instance), I am tempted to set them all to V6, but if you're trying to attract clients and they like their old V3 browser, you had better keep that fact in mind.

✔ **Font:** Select a font to appear on the editing page, the colors used for characteristics of HTML coding, and printer settings. Consider applying different colors to different HTML properties so that coding and debugging are easier. You can change the colors on the special Source view toolbar and context menu as well.

✔ **Color:** Pick colors for syntax highlighting and different page elements. Experiment with different colors and numbers of colors. Important elements to be sure to include in color highlighting are Media and Links at a minimum. In that way, your media (such as your graphic images) and your links codes are highlighted. Because both links and media are common places for code to go haywire, it helps to make them stand out. However, I usually select the Detailed selection because I want to see several key elements of the code stand out, including Media and Links, URLs, and Server Side code. If you change your mind in Source view, all you have to do is change the coloring with the Source toolbar or context menu (see Figure 6-6 in the following section).

✔ **Printing:** Select from the Printer Specific and Special Fonts settings. Generally, I set these options to be different from what's on the screen. Unless you're using a color printer, I suggest that you leave the Syntax Highlighting option unchecked and go with the option labeled Bold Typeface for Tags. Line numbers I find generally in the way, but for long scripts they can be useful. Also, I like a font like Courier because it is monospaced (that helps distinguish code elements from one another).

Changing the Way Code Looks

If you change views in the GoLive 6 document window, the context-sensitive toolbar changes. However, Source view is a bit different, and you have to first open it from the Source context-sensitive menu:

1. **Open Source view by clicking the Source tab in the document window.**

   Now you see your code. Position your mouse over the code.

2. **Right+click (in Windows) or Control+click (on the Macintosh) and then choose View⇨Toolbar.**

   The Source toolbar, as shown in Figure 6-6, appears *in the Source view window* and not on top of the document. It's a wholly separate toolbar and not a context-sensitive one, like the main toolbar.

The Source view toolbar is unique because its functions affect the appearance of HTML source code in Source view, not how the Web page itself looks. You can toggle features on and off by clicking the buttons on the toolbar. The following list describes the functions of each button on the Source view toolbar, beginning on the left:

- ✔ **Check Syntax:** Opens at the top of the Source view window, showing errors and warnings.

- ✔ **Colorize Nothing:** Doesn't color any of the HTML code.

- ✔ **Colorize Detailed:** Warns you if you make a coding mistake that's unacceptable in all browsers or versions (such as including a closing tag without an opening tag). The warning appears with a red ball next to it in the Syntax window. Toggle this button on or off to display errors. (I leave mine on all the time!)

- ✔ **Colorize Elements:** Appears if one of the selected browsers or a selected version doesn't recognize a tag.

- ✔ **Colorize Media and Links:** Colors only media (movies, graphics) and links.

- ✔ **Colorize Server Side Code:** Colors code such as ASP (Active Server Page), PHP, ColdFusion, or other server-side code. *Always* color server-side code if you're working with it so that you don't get it mixed up with the client-side code. GoLive 6 generates lots of code, and if server-side code is part of that generation, you want it to stand out. Server-side code communicates with the code in the various server configurations, such as Common Gateway Interface (CGI). If you use the Dynamic Link software, you see your code generated in the source. Therefore, you may find having a special color for the server code useful.

- ✔ **Colorize URLs:** Colors URLs, filenames, and addresses.

- ✔ **Word Wrap:** Makes lines of HTML code wrap around rather than scroll off the right side of the window.

- ✔ **Line Numbers:** Appears along the left margin of the window to identify lines. Each line has a separate number; wrapped text is not considered a separate line. (Don't worry — line numbers are not left on your Web pages. If they were, they would totally distort them.)

Whether you're an old hand at coding HTML in text editors or a novice to HTML coding, you're sure to find Source view helpful. Source view is as easy to use as a text editor is, and it formats HTML so that the code is easier to debug and edit.

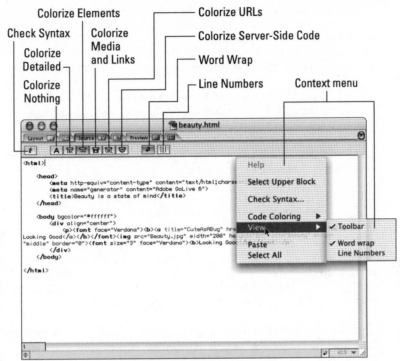

Figure 6-6:
The Source
View toolbar
and Source
View
context pop-
out menu.

Mac users may want to think about investing in a two-button mouse. Context
menus seem to be all the rage these days, and rather than have to press the
Ctrl key plus click your mouse, you will find it more convenient to just right-
click the mouse to get your menu. Usually, you can find a two-button mouse
for the Mac that comes with a scroll wheel as well.

Speaking in Tags

HTML is a language that uses tags to describe a page; it uses a set of tags to
tell objects on pages where to go. HTML gives a page *formatting* (also known
as *markup*) and incorporates links to other sources of information — usually
other Web pages. Those links are known as hyperlinks, or hypertext, which
explains the name HyperText Markup Language. There's nothing really too
exotic about it.

A *tag* is a code that instructs the browser how to convert text, graphics, and links. You identify a tag by its enclosure in arrow brackets (also known as angle brackets, greater-than/less-than brackets, or "those pointy things.") The first tag you see on a Web page, for example, is <HTML> (refer to Figure 6-2). That tag tells the browser that what follows is an HTML document.

Some tags have start and end identifiers that mark text for a particular application. Italicized text, for example, opens with the <I> tag and closes with the </I> tag. All the text between those tags is italicized. The slash mark (/) always denotes the ending tag. Both tags together make up a *container*. The materials you want to show with the tag characteristics are placed into the container (you know, between the tags.)

Other tags have only a single state. For example, the tag that calls up an image, <IMG>, uses a start tag but no end tag. Figure 6-2 contains a line of code that begins with <IMG....>, but the tag has no end tag with the same code. A few tags, such as the paragraph tag, <P>, sometimes have end tags, </P>, as you see in Figure 6-2. GoLive automatically generates them no matter what — in other Web pages, however, you find plenty of <P> tags but no </P> tags. Given the likely future development of HTML, using closing containers is a very good idea, even if one is not required.

You can write or edit HTML scripts in text editors, such as Notepad in Windows or SimpleText on the Macintosh. If you want to do some simple editing, such as changing a page's background color, you can load one of the basic text editors and make the changes. Using a simple editor is a good idea if you have other programs loaded and memory is tight. However, most of the time, straight HTML editing in Source view is much more effective because of the syntax-checking and code-formatting capabilities in GoLive.

Containers and nests

If text and code lie between start and end tags, they're in *containers*. For example, look at the following line of code from Figure 6-2:

```
<h1>My Dog Fred </h1>
```

This line shows a container beginning with <h1> and ending with </h1>. The <h1> (or <H1>, if you like to use caps) stands for *Heading 1,* and all text within the <h1> container takes on the format of Heading 1. The text *My Dog Fred* lies within the container. (I need to contain Fred!)

In Figure 6-1, the text, graphic, and link are all centered on the page. That's because they're in the container that the tags <center> and </center> describe. Within the <center> container are other tags that also use start and end tags. They're *nested* inside the <center> container.

Mixing nesting code is a common problem in editing and creating HTML code. If a tag opens in a container, it *must* close in the same container. Notice in Figure 6-2 that the container for *My Dog Fred* opens and closes within the <center> container. If it opened in the <center> container and closed outside of it, you would see an error and the Web page wouldn't work. The following examples show the right and wrong way to nest tags:

Right:

```
<center> <I> <h3> Look at this! </h3> </I> </center>
```

Wrong:

```
<center> <I> <h3> Look at this! </center> </h3> </I>
```

In the wrong example, notice that <h3> is nested in two containers: <center> and <I>. That means that </h3> should come before *both* </I> and </center>.

When fine-tuning your HTML code, mixing up the nesting sequence is easy. As GoLive automatically creates HTML code, it never makes nesting-code errors. So if you edit your Web page code, be sure that any changes you make nest all the tags correctly. If your page disappears after some fine-tuning in Source view, check to make sure that your nests are set up right.

Leaving in part of a container while deleting the rest of it is another common nesting and container error that frequently happens during editing. For example, if you decide to get rid of italicized text, you may just go in and remove the opening <I> tag and leave in the closing </I>. If you make the change while working in Layout view, GoLive 6 removes both tags automatically; but in Source view, you must remove both of them yourself. Leaving part of a container can cause your page to be formatted in a way you do not want or intend.

One of the greatest things about HTML is that it's *not case sensitive:* You can write the code in uppercase, lowercase, or a combination of cases. So, you can type <B> or <b> or even <br> or <Br>. Live it up with this loosely coded tag language! However, you have to watch it as far as making references to a file in the real world of servers. Unix servers (including the ubiquitous Linux servers) are case sensitive. So a link to greatPlace.html cannot be referenced as GreatPlace.html in your HTML code or else it crashes like a demolition derby.

You've Got Attributes!

Some tags have attributes. An attribute in the context of HTML is something like a parameter — a variable value to set and change. For example, the <body> tag has several attributes, and I use the following attribute in the sample Web page script shown in Figure 6-2:

```
<body bgcolor="#ffffff">
```

The attribute is the background color (bgcolor), and the value of the attribute is the color white. Other <body> attributes include the color of the links, visited links, and active links. If you include no attributes for <body>, GoLive uses the default values: a gray background, blue links, purple visited links, and red active links.

Another tag in the sample Web page script that displays an attribute is the <IMG> tag. Here, the attributes belong to the image called in by the tag.

```
<img src="Beauty.jpg" width="200" height="315" alt="Beauty"
       align="middle" border="0">
```

The attributes are height, width, alt, align, border and src. The image name Beauty.jpg is the value of the attribute src, and the height and width values are culled from the size of the graphic. The src attribute names the *source* of the file being brought into the Web page. The src value can be the name of the graphic file alone if the Web page and graphic are in the same folder or a full URL, such as the following:

```
"http://www.outermongolia.com/recipes/yakbread.html"
```

If you change the attributes of a graphic's dimensions, it distorts unless the changes are proportional to the original values. Similarly, if you change the src value but don't change the height and width values, the new image also distorts. The align attribute places adjacent text at the top, middle, or bottom of the graphic, and the border attribute simply adds a border around the graphic to the specified points. Finally, the alt attribute, which is too often overlooked, alerts the viewer that the graphic will appear. The moral to this story is to be careful in changing attributes unless you know what can happen. (Either that or goof around with attributes on pages you don't care about to determine more about how they affect your page — that sounds like more fun.)

Telling What's on Your Pages

The first part of an HTML script is usually the head. Spotting it is easy because the <HEAD> </HEAD> tags contain it. The title goes here, along with other code not shown directly on the Web page. Common tags you find in the head section include <META> tags, <TITLE> tag, and JavaScript function definitions. You use the <META> tags to tell the world what's in your Web pages. Search engines use <META> tags to locate various topics and page contents. For example, the following <META> tag tells the search engine the contents of my page:

```
<meta name="keywords" content="dogs, training, big">
```

GoLive automatically generates <META> tags for the character set, the file format, and the generator named Adobe GoLive 6.

To describe what is on your page beyond the keywords, use the following <META> tag:

```
<meta name="description" content="We find the beauty within
         you and bring it out for others to see000.">
```

Keep in mind that GoLive, and not your own tedious coding, generates most of the HTML code seen in the script's head. In fact, one of the Objects palette tabs is the Head, which includes icons for all the different things you can drag and drop into the Head area of Layout view. That little arrow next to the page icon in the upper-left corner of Layout view toggles the Head area open and closed. You can fill the Head with lots of valuable information, including <META> tags that don't appear on the Web page but can affect other aspects of the page.

Declaring Your Page's Look

As soon as your Web browser sees the <BODY> tag, it knows that everything in the Body container should appear on the Web page. The attributes of the opening <BODY> tag affect the entire page, and you can override them only by using specific containers that tell the browser to do otherwise. For example, the following <BODY> tag declares that the page will have a tan background color, firebrick links, and red text:

```
<Body bgcolor="tan" link="firebrick" vlink="firebrick"
         alink="firebrick" text="red" >
```

If you develop a color scheme you like, rather than define the majority of your work by using individual font color changes, just put it all in an attribute of the <BODY> tag.

Before you become too enamored with the tags that define different HTML style features, take a look at Cascading Style Sheets (CSS) in Chapter 10. In the not-too-distant future, the dominant way of defining style, including color, will be with CSS. CSS will be the formatting- and style-definition tool most often used for not only HTML, but also XML, PHP, ASP, and just about every other Web language.

Formatting Tags

On the Source palette, you're likely to run across one or more HTML formatting tags. The good thing about the tags is that they provide a consistency across platforms, monitors, and browsers. The bad thing is that they're severely limiting.

Heading tags

HTML provides six heading tags. Each tag begins with an *H* followed by a number. The largest heading is <H1>, and the smallest is <H6>. All the H tags add bold text and a paragraph space to the text block. Think of these tags as containers that affect blocks of text rather than single characters. A typical heading container appears as shown in the following example:

```
<H2> This is the second largest heading. </H2>
```

Style tags

Styles are also rather limited in HTML (nothing fancy here). The following list displays an example of bold, italicized, and underlined styles, and each includes its opening and closing tags:

<B>: **Boldface** </B>

<I>: *Italicized* </I>

<U>: <u>Underlined</u> </U>

You use other styles in HTML less often, but they may come in handy in certain applications. (The last of these I hesitate to provide because its use annoys the viewer.) The following list displays these additional styles and their tags:

<STRIKE>: ~~Strikethrough~~ </STRIKE>

^{: ^{Superscript}}

_{: $_{Subscript}$}

<BLINK>: The text blinks ... </BLINK> ... until the viewer exits the page screaming.

Using the <FONT> tag and its attributes is another, far more flexible way to style how your code looks. Basically, the <FONT> </FONT> container has three attributes; color, size, and font. The color values can be either the

6-character hexadecimal values for the color or one of the reserved HTML color words. (Hexadecimal values are a base 16 numbering system from 0 to F that your microprocessor finds friendly.) Font size is a value from 1–7, but these values have nothing to do with point or pica size. The following line illustrates a <FONT> container employing all three attributes:

```
<FONT color="green" size="3" font="verdana">
```

You can use any one or a combination of attributes in the same tag. If you change the color, size, or font of even a single letter in the GoLive 6 Layout view, GoLive 6 generates a <FONT> container that it reveals in Source view.

Alignment tags and attributes

The alignment tags and attributes work with both text and graphics. You accomplish most of the general alignment in combination with either a heading tag — such as <H3> — or a paragraph tag, <P>, in which alignment is an attribute. One tag, <CENTER>, works as a container with </CENTER> and has no attributes. The following examples show different alignment options in HTML:

```
<P align="left"> All of this is to the left. </P>
```

```
<H3 align="center"> The middle of the road. </H3>
```

```
<P align ="right"> Is this too conservative? </P>
```

```
<Center> Front and Center </Center>
```

In Chapter 10, when I talk about Cascading Style Sheets, you find a far richer selection of alignment options, including margins and indents. However, don't neglect some simpler formats available in the meantime.

Basic lists

The Ordered and Unordered lists constitute the two basic HTML lists. The *Ordered* list generates a sequential set of numbers, and the *Unordered* list appears something like a bulleted list. Each list works with two types of tags. The first tag defines the container as either an Ordered list (<OL>) or an Unordered one (<UL>). Each item in the list is tagged with (<LI>) with an optional (</LI>) at the end of each item. (Usually, coders just leave off the closing </LI> tag because the <LI> at the beginning of the next line accomplishes the same thing.) You must, however, use a closing list tag in the form of either </OL> or </UL>. You can set attributes for specific values or starting points as shown in this example:

```
<OL>
<LI value=4> Four score and
<LI value=20> Twenty Years
<LI> Is a long time
<LI> To figure out what that means!
</OL>
```

On the Web page, you see the following:

```
4. Four score and
20. Twenty Years
21. Is a long time
22. To figure out what that means
```

Coding links

The two basic kinds of link codes apply to graphics files and other Web pages. First, you initiate *hyperlinks* (or just plain *links*) by using the <A> tag followed by the HREF attribute. You need to terminate the hyperlink by using a closing tag, </A>. The HREF is the *H*yperlink *REF*erence that can be any page's URL, from a page in the root folder to a site in Outer Mongolia.

Cutting off the </A> tag is a common error in editing HTML code. If you change the hot spot text or graphic, sometimes you clip the </A> tag as well. That's probably because the closing </A> tag seems divorced from the beginning tag that usually begins with <A HREF...> rather than simply with <A>. And while discussing a warning around <A> tags, I probably need to add that in editing HTML, you can also clip out the hot spot words or graphics that the <A> container surrounds if you're not careful.

The most common link is simply one to another URL, as the following example shows:

```
<A href="http://www.adobe.com"> Click here. </A>
```

A link that includes the full address of the target is called *absolute addressing*. The good thing about absolute addressing is that the link is followed no matter where you move your page relative to your site. The problem with absolute addressing is that if you move your site and you have absolute addresses to your site links, you'll have to go and change them all. Fortunately, GoLive 6 takes care of the link issues if you use Site view and use the GoLive tools to make your links.

Relative addressing occurs when a link is relative to a given page and not to an absolute address. Two pages in the same folder can address one another by simply entering the filename (hotStuff.html, for example), or they can address one another by references to the folders in the site relative to their own position in the site.

If you have several folders in your site and your script calls for links to pages in different folders, you see different references to the file and their folders. The following three examples show the basic types of references to different levels:

- **Link to a level down:** The link is to a folder that the folder in which the linking Web page resides *contains,* as in the following example:

```
<a href="Bottom/botFld.html">Link below.</a>
```

- **Link to the same folder:** The link is to a file in the same folder, as in the following example:

```
<br><a href="level.html">Link level.</a>
```

- **Link to a level up:** The link is to a folder that *contains* the folder in which the linking Web page resides, as in the following example:

```
<br><a href="../topFld.html">Link above</a>
```

The links to an image file follow the same rules of reference as to links to other Web pages. In the sample page shown in Figure 6-2, the reference is to a file in the same folder. However, where all graphics are together in a media file residing in a folder within the folder containing the Web page calling (linking) the graphic file, the reference would have to name the folder and then the filename. For example, if all your graphics are in a folder named (quite originally) *graphics,* for example, first you name the folder and then the particular file. The following line of code, for example, makes this connection:

```
<IMG src="graphics/cow.jpg">
```

The graphic file `cow.jpg` is found in the folder `graphics` that resides at a lower level than the Web page that calls the page.

You can call a graphic file from anywhere on the Web. The problem is that somebody might file a copyright infringement lawsuit if you do. Having a link to someone else's page is one thing (that's okay), but if you just reference a single graphic file you like and integrate it into your page, you may be infringing on a copyright — even if you never take the graphic off the person's server!

Coding in Outline View

The other view in the document window where you enter HTML code is *Outline view.* This view is very different from Source view, and the context-sensitive toolbar transforms into the Outline toolbar. In this view, the sample Web page displays a unique look, as shown in Figure 6-7.

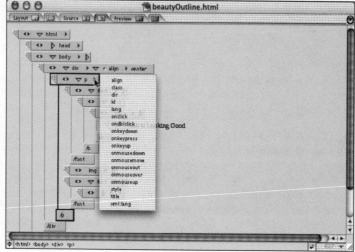

Figure 6-7:
Outline view
clearly
shows the
hierarchy of
the coded
page.

The idea behind Outline view is to provide the designer with a way to enter HTML code while not having to write a single line of code. You can enter not only tags, but also attributes and their values. Using Outline view is virtually a whole new way of thinking about coding HTML. For tweaking attributes and fine-tuning many of the page elements, this view may come in handy. However, it takes some getting used to, and for old hands at coding HTML, it may seem a bit unusual. You really need to consider Outline view along with the Outline toolbar, so please check out Figure 6-8 before forging ahead.

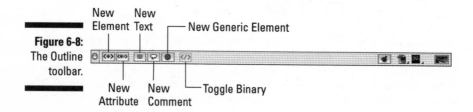

New   New
Element   Text   ┌─ New Generic Element

Figure 6-8:
The Outline
toolbar.

New   New   └─ Toggle Binary
Attribute Comment

Adding tags

To get started using Outline view, you need to use the Outline toolbar and understand how to insert HTML tags. Follow these steps:

1. **From the document window, click the Outline tab (the fourth from the left.)**

   You see a stylized set of tags showing the hierarchy of the coding system. Note the lines connecting the beginning and ending tags of the container.

2. **In the Outline view window, select one of the HTML elements where you want to insert an HTML tag.**

3. **Click the New Element button on the Outline toolbar.**

   An untitled tag appears at the insertion point.

4. **Take one of the following actions:**

   a. Type the name of the tag to replace the untitled tag label.

   or

   b. Deselect the untitled tag and right+click (in Windows) or Ctrl-click (on the Macintosh) the name.

   Be careful the first time you try this step. Up jumps a pop-up menu with a database of HTML tags.

5. **Select one of the tags in the menu, and it inserts itself into the script.**

   If you want to close a container, just select the opening tag and then add a slash in front of it after it appears in Outline view.

Because GoLive 6 advertises its Outline view as enabling you to create HTML code without needing to write it, you may wonder why you have the option to type the name of the tag. If you know the right code to key in, you can just type it. On the other hand, rather than key the code, you can just select an HTML tag from the pop-up menu. You must know which tag to use from the pop-up menu, however, and so, although you do not have to type any HTML, you sure as shootin' need to _know_ what the tags will do. The value of Outline view lies in its clarity of structure and its providing appropriate choices when it comes to attributes you may choose to add. If you want to delete an Outline view tag, choose Edit⇨Clear from the menu bar.

Adding and modifying attributes

You can use one of two methods to modify or add an attribute to an existing tag in Outline view. Because the methods are so different, I discuss each one separately. Go to Outline view as shown in Step 1 of the preceding section, and follow these steps to use the first method:

1. **Identify and select in Outline view of the document window the tag to which you want to add an attribute (or for which you want to modify an existing attribute).**

2. **Click the arrow to the right of the Tag name in Outline view to display a pop-up menu and select an attribute from the menu.**

   Depending on the tag, you have a few or many attributes from which you can choose. You can choose more than one attribute by repeating the process for each attribute you want to add. A rectangle appears around the selected attribute, and, if appropriate, you may write in the rectangle. (See Figure 6-7 for an example of attributes associated with the <P> tag.)

3. **If you're adding an attribute, click the arrow to the right of the attribute name to open a menu displaying the attribute's possible values. Then select the value you want for the attribute.**

   If the attribute is a color, a color box appears. Open the Color palette (choose Window⇨Color to open it if it's not already open or click the Color tab at the side of the screen if it's docked) and drag a color from the Color palette to the color box to add a color value. You can also type the color name or a hexadecimal color value in the box. If the attribute uses a wide selection of values, as is the case of the height and width of an image, just select the value and type any specific value you want.

For learning how to write HTML, I think that you will find this method of modifying and adding attributes much easier and useful than adding tags in Source view. It's also a good way to discover which attributes associate with various tags.

The second method of adding attributes involves using the Outline toolbar:

1. **Select in Outline view of the document window the tag to which you want to add an attribute.**

2. **Click the New Attribute button on the Outline toolbar (the second from the left).**

3. **Type the name of the attribute you want to add over the** attr **abbreviation that appears where you placed the New HTML Attribute.**

   For example, if you selected the body tag and clicked the New HTML Attribute button, you could type link and you would see a little color box appear next to it. Now that you have the attribute in, you can put in the value for the attribute, which in the case of link is a color. (I sort of liked the color plum.) If you add an unknown or illegal attribute, no values appear. GoLive 6 prevents you from making a mistake. Nice touch.

Adding more content and tags with Outline view

The remaining buttons on the Outline toolbar provide ways to add text, comments, and non-HTML tags. The toolbar also includes a button for showing one or both ends of a container — the binary toggle. See the toolbar in Figure 6-8 for button references for the following buttons:

✔ **New Text:** Select the area above where you want to add text and click the Add Text icon on the toolbar. Write in all the text you want in the inserted window that appears when you press the Add Text button. Be sure that you add the text in the <BODY> container and not in the Head area.

✔ **New Comment:** Select the area above where you want to add a comment and click the Add Comment icon. You can add comments anywhere you want in the script. The comments are just to help you remember what you're doing in the script and don't appear on your Web page.

✔ **Generic Element:** The tags you add by using this button aren't HTML tags but rather tags from ASP, XML, or some other non-HTML scripting language.

✔ **Binary Toggle:** Click the binary toggle icon to show and hide the closing tag. "Why do this?" you may ask. It saves screen space and you can see more of the script.

Part II
Looking Good: Designs That Delight

The 5th Wave   By Rich Tennant

"You know kids — you can't buy them just any Web design software"

In this part . . .

Just when you thought "This is as good as it gets" in Web site development, you are now about to enter the second realm of mind-blowing enhancements that you thought only a genius could do. But, no! You'll find that you can match colors with Picasso, create more forms than a tax attorney, and even partition your Web page into separate parts so that you can display different elements at the same time. (Those in the know refer to those partitions as *frames*.) That's not all! This part has CSS — those magic Cascading Style Sheets that you could never fathom and now are as easy as a point-and-click.

If you're frustrated by the way HTML deals with formatting text, you'll love CSS. You define the font, its color, its indent, its margin, the background color, and every other CSS feature by simply selecting what you want from one of the handy GoLive windows. You get control over unruly formatting quickly. Oh, and by the way, in this part you'll discover that after you create a to-die-for style sheet, you can import it to other sites and reuse it.

Chapter 7

Color, Color, and More Color

$\bullet$ $\bullet$

In This Chapter

▶ Selecting and mixing colors for a Web site

▶ Using the Text toolbar's Color Well button

▶ Copying colors

▶ Creating and using custom colors

▶ Creating site colors

▶ Using background colors

▶ Creating and using background images

$\bullet$ $\bullet$

GoLive 6 makes adding color to your Web page easy by giving you color wells and a Color palette with nine different coloring options. Further examination of the humble Color palette also reveals features that make GoLive 6 more than just a nifty way to add color to a Web page. More revelations are in store! (Film at 11.)

Getting a Mix of Color

To access the Color palette, either click the Text Color well in the center of the Text toolbar or a color well in one of the Inspectors or choose Window⇨ Color. The Color palette displays nine buttons to use for selecting or mixing colors. (If you can't see the buttons on the Color palette, click the arrow in the upper-right corner of the palette to reveal a drop-down list. At the bottom of the list, select the Show Buttons option, placing a check mark in the box.) All the color buttons work the same way in adding a color from the palette's Preview pane (the largest frame on the left side of the Color palette). Each button, however, uses a different method to mix the color. The following list examines each button, from left to right:

✔ **Grayscale Slider:** A slider enables you to pick a percentage of black in a color.

✔ **RGB Sliders:** Color mixes as a decimal percentage of red, green, and blue.

- ✔ **CMYK Sliders:** *CMYK,* or *"Process,"* provides four sliders that enable you to mix percentages of cyan, magenta, yellow, and black. Because CMYK is for color on paper and not on computer screens, it may not meet your expectations, but many sources of color codes are in CMYK, so you may find this color mixer very important. (See the Tip at the end of this list.) The pull-down menu indicated by an arrow in the upper-right corner of the Color palette contains a *Percent Values* selection when you want to use percentages rather than decimal values.

- ✔ **HSB Wheel:** Hue, saturation, and brightness are the three variables selected in the HSB wheel. Click the color ball to get the color you want and then move the slider to make it lighter or darker. (The pull-down menu indicated by an arrow in the upper-right corner of the Color palette contains a *Percent Values* selection if you want to use percentages rather than decimal values.)

- ✔ **HSV Picker:** This option sets the hue, saturation, and value to create a color. The outer ring enables you to set the hue by dragging a little box around the ring. Drag the horizontal axis on the inner rectangle to set the saturation, and the vertical axis to set the value.

- ✔ **Palettes:** To the right of the default set of color swatches is a pull-down menu. On the menu, you may choose from 256 colors, 16 colors, 16 grays, desktop colors, and custom colors. The number of colors helps determine the size of the file — the more colors, the larger the file. Custom colors are important for applications where you want a limited set of colors for your color scheme.

- ✔ **Web Color List:** These colors are the 216 Web-safe colors which ensure that the color you see on your Web page looks the same to everyone regardless of the computer or monitor they use. (Well, if the monitor is incorrectly adjusted, the viewer' doesn't see the colors correctly.)

- ✔ **Web Name List:** If you like to choose your color by name, this button is the one for you. Although color names such as orange, gray, blue, and purple are clear enough in meaning, how those colors as DarkSeaGreen, Peru, Moccasin, and DodgerBlue may appear, however, is anyone's guess. (Folks in Los Angeles and Brooklyn may know what DodgerBlue looks like — da bums!) If you choose fuchsia or magenta, you get the same color.

- ✔ **Site Color List:** This button works only if you have the Site window open. This feature enables you to have consistent colors throughout your site. For more information on installing colors on the Color tab of the Site window, see the section "Storing a Color Set in the Site Window," later in this chapter. (The fourth tab on the Site window selects the color view.)

The best way to make the jump from color combinations in art and design to the Web is with Leslie Cabarga's books, *The Designer's Guide to Color Combinations: 500+ Historic and Modern Color Formulas in CMYK* (North Light Books, 1999) and *The Designer's Guide to Global Color Combinations: 750 Color*

Formulas in CMYK and RGB From Around the World (How Design Books, 2001). Not only can you learn a good deal about color combinations and color combination arrangements, the colors are also presented in a context of their use. You get a much better idea of how colors go together than you do from looking at color wheels and gradient rainbows. Also, you get the color codes for the different combinations, saving a good deal of development time.

Tickled #FFC0CB: Color on the Web

Your Web browser interprets color through *hexadecimal codes* (used in a base 16 numbering system that your computer relates to). If I were tickled pink, I would be tickled #FFC0CB as far as my Web browser is concerned. At one time, when the majority of computer monitors used 8-bit color, only a certain subset of colors was assured to be "safe." In this context *safe* refers to looking like the color you designed into your site. However, because 16-, 24-, and 34-bit are now the most common type of monitors shipped with computers, the necessity of Web-safe colors has waned. However, if your audience is likely to have older monitors, by all means pay close attention to the following section.

Practicing safe Web-page coloring!

The 216 Web-safe colors derive from the common values that all 8-bit monitors can read. What looks a certain way on your Web site on your computer looks the same on everyone else's — from the old 8-bit monitors to the newest 64-bit.

In Chapter 1, I discuss the Web Color List button on the Color palette. Now you get to see what makes those colors so safe.

Using the Web Color List button on the Color palette is the best way to ensure that your colors are truly Web safe. In fact, if anyone other than you and your cat looks at your site during development, keeping a Web-safe palette is important.

You can mix colors in many different ways, and folks with an artistic and graphic-design background often display a decidedly non-Web way of thinking about color. GoLive 6, however, enables people who're smart about color and color mixing to more easily obtain the exact colors they want for their Web-page development. That's why GoLive 6 offers so many buttons on the Color palette. The following section examines the three main numbering systems you use for entering color on the Web. So, no matter whether you're new to graphics or are an experienced graphic designer or artist, this section has something for you.

Magic Web values

If you want an exact color match, you can use the values for the *RGB* (Red, Green, and Blue) palettes. Three different sets of values define Web colors. First, in the native language of HTML, you have sets of six hexadecimal values. You express these values in terms of 16 alphanumeric values from 0 to F. In an HTML color value, for example, you may see the number CC9933. That number tells your computer to create a color containing the following values:

Color	Hex	Decimal
Red	CC	204
Green	99	153
Blue	33	51

Most Web and graphic tools perform all the numeric conversions for you, and the only real knowledge you need is to duplicate the value. So, if you see the color value CC9933 and you use that same value in another graphic, you know that you get the same color.

Even if you never understand hexadecimal numbers, you can copy them to your Web page. What's more, if your RGB colors use the following set of numbers, they're Web safe:

00 33 66 99 CC FF

Safe hexadecimal values

Any RGB combination of those values is safe on any Web browser. The value 666699 or the value FFCCFF, for example, is safe, but FFC0CB (pink) isn't, although HTML accepts it as a legitimate color. The following HTML example works like a champ, although it's not Web safe:

```
<body bgcolor="LemonChiffon">
```

So, although LemonChiffon may look good enough to eat on your computer, the way that color comes across the Web to the computer of some poor lady in Sheep Dip, New Zealand, with an 8-bit monitor may end up dazing and confusing her.

The second button on the left side of the Color palette provides RGB colors in percentages — a mixing procedure familiar to graphic artists. Fortunately, mixing Web-safe colors by percentage is even easier than working with hexadecimal values because the percentages are all units of 20 (all except 0, that is). Just remember to count by 20 as you set the percentages of RGB, as the following example shows, and your colors are sure to remain Web safe:

0 20 40 60 80 100

All CMYK values are rendered in percentages, and if you're not doing so, you should. When you enter the percentages for Web-safe colors in CMYK, you will still get the Web-safe RGB colors. However, CMYK (subtractive) and RGB (additive) use a different mixing scheme, and so the percentages you mixed in CMYK may look strange in RGB (and *vice versa*), but they both work for Web-safe colors.

Safe decimal values

Another way to select RGB values is to use decimal values (not percentages) rather than hexadecimal value. To access percentage values, you need to click the arrow in the upper-right corner of the Color palette. A drop-down list appears, where you can toggle percentage values on and off. If you prefer to use decimal numbers rather than percentages, the following are Web-safe:

00 51 102 153 204 255

GoLive 6 includes decimal values for Windows users because you may be working with graphics that you want to match to a color scheme you develop in GoLive 6. The graphic-editing system (such as Adobe Illustrator or Photoshop) may provide colors that they represent in decimal values. (Remember that fact and keep this book handy whenever you wander over and start cranking up your drawing program.)

A simple trick to use to make sure that your mix of colors is Web safe is to select or mix any color you want on your favorite Color palette button. After you get the color mix just the way you want it, click the Web Color List button (that's the Web-safe one) and see whether the one you're mixing up matches a Web-safe color. If not, pick the color closest to it. Or, you can just go to the RGB button (the second from the left on the Color palette) and see whether all percentages are either 0 or a factor of 20.

Coloring Text By Using the Color Well

Notice the Text Color well button in the center of the Text toolbar — the ninth button from the left. (It's the one that looks like a little box or window.) Other color wells appear on the Inspector palette, enabling you to color different objects in GoLive 6. (Chapter 5 describes how to use color wells in tables and cells.) You can use the color wells with all the different buttons of the Color palette, except Site Colors. The Text Color well button on the Text toolbar works just the same as all the other color wells. By using the Text Color well, you can watch your text change colors as you click away on the Color palette.

To color text by using the Text Color well button on the Text toolbar, follow these steps:

1. **Open a page by choosing File⇨New from the menu bar or by pressing Ctrl+N (in Windows) or ⌘+O (on the Mac).**

   A new, blank page appears in Layout view of the document window.

2. **Type a line of text on the new page in Layout view.**

3. **Select the text you typed in Step 2 and then select Header 1 from the Paragraph Format drop-down list on the far-left side of the Text toolbar.**

   You want your text nice and big so that you can see it change colors.

4. **Click the Text Color well *once*.**

   If it's not already on the screen, the Color palette appears.

5. **Select any of the Color palette's buttons.**

   The coloring scheme of your choice appears on the screen.

6. **Select any of the colors on the Color palette.**

   Not only do the colors on the Text Color well button change, but the selected text changes colors too.

Coloring text by using the color wells is a little quicker than dragging colors from the Color palette to the selected text. Try different combinations of text colors with background colors and link colors. Take the time to get it just right because poorly chosen colors can ruin even the most sophisticated of Web pages.

Matching Your Web Page to Your Graphics

One of the greatest features of GoLive 6 is its color-copying tool. You can match to the color of an existing object the color of any object you add to your Web page (including text, background color, or graphic image). To do so, just follow these steps:

1. **Choose File⇨Open or press Ctrl+O (in Windows) or ⌘+O (on the Mac) and then select the page containing the colors you want to copy from the Open dialog box that appears.**

   The page appears in Layout view of the document window.

2. **Choose Window➪Color from the menu bar.**

   The Color palette appears on the screen.

3. **Click either the Web Color List button (seventh from the left) or the Palettes Color button (sixth from the left) on the Color palette.**

   I prefer to use the Web Color List button because after I match a color, I can choose to make it Web safe if I want by selecting from that button the color that's closest to the one I'm matching. (I gotta tell you, though, I've been less likely to worry about Web-safe colors as 8-bit monitors begin appearing in computer museums rather than on desktops.)

4. **Place the mouse pointer on the swatch area of the button.**

   On the Web Color List button, the swatch (it looks like a patch quilt of all different colors) is on the left side of the window. On the Palettes button, the swatch takes up most of the window.

5. **Press the mouse button (the left mouse button on Windows PCs) until you see the pointer become an eyedropper.**

6. **Holding the mouse button down while in Layout view, drag the pointer over the area on your page for the color you want to match.**

   The color in the Preview pane changes as you move the eyedropper pointer over the areas on your page. The color in the Preview pane picks up the color you drag the eyedropper over. (Just for fun, move it anywhere on your computer screen and watch it pick up the colors there and display them in the Preview pane.)

7. **After you use the eyedropper pointer to match the color you want to use, release the mouse button.**

   The color over which you're holding the eyedropper pointer as you release the mouse pointer stays in the Preview pane, and now you can drag and drop the color from the Preview pane to color anything you want on your page. (You can't change the color on a graphic image, however.) Figure 7-1 shows how to select a color from a graphic image on the page (the monk) by moving the eyedropper pointer over it so that the same color appears in the Preview pane of the Color palette. By collecting colors from the robot, you can create a page using the robot's color scheme for your text and links.

In cases where you have a large dominant graphic figure, you can often collect an entire color scheme for a page or even a site by using the color-copying feature of GoLive 6. You need not use all the colors, and sometimes copying colors from a central graphic may not work. However, integrating colors in your text and graphics is one way to make use of color on your page in a pleasing manner.

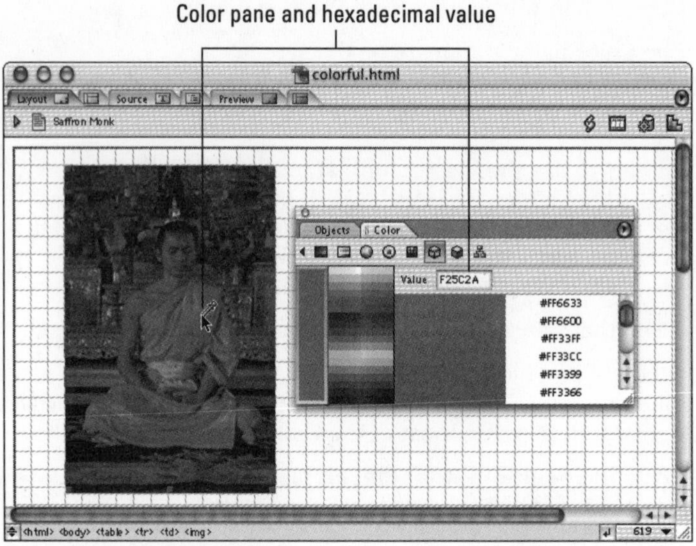

Color pane and hexadecimal value

Figure 7-1:
Copying
color from
a graphic
image — in
this case, a
Buddhist
monk — to
the Preview
pane of
the Color
palette by
using the
eyedropper
mouse
pointer.

Customizing your color scheme

If you go to all the work of creating a color scheme from a graphic, you probably want to save the color scheme so that you can use it on your site or on other pages. GoLive 6 provides an easy way for you to do that. The Custom palette on the Color palette is a well-hidden but valuable tool that you can use for such a purpose. To save your color scheme on the Custom palette of the Color palette, follow these steps:

1. **Choose Window⇨Color from the menu bar.**

   The Color palette appears on your screen.

2. **Click the Palettes color button (sixth from the left).**

   A set of color swatches appears.

3. **Click the arrow in the upper-right corner of the screen to open a drop-down list and then select Custom from that list.**

   A black color grid with 36 black cells for color swatches appears on the Color palette. You can drag any color from the Preview pane to any of the 36 cells to store a color selection.

4. **Color your Web page by using colors you capture from a graphic image, as I describe in Steps 3–6 in the preceding section.**

   You can store in your custom palette each color you copy from your graphic. After the selected color from the graphic appears in the

Preview pane, drag the color from the Preview pane to one of the black custom cells. (Of course, if you select black from the graphic, you have no need to drag it on top of an existing black one.)

After you have your custom palette completed, you can use it to color the remaining text on your page. You may even want to drag the colors to the Color tab of the Site window and use them as site colors. (See Chapter 11 for details about setting site colors.)

Transferring color schemes from outside sources

Some excellent design books dealing with color sets provide the values for different sets. If the values for the color schemes are in RGB (Red, Green, Blue) or CMYK (Cyan, Magenta, Yellow, blacK), you can easily transfer them to your Custom color palette. As I mention in the section "Getting a Mix of Color," at the beginning of this chapter, Leslie Cabarga's books *The Designer's Guide to Color Combinations* and *The Designer's Guide to Global Color Combination* describe percentage colors (CYK) and decimal color values (RBG) for a wide range of color sets. To transfer one of these sets to your Custom color palette, follow these steps (as they lead you down the #FFFF00 Brick Road):

1. **Choose Window⇨Color from the menu bar.**

   The Color palette appears on the screen.

2. **Click the Palettes button on the Color palette.**

   The top palette is a color grid with swatches of 256 colors.

3. **Click the arrow in the upper-right corner of the screen to open a drop-down list and then select Custom from the list.**

   A black color grid appears on the Color palette with 36 cells where any color can be added by dragging the color from the Preview pane of the Color palette.

4. **Select CMYK Sliders by clicking the third button from the left on the Color palette.**

   The CMYK Sliders appear, displaying four sliders, one each for cyan, magenta, yellow, and black. To the far right of each slider is a text box, where values appear as the sliders are moved.

5. **Click the arrow in the upper-right corner of the screen to open a drop-down list and then select Percent Values from the list.**

   You can add values in either decimal or percentage in the text window next to each slider.

6. Enter the values shown in the following table into the text boxes next to each of the CMYK sliders.

I found it much easier to type the color values than to use the sliders to get exactly the right value for each of the four colors. However, if dragging the sliders is easier for you, by all means use the sliders:

	C	M	Y	K
Color 1	39	5	11	0
Color 2	93	26	46	11
Color 3	19	30	77	6

After you enter a value for each color, it appears in the Preview pane of the Color palette. Click the Palettes button (the sixth from the left) on the Color palette and you see the same color in the Preview pane of the Custom palette. Drag these colors into the black cells until all three colors are there.

This color set comes with a good Web designer's seal of approval, so you can rest assured that the colors will look really smart when you use them to color your page. Use one for a background, one for headline fonts, and one for body fonts. Or, you could use one for the page background and one for a table background, making color a central and interesting part of your page.

GoLive 6 preserves the Custom palette you create on the Palettes button of the Color palette. The next time you open GoLive 6 and select the Custom Color palette from the menu on the Palette button, you see all the color sets you've entered. If you're working on a big project, keeping a Custom palette saves you lots of time. If you want, you can put these customized color sets right into Color view of your Site window, as I explain in the following section.

Storing a Color Set in the Site Window

Color is key on the Web. Color is one of the main elements that ties together all the different pages in a site, as well as all the elements on the individual pages that make up the site. A Web site displaying a consistent set of colors feels cohesive to the viewer. You need to work up a color scheme with care, but after you do establish a color set on your site, you want one that's easy to use.

That's certainly the case with any color scheme you create in GoLive 6. Using the Color tab of the Site window, you have a place where you can store the set of colors you plan to use on your site. After your site colors are determined and safely tucked away on the Color tab (or view) of the Site window, your color work is virtually complete. Besides, all the colors stored on the Colors tab of the Site window can be accessed through the Site Color List of the Color palette.

Follow these steps to formulate a color scheme on the Color tab of the Site window:

1. **Choose File⇨Open or press Ctrl+O (in Windows) or ⌘+O (on the Mac) and then select a site from the Open dialog box that appears.**

   The Site window appears on the screen. Depending on what view or tab you had selected before closing the site, different site views appear. If you don't have an existing site, you can create one by choosing File⇨New Site⇨Blank. (With a new site, Files view of the Site window appears first.)

2. **Click the Color tab in the site window.**

   Color view appears. GoLive 6 may have automatically placed colors there, and you see them with untitled names.

3. **Choose Window⇨Color to open the Color palette.**

   After you open the Color palette, click any button with which you want to work. A safe bet is to select the seventh button — Web Color List.

4. **Create or select a color on the Color palette.**

   Enter color values on one of the slider palettes or choose from a swatch selection by clicking the swatches. Whichever method you use, the color appears in the Preview pane of the Color palette.

5. **Place the mouse pointer in the Preview pane of the Color palette, press and hold the mouse button, drag the color into the Name column of Color view in the Site window, and then release the mouse button.**

   A new color box now appears in the Name column of the Color tab, as shown in Figure 7-2. This color carries the label `untitled color`. You can give it any name you want. Even the colors from the Web Name List button now — alas — appear untitled in the Name column. (They do, however, retain their original names in the HTML Name column.)

After you have your colors in the Site window, give them names that are easy to remember. Most colors display no names in the Site window until you give them names yourself — GoLive 6 identifies them only by their hexadecimal values.

If you use a name reflecting the nature of the Web site, that identifier helps you to remember the purpose of the original color set. In the sample Site window shown in Figure 7-2, I copied colors from the robot image shown in Figure 7-1 for use as a theme for the entire site. Hence, I name each color as a "monk color."

Matched color transfer

Figure 7-2:
Site colors
can be
dragged
from the
preview
pane of
the Color
palette to
Color view
of the Site
window and
named to
reflect their
use or
source in
the site.

Using Site Colors to Paint Your Pages

After you select and store your site colors, you use them to color your Web page. If you limit the color scheme for your Web page to the selected color set for that site, your pages and site look professional. To select site colors, follow these steps:

1. **On the File tab of the Site window, open a Web page for that site by double-clicking the page's icon.**

   As you create a site, it automatically creates an index.html page file, and you can open that file or any other file in your site by clicking its icon on the Files tab.

2. **Choose Window⇨Inspector.**

   The Inspector appears on the screen.

3. **Choose Window⇨Color to open the Color palette.**

   The Color palette appears on the screen.

4. **Click the Site Color List button on the Color palette.**

   You now see all the colors you dragged to the Colors tab of the Site window, as described in the preceding section. The names appear in a list and are either the ones you gave them or `untitled color` (see Figure 7-3).

5. **Select an object on your Web page to color by clicking it.**

   You can select individual passages of text to color or go for a more global approach by using the Page button in the upper-left corner of Layout view of the document window. Clicking the Page button sets the Inspector to its Page mode. Click the Page tab in the Page Inspector to find color wells for setting default colors for text, links, and background colors. For more information about the Page tab of the Page Inspector, see the section "Setting the Tone with Background Color," later in this chapter.

6. **Click the color well for the object you want to color in order to activate it.**

   Text uses the Text Color well button on the toolbar. You find the color wells for other objects in the Inspector.

7. **Choose a color by clicking it in the Site Colors List on the Color palette.**

   With a custom set of colors, you don't have to hunt for the color or jockey the sliders into place. The color in the color well changes, and so do the objects you select or target (as, for example, you do with links) to color.

You can also drag the colors directly from the Colors tab of the Site window to the selected objects on the Web page. Dragging is awkward, however, because you must flip back and forth between Layout view of the document window and the Colors tab of the Site window. By using the Color palette, you don't need to bother with switching back and forth because the palette shares the screen with Layout view of the document window. My word to the wise: Life is complex enough. Make things easy on yourself and use the Site Colors List on the Color palette (unless you're showing off for friends; then, doing things the hard way is okay!).

If you take the colors from graphic images in your Web page to use as site colors, the combination provides both page and site integration. Figure 7-3 shows a page that gathers all its site colors from a key graphic image on the page. After you select all the colors from the image, you can use them as the text and link colors to create a seamless color integration of graphic, page, and site elements.

Figure 7-3:
Copying
colors from
a graphic
image for
use as site
colors on a
Web page.

Setting the Tone with Background Color

You want viewers to see but not notice a Web page's background color. The color sets the tone for the page, but you need the content of the page to contrast with the page's background color. A dark background calls for light-colored text and images so that these elements remain visible, and a light-colored background needs darker text and images to create contrast.

Design and style issues aside, coloring the background of your page in GoLive 6 is easy; just follow these steps:

1. **With GoLive launched, choose File⇨New from the menu bar.**

   A new page opens in the document window.

2. **Choose Window⇨Color from the menu bar to open the Color palette.**

   The Color palette appears on the screen.

3. **Choose Window⇨Inspector.**

   The Inspector appears on the screen.

4. **Select the Web Color List button (seventh from the left) from the Color palette and click the color you want to use.**

   Because the background color affects a large area of the page, you want to make sure that you use a color that best sets the "feel" for your site.

5. **Click the Page button in the upper-left corner of the document window, right next to the Page button.**

   When the Page button is clicked, the Inspector becomes the Page Inspector.

6. **Click the color well in the Background row of the Page tab of the Page Inspector and then click to choose from the Color palette the color you want for the background color.**

   The background changes to the new color you selected on the Color palette. With the color well, you can keep clicking different colors until you get just what you want.

 Go to a bookstore or art-supply store and invest in a good book on colors. The more you know about good color combinations, the better off you are in designing pages. You may also want to look online for software that helps you in choosing color sets. Check out www.hotdoor.com on the Web for an Adobe Photoshop plug-in known as Harmony. It helps you select appealing color sets.

Keeping Up Your Background Image

Besides adding a background color, you can add a background image to your page. Any Web graphic you choose can serve as a background image. The browser tiles the image so that it repeats itself in the background of the Web page.

You need to select a background image before you can apply one to your page. Finding or creating the right background image is important. Because a background image acts like tiles on the floor, the wrong background image repeating countless times can look more than awkward. Remember that your Web page must load the graphic file, so try to pick one that is "light" — one with a small file size. You also want to use only a JPG or GIF file for your background image. After you find the file you want to use as your image, follow these steps to add it to the background of your page:

1. **With GoLive launched, choose File⇨New from the menu bar.**

   A new page opens in the document window.

2. **Choose Window⇨Inspector to open the Inspector or undock it by clicking the Inspector tab at the edge of your screen.**

   The Inspector appears on the screen.

3. **Click the Page button in the upper-left corner of Layout view of the document window.**

   The Inspector turns into the Page Inspector.

4. **Click the Page tab of the Page Inspector.**

   The Page tab appears. Near the bottom of the Page tab, you see the Image window.

5. **Click the Image check box in the Background row directly beneath the color well to put a check mark in it.**

   The Link text box in the Inspector activates and you see (Empty Reference!) in the text box.

6. **Enter in the Link text box the path to and the name of the file you want to use as a background image, or click the Browse button — the one with the folder icon — to find the file on your computer.**

   You can also click the Point-and-Shoot button in the Inspector to select the file from the Files tab of the Site window. Just click the Point-and-Shoot button and drag the point-and-shoot line to the graphic file on the Files tab of the Site window. As soon as you select the file for the background, the image appears in Layout view, tiled as the background for your page.

A graphic background can add depth and interest to a page. Alternatively, the background can camouflage all your efforts. (If you've surfed the Web, you probably have seen sites where the Webmaster decided that he needed a cool graphic but neglected to consider the fact that it would hide the site's content.)

Chapter 8

Good Form: Buttons, Boxes, and Lists

Forms provide the Web surfer with a means to enter information into your Web site. The information can be relayed with text elements, selections from pull-down menus, and different types of buttons. The more interactive a Web site is, the more the visitor is involved in the site. Because forms are the primary way users enter feedback, forms are central to Web site planning.

The Line Forms at the Right

Web pages often incorporate forms for viewers to fill out, and GoLive 6 makes creating and using such forms a snap. Many different forms are available for use on the Web, and some things that may not look like forms actually are forms. Some forms consist of little (or big) windows in which the viewer writes. Other forms offer buttons for the viewer to click, press, and pound — well, at least to click. Still others consist of menus and drop-down lists you can put where you want on the page.

Creating your forms is the easy part. Making those forms accomplish some specific task requires a bit more help from GoLive 6. A number of buttons on the Objects tab of the Objects palette can prove to be a big help to you in getting your forms going. Some simple JavaScript programs help extend the useful and creative aspects of forms as well. GoLive 6 writes the JavaScript to resize the window when a button is selected so that the user can control the window size.

One major use of forms on your Web site is to establish a link with a server. Usually, you form these links by using CGI (Common Gateway Interface), PHP, ASP, or some other type of communication link that uses special programming. Unless you know how to program in PHP or one of the other server languages, you need to hire a programmer who does. By using GoLive 6, however, you can create forms that make the site ready to communicate with the server.

Web designers routinely use forms for sending information through what's called the back end or server-side scripts.

If your job is to design Web pages by using GoLive 6, concentrate on how the page will look to the user and how to communicate to the user. Don't worry about how you're going to use the PHP and JavaScript or script them to use the data indicated by the radio buttons and check boxes. That's not your job. Get a clear idea of what the page must do and how it must work to make it look good. What's important at this point is for designers to maintain good communications with the programmers who later add the PHP, ASP, or JavaScript to the site.

An Entire Palette of Form Elements

You use the Form tab of the GoLive 6 Objects palette to place any number of different form elements on your page. The form element goes inside a form *container* represented by a single form icon. Each of the form elements has its own icon. Placing a form element is as simple as opening up the Objects palette (by choosing Window⇨Objects) and then dragging the icon of the form element you want from the Form tab to your Web page. The following list gives you the details on each icon on the Form tab and what it represents on the form itself. (The order of these icons begins with the first one on the left and proceeds to the right in order of placement on the Forms tab of the Objects palette.)

- ✔ **Form:** Placing the Form icon on your page creates a *form container*, a kind of box where you place all the other *form objects* in this list. The Form icon contains both the beginning and ending HTML tags of the form container, which ensures that the HTML code written into the form objects on this list gets carried out. (In Chapter 6, I describe how containers use both start and end tags.)

✔ **Submit Button:** Placing this icon within the form container on your page creates a Submit button, useful for sending the information in the form to somewhere else. Usually, this information goes to a CGI program on a server.

✔ **Reset Button:** Placing this icon within the form container on your page creates a Reset button. A viewer can use a Reset button to clear all the data she entered in the form. (Think of it as a Zap button. *Zap!* — the info is all gone!)

✔ **Button:** With this icon in your form container, you may end up with a simple button on your form. I say *may* because this particular button works only when the viewer is using Internet Explorer 5 or Netscape Navigator 6; earlier versions of these browsers don't support it.

✔ **Input Image:** The Input Image icon is just like a button icon except that you select which image you want to put on the button. When you place the Input Image icon on the Web page, a graphic placeholder appears and you can then, by using the Form Image Inspector, place the graphic just as you would place a graphic on a standard image placeholder (as described in Chapter 2).

✔ **Label:** A Label element in a form is associated with a text field. Basically, the Label element is a button that, when pressed, selects the text field. When you design a Web page by using the Label element, you use the Form Label Inspector to make a connection between the Label element and the text field. A point-and-shoot button on the Form Label Inspector makes connecting the Label element with a text field easy because you just drag the point-and-shoot line to the text field you want the Label element connected to. You want to use a Label element judiciously because not all browsers or versions of browsers support this object. Clicking a label on a form selects, or brings into focus, whichever field the label describes. (If a field is *in focus,* that field is selected.) This type of object can prove useful if you have several different text fields on a form; the user needs only to click the label of a specific field to prepare that field to receive text.

✔ **Text Field:** Placing this icon within the form container on your page creates a text field, great for when you need to add small areas of text to a form, such as fields for a respondent's name, address, and phone number. Drag and drop the Label icon I describe in the preceding paragraph inside the form container and next to a text field on a form, and you have a labeled text field.

✔ **Password:** Placing the Password icon within the form container on your page creates a text field for entering a password. For commercial sites, Password objects can act as gatekeepers to specific sections of your site.

✔ **Text Area:** If you want the viewer to enter a good deal of text, such as an entire paragraph, place the Text Area icon within the form container on your page to add to your form an area where the viewer can write down her thoughts, ideas, complaints, and feelings.

✔ **Check Box:** Use the Check Box icon's checking feature to provide a user with more than one choice to select. You can determine the status of a check box (as checked or not) by using a JavaScript function that compiles a record of which check boxes contain a check and which don't.

✔ **Radio Button:** If you want the viewer to enter only one choice, place the Radio Button icon within the form container on your page to place this object on a form. On a single form containing radio buttons, clicking one button to turn it on automatically turns the others off (as in "Click one: Male, Female").

✔ **Popup Menu:** A pop-up menu provides the viewer with several choices on a menu that appears wherever the form element was set up, seemingly out of nowhere. You use these menus to set several links into a very small place or to provide the user with a selection of different page actions. For example, you may use the menu to link users to pages for men's, women's, or children's clothing.

✔ **List Box:** Similar in function to the pop-up menu in providing the user with several choices, the List Box object, on the other hand, keeps all its choices right there on-screen at all times. Place the List Box icon within the form container on your page if you want the viewer to see all the options at one time without having to open the menu.

✔ **File Browser:** You use the button and text window this icon creates to view the contents of a PHP file on a server. You create the path of the file browser to the file browser PHP program with the Form File Inspector. When you press the button, the contents of the PHP file appear in the text window.

✔ **Hidden:** The Hidden text window element created by the Hidden icon is great for storing data that visitors can use interactively in the Web-page design. Because the form is hidden, you can put as much information in it as you want without taking up real estate on the viewable portion of the page. Hidden elements are useful if you're storing data that someone can open on-screen only if necessary. Using Hidden elements helps keep the screen clear and clean so that the viewer can focus on what he needs. I like to think of Hidden elements as underground storage tanks.

✔ **Key Generator:** The Key Generator object applies to only the Netscape browser. It generates three key sizes from which to choose. You then use the selected size to generate an encrypted challenge. Any key does the job.

✔ **Fieldset:** Place the Fieldset icon within the form container on your page to visually group any of your form elements in a certain area on your form. It works only in Microsoft Internet Explorer Version 4.0 and later, but be careful in using it on the grid. (The grouping mechanism in the Fieldset object likes to generate its own grid.) Using the Fieldset object to visually group form elements aids viewers in responding to data in the forms or that users enter into the forms. When viewed in Internet Explorer, the grouped fields appear in their own window on the page.

Whew! The preceding list describes *many* forms, and although some are marginal because they're browser specific, you can make your pages do plenty by using the forms GoLive 6 generates. To get more use from your forms, you need either some JavaScript that GoLive can automatically generate for you or some back-end (server-side) scripts, like PHP and ASP, that can be developed using Source view or generated using dynamic links.

The User Gets a Word In

Two types of text elements, *Text Field* and *Text Area,* enable you to create a page where the viewer can type words, numbers, or anything else she wants. In the world of PHP and PHP, this type of text goes to a server for processing. If you set up an eBusiness by placing order forms on your Web pages, for example, you may use a Text Field element to enable the viewer to type into a field on the form the kind of products she wants. The word the user types into the Text Field element then goes to the server for comparison against your company's inventory. The server then returns a response page to the viewer, informing her whether that particular item is available.

Name, please: The Text Field element

Setting up a Text Field element consists of two basic parts: First, you must put the element on the page where you want it, and then you must provide values for its attributes. In computerese, an *attribute* is a characteristic or property of a form or element. A text element, for example, has attributes of name and size. The *value* is a property of the attribute. If you use a text element to enter two-letter abbreviations of state names, for example, the value for the attribute *name* may be State and the value for the attribute *size* may be 2. Follow these steps to set up the Text Field element on a Web page:

1. **With GoLive 6 launched, choose File⇨New from the menu bar to open a new page.**

   A new page appears in the document window.

2. **Choose Window⇨Objects from the menu bar to open the Objects palette on-screen.**

3. **Click the Form tab on the Objects palette.**

   The Form tab is the third one from the left on the Objects palette.

4. **Drag the Form icon (first one on the left) from the Objects palette to the open page.**

   A rectangle appears on the page. This rectangle is the form container.

5. **Drag the Text Field icon (seventh from the left) from the Objects palette to the page and drop it inside the form container.**

   The Text Field element is now where you want it on your Web page. In Layout view, you see the outline of the form rectangle around the Text Field element, but on your Web page you do not (see Figure 8-1).

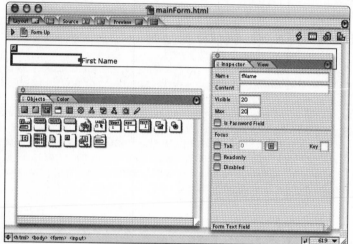

Figure 8-1:
A Text Field element inside a form container with a text label.

Adding values

After the Text Field element is in place, you need to adjust it to the size you want and fill in values for the attributes. Follow these steps:

1. **Make sure that you have a page open in Layout view of the GoLive 6 document window.**

2. **Hide the Objects palette by pressing Shift+Ctrl+Tab (in Windows) or Shift+Ctrl+Tab (on the Macintosh) anywhere on the page.**

   Hiding the palettes that you don't need visible on-screen is a good idea so that you don't clutter the screen too much while you're working. (Note that the sequence on the Mac includes the Ctrl (*not* the Command key).

3. **Choose Window⇨Inspector from the menu bar.**

   The Inspector appears on the screen.

4. **Select the Text Field object on your page.**

   The Inspector becomes the Form Text Field Inspector.

5. **In the Name text box of the Form Text Field Inspector, enter the name of the form.**

   Usually, giving the form a name that approximates what the viewer types in it is a good idea. A zip code form you name **Zip,** for example, helps you to remember the purpose of the form. The name is referenced as a unique element name in the form, so be sure that each Text Field element has a unique name within the *same* form. Note also that the name becomes the fieldname of a database that could be generated (refer to Figure 8-1).

6. **In the Value text box (in Windows) or the Content text box (on the Mac) of the Form Text Field Inspector, either do nothing (leave it blank) or type what you want to appear in the text box.**

   Generally, you leave this value blank because you want the viewer to enter the value. If you do enter a value name in this text box — for example, **Enter ZIP code here** — the user can overwrite it with what he enters in the text box. I recommend, however, that you just add a label next to the text box telling the viewer what to do rather than put a word or phrase inside the text box to tell him.

7. **Specify the width of the visible text field in the Visible text box of the Form Text Field Inspector.**

   The width of the text field on the Web page gives the user an idea of what to write. You abbreviate states, for example, by using two-letter codes, such as CA, TX, or NY. If the text field for a state is only two letters wide, the viewer has a better idea of what to type in the text field. (She knows that she can't spell out the entire name of the state or even use an abbreviation longer than two letters.) For any text field you designate for a user's name, you want a wider space — one sufficient to contain a person's entire name, whether she uses Kay, Kate, or Kathryn.

8. **In the Max text box of the Form Text Field Inspector, enter the maximum number of characters the text field can accept.**

   As with the Visible text box, you want the Max text box to reflect how many characters you intend the user to enter into the text field on the form. The value in the Max text box, however, terminates any text longer than the amount you set there. With fields you designate for names and similar words of unknown lengths, you can leave this text box blank. For fields you designate for phone numbers, zip codes, and other values of known lengths, specifying the maximum number of characters that users can enter into the field is a good idea. (They can take it to the Max — but no further.)

9. **If you're designating the text field as a Password field, click to select the Is Password Field check box on the Form Text Field Inspector.**

   If you designate a text field as a Password field, bullets (or asterisks) appear in the text box rather than the text that a user is entering. This feature helps the viewer feel secure that no one can see his password.

Setting up your attributes individualizes and clarifies your Text Field elements. By doing so, you not only present the viewer with a clearer set of options but also set the stage for using the information that users will enter. The names of the text fields are used by both JavaScript and the server database to identify fields to use or store the information provided by the people who use your Web page.

Text fields in a single-form container

Suppose that you want to create on your Web page a contact form that asks for a person's name, address, phone number, and e-mail address. You want the form to send this information to the server through a PHP script. If all the text fields are in one form, a single click of the Submit button sends to the right place the information the user puts into the forms.

To make arranging the text fields easier, you can use either a table or the GoLive 6 Grid feature. (For more information about tables, see Chapter 5; for more information about the GoLive Grid feature, see Chapter 3.) As is the case with every other object on a Web page, unless you use a grid or a table, you can never tell just where the objects will appear on the page. Figures 8-2 (showing a form in Layout view) and 8-3 (showing the same form in Preview view) show several text fields in a single container that I position by using a grid I put right inside the form container.

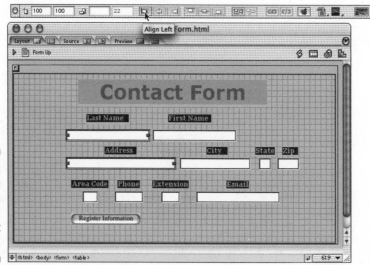

Figure 8-2:
Elements
and labels
on a grid
(in Layout
view).

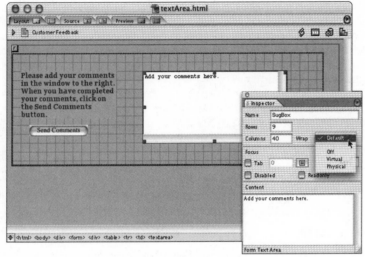

Figure 8-3:
Text area
elements
provide
more room
for viewer
input.

To work with forms and the grid, first drag the Form icon to the page in Layout view and then drag the Grid icon into the rectangle the Form icon creates. Otherwise, all the form elements you place inside the rectangle that the Form icon creates on your page pull to the left and top of the page.

Notice that in Figure 8-2 the grid lies fully inside the Form rectangle — the Form container that the box containing an F in the upper-left corner of the screen denotes. (The F is just an icon label to help you differentiate the form rectangle from the many Text Field element rectangles that reside within the form container.) As you can see in Figure 8-3, the form-container tag and rectangle don't appear on the Web page (and neither does the grid).

In laying out a page of forms, don't forget to use the alignment tools. Notice on the toolbar shown in Figure 8-2 that the alignment tools are available for placing form objects. Figure 8-3 shows the page objects centering vertically and horizontally on the page — thanks to the alignment tools. (See Chapter 3 for details on aligning objects on the grid.)

Text Area elements

Text Area elements are similar to Text Field elements. They have different attributes and uses, however. You employ text fields to gather specific data, and text areas are used for more general or in-depth descriptions or comments. An eBusiness, for example, may employ text areas rather than text fields to gather customer comments about its service or special shipping instructions. You place Text Area elements on a page in the same way as you place a Text Field element, as I describe in the section "Name, please: The Text Field element," earlier in this chapter. The exception is that now you use the Form tab of the Objects palette to place a Text Area icon on your page inside the Form container.

After you place your Text Area icon where you want it, you use the Inspector (with different attributes) to fine-tune the text area. Follow these steps:

1. **With a page open in Layout view, hide the Objects palette by pressing Ctrl+Shift+Tab (in Windows) or Ctrl+Shift+Tab (on the Macintosh).**

2. **Choose Window⇨Inspector from the menu bar.**

   The Inspector appears on the screen.

3. **Select the Text Area element on your page.**

   The Inspector becomes the Form Text Area Inspector. Notice that the attributes are different in the Properties area of the Inspector from the way they are in the same area of the Form Text Field Inspector, which I describe in the section "Adding values," earlier in this chapter. Notice also that *resize points* (or handles) appear on the lower-right corner, bottom, and right side of the text area after you select it. You can push and pull on the handles with your mouse pointer to adjust the text area to any size you want.

4. **In the Name text box of the Form Text Area Inspector, enter the name of the form.**

   Provide a name that reminds you of the text area's purpose. You may, for example, call it **CusCom** or **SugBox** if you're designing it for customer comments or as a suggestion box, respectively. Keeping the names within eight characters reduces the chances of conflict with database programs limited to eight characters. (The name you type in is never seen on the page. It is used by JavaScript and server-side programs to identify a specific form element.)

5. **In their respective text boxes, enter the number of rows and columns you want for the Text Area element in the Properties area of the Form Text Area Inspector.**

   If you push and pull on the resize points to resize the text area, the row and column values appear there with the changed values filled in for you, so you don't need to fill in these text boxes on the Inspector. The default size for a text area is 4 rows and 40 columns — and any other values appearing there indicate that you have already resized the text area. The rows and columns are measured in pixel units.

6. **Use the Wrap drop-down list of the Form Text Area Inspector to select the type of wrap you want for the text that someone enters into the text area.**

Select Default, Off, Virtual, or Physical. To use the visitor's browser's settings, select Default. Selecting Off ignores the columns you enter, preventing wrapping. Virtual and physical wraps force wraps at the column limits. *Wraps* means that the text wraps around in the text window rather than disappear straight out of the window (refer to Figure 8-3).

Now you can post both Text elements and Text Area elements on your page. A Submit button added in the form lets you send all the contents of whatever the user enters in the text area, just like with the smaller Text element. The differences between the two types of elements are subtle but crucial. Using one element or the other depends on what type of information you want the user to enter when she uses your page. Arranging and labeling text areas with the other elements in the form container and on the page as a whole determines how and whether you get from the user the information you want.

Tag containers don't enclose text fields, but they do enclose text areas. The `<Textarea>` and `</Textarea>` tags act as a container surrounding all text that someone enters into a Text Area element. By contrast, GoLive 6 considers all text in a Text Field object as a property of the value attribute of the unary `<Input...>` tag.

Using focus in elements!

The context-sensitive Inspectors for Text Area and Text Field elements also include a Focus text box. The primary purpose of *focus attributes* is to handle the transfer of information that a user enters into a form element from that form element to a server, although the Focus text box does provide some programming aids as well. Programmers use inactive (disabled) elements of forms to keep information in place and buttons inactive until a PHP, CGI, or some other script element activates them. (In Figure 8-1, you can see the Focus section in the Form Text Field Inspector.) The concept of *focus* with text elements is akin to *click* in button elements. Essentially, *focus* refers to the selection of the element — usually it's in use by the user typing information. You need to address each of the following focus attributes:

✔ **Tabs:** The Tab text box and button on the Inspector enable you to decide the order of tab stops on your form. If a viewer uses the Tab key to navigate through a set of elements in a form, you need to make sure that the viewer goes to the next correct element in the form. For example, if the user first enters her last name and then is supposed to enter her first name, you want to make sure that she doesn't tab to some other form element than FirstName. Therefore, you would have LastName with a tab value of 1 and FirstName with a tab value of 2 and so forth through the entire form in the sequence you want the form completed. The last element in the form would have the highest tab value. Type in the text box the tab number you want to correspond with the order in which you want the viewer to tab through your page. If you press the Auto-tab button (the one displaying the pound [#] sign), you can click each tab in the order you want them to appear. A little number in a box appears next to each text field as you click it while you're pressing the Auto-tab button.

✔ **Read Only:** You may want to use a text field or area to leave a message on your Web page or to generate one from a PHP or JavaScript script. In that case, you don't want the user scribbling in the text field. On the Web page, the viewer doesn't see the text area or field — only the message it contains. Check the Readonly check box in the Form Text Field or Form Text Area Inspector with the element selected. (GoLive 6 collapses the two words *Read only* into *Readonly.*)

✔ **Disable:** A field you disable is invisible to the Web-page viewer, so why ever bother to put one on your page if you're going to disable it? (You may well ask!) Sometimes, Web page designers want to disable a field until a visitor meets certain conditions and then have the PHP or JavaScript script remove that field from the disabled list so that it appears (like magic) on-screen before your very eyes. Check the Disable check box in the Form Text Field or Form Text Area Inspector with the intended element selected.

✔ **Content (in Text Area elements only):** Typing a message in the Content text box of the Inspector places a message in the text area on your page as soon as the browser loads that Web page. You can use the data of the Contents text box as a message to the viewer, as information you use in a script, or as a place for JavaScript or PHP scripts to insert information on the page from the server or from some other type of user input. For example, using either JavaScript or PHP scripts, you may want to have different messages appear to remind the user to fill in any empty form elements. The message appears in the text area when a Submit button has been pressed and the script launched by the button finds an empty form element. In turn, a message is sent to the text area reminding the user to fill in all form elements.

Check This Out: Check Boxes and Radio Buttons

Check boxes and radio buttons provide a way for the viewer to quickly respond to fixed-choice questions. Making responding to a question easy for a visitor increases your chance of getting the information you're requesting; that's why so many Web sites supply a set of either check boxes or radio buttons — to solicit information from the viewer. Educators and trainers use check boxes and radio buttons in online quizzes and tests. The information from these objects goes into a PHP, ASP, CGI, or JavaScript script that either returns the results to the user or sends it to a server for further processing. The following sections describe how to add radio buttons and check boxes to your Web-page forms.

Adding radio buttons to your page

To get radio buttons to work the way you want, you must first place them on your Web page and then define them appropriately so that GoLive 6 knows exactly what to do with them. (Labeling your radio buttons — that is, adding text next to each button on your Web page to define the button for a user — is a separate step, and I cover it in the section "Labeling your radio buttons and check boxes," later in this chapter.)

To place a radio button on your page by using GoLive 6, follow these steps:

1. **With GoLive 6 launched, choose File⇨New from the menu bar to open a new page.**

   A new page appears in the document window.

2. **Choose Window⇨Objects from the menu bar to open the Objects palette.**

3. **Click the Form tab (third one from the left) on the Objects palette to select it.**

   The form and element icons all appear on the Objects palette.

4. **Drag the Form icon (first one on the left) to your page in the document window.**

   The form container appears on your page as a long rectangle. It fills the width of the page and then expands downward as you add elements to the form container.

5. **Drag the desired number of Radio Button icons (eleventh from the left) from the Form tab of the Objects palette and drop them in the form container on your page.**

   As soon as you drop the icons, they appear as radio buttons.

6. **Select a radio button on your page by clicking it.**

   The selected button now displays a square around it, indicating that you selected it. (Select only one button at a time because you must set each button's attribute individually. If you try to grab more than one at the same time, GoLive 6 doesn't allow it.)

7. **Choose Window⇨Inspector from the menu bar to open the Inspector.**

   The Inspector becomes the Form Radio Button Inspector. You can now use the Inspector to work on the selected radio button. (Remember that you must select each button in turn to work on it.)

8. **Enter a one-word description of the category of responses you expect to get in the Group text box of the Form Radio Button Inspector.**

   The Group text box holds the key to using radio buttons on your form page. A *group* is a set of radio buttons of which the user can select only one. (Users can make only one choice among a set of radio buttons in a single group.) A multiple-choice test, for example, may contain ten questions. Each question offers a *group* of radio buttons next to the possible answers, and only one answer among them is correct. You can, therefore, select only one button. For example, you might name one group Gender for a question about gender and name another one Income for a question about income categories. If the user first selects one radio button in a group and then selects a second button, that second action deselects the first button. No matter how many choices a group may offer, a user can choose only one. (Is that your *final* answer?)

9. **Enter a one-word description of the value for each button you're associating with the Group in the Value text box of the Form Radio Button Inspector.**

   Several buttons can belong to the same group, but each button in the group must have a unique value. A group you name Gender in Step 8, for example, can have two buttons under the group name Gender. You want to assign one of the Gender buttons a Value name of **Male** and the other a Value name of **Female**. (You select each button individually and type the appropriate names in the Group and Value text boxes of the Inspector.)

That's all there is to creating radio buttons. Be sure to use them only when you want just a single response. (If you want more than a single response to a question, see the next sections on check boxes.) On your Web page, after the user clicks a radio button, only one button in each group stays selected. If the user selects more than one, he deselects the other (turns it to the Off position). A JavaScript, PHP, ASP, ASP.NET, CGI, or other script returns the value of a selected radio button for use in tabulation. For example, you may want to tabulate the number of men and women who visit your site or some other characteristic of the folks who visit your site.

Placing check boxes on your page

Web page designers use a check box whenever they assume that the user may make more than a single choice for a category. A particular Web page design may, for example, include questions about recreation and offer check boxes for the visitor to select for different types of activities. Setting up check boxes on your Web page forms is similar to setting up radio buttons, with just a few key differences.

To place a check box on your Web page by using GoLive 6, follow these steps:

1. **With GoLive 6 launched, choose File⇨New from the menu bar to open a new page.**

   A new page appears in the document window.

2. **Choose Window⇨Objects from the menu bar to open the Objects palette.**

3. **Click the Form tab (third one from the left) on the Objects palette to select it.**

   The form and element icons all appear on the Objects palette.

4. **Drag the Form icon (first one on the left) to your Web page in the document window.**

   The form container appears on your page as a long rectangle.

5. **Drag the number of Check Box icons (tenth from the left) you want on your page from the Form tab of the Objects Palette and drop them in the form container.**

   Little, square check boxes appear where you drag and drop them in the form container.

6. **Choose Window⇨Inspector from the menu bar to open the Inspector.**

   The Inspector becomes the Form Check Box Inspector. You can now use the Inspector to work on the selected check boxes. (Remember that you must select each check box in turn to work on it.)

7. **Click a check box on your page to select it to work on.**

   The Inspector becomes the Form Check Box Inspector.

8. **Enter a one-word description of the category of responses you expect to get in the Name text box of the Form Check Box Inspector.**

   Unlike with radio buttons, when the user selects only one value from a group, she can select several check boxes with the same name. Naming several check boxes with the same name, **Recreation**, doesn't mean that the user can select only one check box. Rather, the user can select each check box with the same name and a different value. For example, if you want input about gender, you want only a single choice. However, if you want to know about the different types of recreation a person is involved in, you should make several choices available. The essential difference between Radio Button elements and Check Box elements is that with radio buttons, a user can select only one with the same name (group); with check boxes, she can select several that have the same name.

9. **Enter a one-word description you're associating with the name of the selected check box in the Value text box for each check box.**

   A set of check boxes with the same name can have as many different values as you want (the only limit is the number of check boxes), and the user can select as many of the check boxes as he wants. Among the check boxes that you name Recreation — in the Name text box of the Inspector, for example — you may assign such different values as **Hiking**, **Swimming**, and **Skydiving** in the Value text box. The user may participate in all those types of recreation and, therefore, want to check all the boxes.

Creating check boxes and radio buttons in GoLive 6 is easy. The names and values you provide for these elements are used in linking to server databases or with JavaScript to present calculated data on the screen. Just remember that when you want the user to enter a single choice for a question, use a radio button, and when several responses are possible, use the check box.

Labeling your radio buttons and check boxes

Labeling radio buttons and check boxes is important because, unlike what you can do with some other buttons, you can't place a label in the radio button or check box itself. The easiest way to label radio buttons and check boxes is simply to type a name next to the button. You can use the grid to make everything look neater and make your designing tasks simpler, especially if you want more than a single column of radio buttons or check boxes on your page. If you're using the GoLive 6 grid, described in Chapter 3, you can drag the Text Box icons next to the radio buttons and check boxes on your form for use in creating labels.

Making the Buttons Behave

Using a Form Button element is one way to put on your page an object to be used to initiate an action or link to a page. This section examines how to put the button on your page and use it. The Button icon (fourth from the left on the Forms tab of the Objects palette) generates a button element on your page when you drag and drop it there. It's only one of the button elements, and, ironically, it is a bit troublesome at the time of this writing (see the following Warning paragraph). Therefore, rather than use the unadorned Button element, I want to use the Submit and Reset buttons as "normal" buttons. In other words, you see how to make a normal button from a specialized button element in this section and put it to use on your Web pages. However, before doing that, I want to show you ever so briefly what you *can do* with the Button elements.

Netscape Navigator Version 6 and later and Internet Explorer Version 5 and later recognize the GoLive 6 Button element. Earlier versions of either browser show only the label with no button on the page.

When you use the Button element by dragging its icon (fourth icon from the left on the Form tab of the Objects palette), you have a unique advantage: It's the only button that offers some flexibility of appearance in working a button into your design without requiring you to import a special graphic as an image. By clicking the text area of the button image on your Web page, you can type any name you want and format the text just as you would any text, as described in Chapter 2. You can even use Cascading Style Sheets to create special background colors for the text on the button. (For more information about Cascading Style Sheets, also known as CSS, see Chapter 10.)

Because this button is somewhat problematic now for cross-browser use, I forgo a detailed description of the process for getting it on your page and using it. However, if you follow the steps in this section for using the other buttons, other than the name being derived from the value attribute, the process is almost identical. Use it with the knowledge that many viewers will never see it as a button. Also, as the following paragraph points out, other form elements can be thrown out of order when this button is used.

Forms are *arrays,* and you associate a number with each element in a form, beginning (automatically) with *0* and incrementing the number with each form object you add to the form — that is, all the objects you place in the form container on your page. So, if you have 10 elements in your form, they are automatically recognized from 0–9. (This has nothing to do with either the user or designer; it's built into HTML.)

In using code, programmers sometimes refer to an element in a form by its number rather than by its name. If one browser doesn't recognize a tag such as `<button...>` (which is used by the button element) as a form but another browser does, the element numbers get all thrown out of whack. If, for example, you have three check boxes, a text area, a `<button....>` tag, and a text field on a page, in that order, Netscape Navigator counts the text field as element 4. (Remember that it counts the first check box as 0.) Internet Explorer, however, counts the text field as 5 because it counts the `<button....>` tag as 4. If you're using JavaScript or a server-side script on your page, these types of differences can result in catastrophic messes.

So the problem isn't only that in one browser you see a button and in the other browser you see only text where you place the button. Rather, if you enter the same data into the forms but the programmer uses numbers rather than name references with the forms and the form elements, the set of information that the scripts on different browsers collects is entirely different in the two browsers.

What if you really want just a plain-vanilla button and you don't want to mess with HTML code to create it? The Button icon, fourth from the left on the Form tab on the Objects palette, really isn't an option if you want to keep the folks using earlier versions of Netscape Navigator happy, but you do have a way to get around this mess. Follow these steps:

1. **With GoLive 6 launched, choose File⇨New from the menu bar to open a new page.**

   A new page appears in the document window.

2. **Choose Window⇨Objects from the menu bar to open the Objects palette.**

   The **Objects** palette appears on your screen.

3. **Click the Form tab (third one from the left) on the Objects palette to select it.**

   The form and element icons all appear on the Objects palette.

4. **Drag the Form icon (first one on the left) to your Web page in the document window.**

   The form container appears on your page as a long rectangle.

5. **Drag the Submit Button icon (third icon from the left) into the form container on your page.**

   Earlier versions of both Internet Explorer and Netscape Navigator recognize the Submit button, so it's a good place to start for creating a new button. When you release the icon on the page, you see a button with a Submit label on it. Select that button.

6. **Choose Window⇨Inspector from the menu bar to open the Inspector.**

   The Inspector becomes the Form Button Inspector.

7. **In the Name text window of the Form Button Inspector (where it reads** submitButtonName)**, replace the name with the name you want for the button.**

   This name is the one that programmers use to reference the button. Make this name a single word, but make sure, too, that it's one that identifies what the button does. You may, for example, use a button to launch a calculation script. If you name that button Calculate, you can more easily determine what script to link to that button.

8. **In the Button portion (near the top) of the Form Button Inspector, select Normal for the button type.**

   The name on the button changes from Submit to Button. At last! A plain, simple button.

9. **Click the check box next to the Label text box of the Form Button Inspector and enter the message you want to appear on the button.**

You want this label to tell the user what to do. The label `Click Here` in the context of the other objects on the page is usually clear enough. If you have lots of buttons on a page, however, entering a more specific label, such as **Click here to calculate taxes**, in this text box better clarifies the button's job.

The procedure to make a normal button from a Submit button is fairly simple, and it would be even simpler if you didn't have to change the Submit button into a generic button element. However, you now know how to make your own button; and don't think that because you have to cobble it out of a Submit button that there's anything unusual about your button.

After you create one Normal button by reconfiguring a Submit button, copy as many as you need and paste them to your page. Just select the completed Normal button; choose Edit⇨Copy and then choose Edit⇨Paste and keep on pasting until you have all you want. Then just change the names and labels.

Working with Lists and Menus

You find two main kinds of menus or lists — list boxes and pop-up menus — on the Form tab of the Objects palette. You can use either one to give the viewer a choice of options. The designer can designate the selections on a menu or list anything that he can either link to or create dynamically on the page. (You actually have two sources for the pop-up menu: one from the Form Tab and the other from the Smart tab of the Objects palette.) I describe the list box first, in the following section, because it's the least complex of the two.

Using the list box

In a list box, a number of options for a user are always visible on-screen; the view never limits a visitor to just one option, as is the case with a pop-up menu. All the viewer needs to do is select one or more choices, and any scripts in the page use these choices. Follow these steps to set up a list box on your Web-page form:

1. **Begin with a page open in Layout view of the GoLive 6 document window.**

2. **Choose Window⇨Objects from the menu bar to open the Objects palette.**

   The Objects palette appears on your screen.

3. **Click the Form tab (third one from the left) on the Objects palette to select it.**

   The form and element icons all appear on the Objects palette.

4. **Drag the Form icon (first one on the left) to your Web page in the document window.**

   The form container appears on your page as a long rectangle.

5. **Drag the List Box icon (thirteenth icon from the left) into the form container on your page.**

   You see the List Box with First, Second, and Third labels in its window. The List Box object is automatically selected as you first place it in the form container on your page. Leave this object selected.

6. **Choose Window⇨Inspector from the menu bar to open the Inspector.**

   The Inspector becomes the Form List Box Inspector.

7. **In the Name text box of the Form List Box Inspector, provide a name for the list box to identify its purpose.**

   Use a name that you or a programmer can quickly understand. If you're listing a selection of fruits, for example, enter **Fruit** as the name of the list box.

8. **In the Rows text box of the Form List Box Inspector, specify the number of rows you want visible on-screen.**

   If you want the user to see all items without scrolling, enter a number of rows that is equal to the number of selections you intend to show in the list box. If you want to take up only a certain number of rows on the page, regardless of how many items are on the list, enter that number; the viewer must scroll down through the list box's contents to bring the rest of the items into view.

9. **Click the Multiple Selection check box of the Form List Box Inspector if you want to enable the viewer to select more than a single item from the list at one time.**

   Using a list box is a good way to entice an e-customer to make more than a single choice, so don't ignore the Multiple Selection check box. Of course, if the list box shows dress sizes, don't confuse the user by enabling her to choose more than a single size for each item. (Hmmm, I think that I need a size 8 petite — yeah, right!)

10. **In the Label column in the Focus area of the Form List Box Inspector, start filling in the entries for your list by selecting a row and typing the name of your entry in the text box below the column. Repeat this action for every entry you want to add to your list.**

    These labels you type appear as selections in the list box. You want to use labels that clearly describe the choices. Click the check box in the right-most column next to each item if you want an item automatically selected on startup. If you have a list of fruit, examples of what you may enter as labels include **apricots**, **apples**, **oranges**, and **pears**. See Figure 8-4 for a list-box selection in the Form List Box Inspector consisting of different cameras. (Yes, you can still find film cameras! They're not all digital — yet.) If you want more rows, just click the New button at the bottom of the Form List Box Inspector.

11. **In the Value column of the Focus section, type in the text box at the bottom of the column the value you want to associate with the label.**

    Depending on the nature of the item and how the script or program will use the information, you can enter just about any text or number you want as the value. In Figure 8-4, the value simply refers to the placement of the item in the list. Often, you give the label name to the value, too. What you enter as a value here, however, really depends on what information you want the selection to send to the script.

12. **Use the Delete and Duplicate buttons at the bottom of the Form List Box Inspector to delete or duplicate any of the selected label and value pairs.**

    You may, for example, want to duplicate a label and then either make small edits to each name (changing *Cars* to **Cars1**, **Cars2**, and **Cars3**, for example) or give different values to the same label. Labels and values are deleted as pairs. To change a label or value, just type another name in the text windows at the bottom.

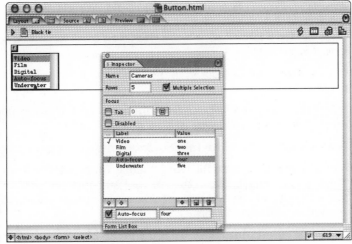

Figure 8-4:
Labeling
items for a
list box in
the Form
List Box
Inspector.

With all the selectable form elements available to you, you can show the initial element in the selected mode by using the Selected check box in both the Form Radio Button and Form Check Box Inspectors to automatically select an item on startup. Radio buttons and check boxes are filled in or checked, and menus display items already highlighted. By making items appear already selected on their Web pages, e-retailers encourage a specific choice that they want to see a visitor make. A line next to a check box, for example, may read Check if you want to receive news of new products and services. The ever-helpful Web page, however, already displays the check box with a check mark inside.

Pop-Ups and URL Pop-Ups

You can place pop-up menus on your page the same way as you place a list box, except that you use the Popup Menu icon (the twelfth from the left) and the Form Popup Menu Inspector. The major difference between pop-up menus and list boxes is that pop-ups generally show only a single message and the user clicks the vertical arrows at the side of the box side to reveal the rest of the selections.

GoLive 6 does provide an interesting twist on a pop-up menu, however — one that's already rigged with script to jump to a choice of other Web pages. Rather than take the pop-up icon from the Forms tab of the Objects palette, you use the URL pop-up from the Smart tab of the Objects palette. A URL Popup Inspector enables you to enter, browse, or point-and-shoot URLs to your heart's content. Follow these steps to set it up and link away:

1. **With GoLive 6 launched, choose File⇨New from the menu bar to open a new page.**

2. **Choose Window⇨Objects from the menu bar to open the Objects palette.**

3. **Select the Smart tab (second from the left) of the Objects palette to display the ten Smart icons (with a greenish tint.)**

4. **Drag the URL Popup icon into the form container on the page.**

   A pop-up menu bar with the word Choose appears in the form container. The key difference between this element and ones pulled from the Form tab of the Objects palette is that these elements are smart and contain script to do things with forms.

5. **Choose Window⇨Inspector from the menu bar.**

   The Inspector appears, becoming the URL Popup Inspector, as shown in Figure 8-5. You see Label and URL columns in a list box in the Inspector. One label, Choose, appears already filled in for you in the Label column, as does a second label for Adobe Systems, Inc., displaying Adobe's accompanying URL in the URL column. (Figure 8-5 shows several more labels and URLs I added here.)

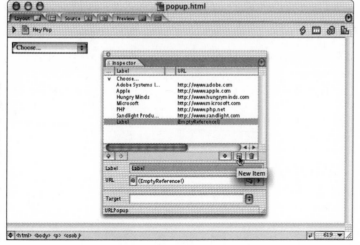

Figure 8-5:
The URL
Popup
Inspector,
displaying
labels and
URLs for
your pop-up
menu.

6. **Select the sample entry,** `Adobe Systems, Inc.`, **on the row below** `Choose` **in the sample list box in the URL Popup Inspector.**

   The label and URL of the sample entry appear in the corresponding text boxes below the list, near the bottom of the Inspector. (In Figure 8-5, a newly added entry is selected.)

7. **Replace the sample label and URL with the label and URL for the Web site you want to add to your menu.**

   Type the label in the Label text box and either type the URL in the URL text box, select the Browse button (the one displaying a folder to the right of the URL text box) to locate a URL, or use the Point-and-Shoot button (the one displaying the spiral symbol, to the left of the URL text box) to select a URL, as described in Chapter 2. (The label simply describes the target URL.) You may, for example, type **PHP** as a label and select the PHP home page, at `www.php.net`, for the URL.

8. **After you replace the sample label and URL, add another line to the list by clicking the New button.**

   Use the New button to add lines for all the URLs and labels you need for the pop-up menu, typing new labels and URLs in the appropriate text boxes for each line. (Note the pointer on the New button in Figure 8-5.)

9. **Click the Delete or Duplicate buttons on selected lines as necessary.**

   If you don't want any of the URL addresses and their labels, just select each one and click the Delete button. You can't delete `Choose` without going into the source code and changing the word *Choose* to one that you want. However, after changing `Choose` to something else, you *can* change it from the URL Popup Inspector. (Go figure.)

Chapter 9

Frame Works

● ●

In This Chapter

▶ Defining frame elements

▶ Why use frames?

▶ Setting up the frame set

▶ Loading the frame set

▶ Naming frames

▶ Adjusting the frame set

▶ Navigating with frames

▶ Adding frames

● ●

*F*rames add a whole new dimension to HTML and Web sites. By using frames, you can organize the look of your Web page in a browser window so that you can display more than a single page simultaneously. Basically, one Web page acts like a latticed window frame with all the glass removed. The empty window frame, divided up by the latticework into separate compartments, is the *frame set*. It specifies the number of frames in a set and the dimensions for each of the frames. No matter what size Web page you bring into a frame, only the portion that fits into the frame is visible.

Defining Frame Elements

GoLive makes setting up and editing frames easy, but it uses a particular terminology when dealing with frames. The following list spells out what GoLive means when it's talking about frames:

✔ **Frame set:** A Web page used to organize and define the frames and to load the initial pages for each frame. Although the borders defined by the frame set do appear on the screen, no other visual content in the frame set file appears on the screen. (Think of the frame set as the director in a movie — he stays behind the camera. The Web pages are the actors that show up in the different frame windows.)

✔ **Frame:** A single window where a Web page is viewed. Any Web page with a URL can appear in a frame. A link to a Web page anywhere in the world or simply in your site folder can bring that Web page into any or all of the frames in a Web page using frames.

✔ **Frame Border/Separator:** A line separating frames within a frame set. Editing tools enable you to control the width and color of frame borders. (Frame borders are removed by having a value of zero.)

Why Frames?

Because you can bring any page into a browser window by clicking a button, you may be asking why you need frames. Plenty of reasons exist, and you're sure to want to use frames in some application or another. Consider the following features of frames:

✔ **Navigation aids:** Many designers use one frame in a set to navigate other Web pages in and out of the framed page.

✔ **Multiple functions:** A Web page with frames can use one frame for calculating values, another frame for displaying products, and another frame for showing inventory. Different pages within the frame set accomplish different jobs.

✔ **Comparisons:** By viewing two or more Web pages simultaneously, you can compare different elements in a Web site. For example, an art historian may display Web pages with different or similar art styles in a frame set. Because you can include different Web pages in a frame set, the juxtaposition of the pages' content creates dynamic comparisons controlled by the viewer.

✔ **Passing data:** Web pages within the same frame set read information from another page and write information to other pages. In this way, data can pass dynamically in Web pages without having to use server-side scripts, such as PHP, ASP, and CGI. By using frames, designers have the opportunity to have multiple databases responding to user input. Designers using PHP, ASP, or CGI can use pages in a frame set to pass data between the server and the client as well.

Other uses no doubt abound, and creative Web page designers find new uses for frames all the time. Fortunately, creating and using frames in GoLive is simple.

Setting Up Your Frame Set

The first step in getting your frames up and running is to define your frame set. GoLive has a separate tab for frames on the Objects palette, and, like everything else in GoLive, it's just a matter of dragging and dropping. Before you define a frame set, you need to set up a new site. Follow these steps:

1. **Choose File⇨New Site⇨Blank from the menu bar.**

   The New Blank Site dialog box appears.

2. **Type a name for the site in the New Site text field; then enter a folder destination in the In Folder text field. Click OK.**

3. **When the Site window appears, click the File tab.**

   File view of the Site window appears. You see one new file, named index.html.

4. **Choose Window⇨Objects from the menu bar.**

   The Objects palette appears.

5. **Click the Site tab of the Objects palette and then drag three new Page icons (the first icon on the left) from the Site tab to the File tab of the Site window.**

   For purposes of helping you understand how the pages work in the context of a sample site for an online news site, I used the names banner, headlines, and new followed by the .html extension. To rename a file on the Files tab of the Site window, either click the right button of the mouse and choose Rename from the pop-up menu (in Windows only) or click the name on the Files tab, pull the mouse away, and type a new name. Also, you can select the file icon and press the F2 key.

6. **Double-click each of the three pages to open them and write something unique on each page to distinguish them from one another.**

   I got a bit carried away and tried to make it look like an online news service. You can make yours as simple as you like. For learning purposes, you may want to give each page a different background color to distinguish one from the other.

7. **Open index.html from the Site window by double-clicking the appropriate file icon.**

   You can rename index.html to any name you want. In this case, I left it as index.html because it is a frame set and *must* be the first of the set to be loaded.

8. **Click the Frames Editor tab in the document window.**

   It's the tab right between Layout and Source in the document window. A drop-down label appears when the mouse pointer crosses it.

9. **Click the Frames tab on the Objects palette — it's the fifth tab from the left.**

   On the Frames tab, you see a number of different frame arrangements. Select one you like. (Note that the maximum number of frames in each set as displayed is three, but you *can* add more frames to a frame set if you want.)

10. **Drag the Frame Set icon you selected into the document window.**

    As soon as you release the mouse button, you see the frames with question-mark file icons. In the Site window, you see the page with a green bug next to it. You haven't done anything wrong. It's just the way GoLive tells you that your frame set needs files. Figure 9-1 shows how the page appears in the document window after the frame set is dropped in.

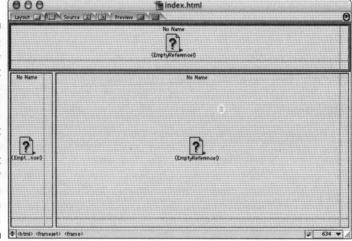

Figure 9-1:
This is how the first page looks after you drag the Frame Set icon into the document window within Frames Editor view.

If you drag a Frame Set icon into Layout view rather than Frames Editor view, you see lots of code on top of the page. It's a signal that you've just put the frame set in the wrong place. Choose Edit⇨Undo or press Ctrl+Z in Windows or ⌘+Z on the Macintosh. Click the Frames Editor tab and drag the icon again.

Loading the Frame Set

Initially, a frame set is as naked as a jaybird. You need to assign pages that will appear in the frame set's frames. Each page in a frame set can be loaded and viewed in a browser separately. The pages that go into a frame set are not slaves to the frame set, and if you know their URLs, you can load the pages independently anywhere in the world. To load the frame set, follow these steps:

1. **Begin with both the File tab of the Site window and Frames Editor view of the document window opened by clicking the File tab and the Frames Editor tabs in their respective windows.**

2. **Choose Window⇨Inspector from the menu bar.**

   Because the Frames Editor is selected, the Frame Set Inspector appears.

3. **Click one of the question-mark icons in the document window.**

   The Inspector becomes the Frame Inspector. Notice that a Point-and-Shoot button is available on the Inspector.

4. **Pull the point-and-shoot line from the Frame Inspector to the file in the Site window that you want to appear in the particular frame of the frame set, as shown in Figure 9-2.**

   After the file is connected to the frame, the file's icon replaces the question-mark icon in the frame window. Repeat this step until each frame has a file associated with it. Figure 9-2 shows the last of three pages being linked to the frame set.

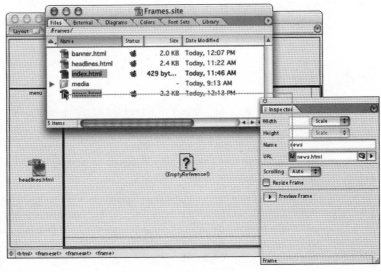

Figure 9-2: A selected Empty Reference icon is replaced with a file in a point-and-shoot selection.

Naming the Frames

Each frame in a frame set needs a name. The name of the frame is totally independent of any HTML file that may appear in the frame. Frames need to be clearly named so that when you want a Web page to appear in a frame, it knows where to go. (All right, there's no need to name a frame with *that* name!) The procedure is simple yet crucial. Here's how to name a frame:

1. **From Frames Editor view of the document window, choose Window⇨Inspector on the menu bar.**

2. **Click a file icon in one of the frames.**

   The Inspector becomes the Frame Inspector.

3. **In the Name window of the Frame Inspector, replace** No Name **by typing a name that describes the frame.**

   The name of each frame should remind you of what you plan to put into the frame or at least serve as a point of reference relative to the frame set. For example, you may want to use one of the frames as a menu bar and name the frame menu. Alternatively, you can name the frames relative to their positions: side, top, and bottom. Use one-word names.

4. **Select and name the rest of the frames.**

   Figure 9-3 shows the Frame Inspector with the name for a frame.

5. **Click the Preview tab (the last tab from the left in Windows) or the Frame Preview tab (the last tab from the left on the Macintosh) in the document window to look at the pages arranged in the frame set.**

   Preview your frame set periodically to keep a perspective on how the page looks. Note that the top frame has a page in it being previewed.

Fine-tuning a frame

The Frame Inspector has a few other elements you may want to use:

✔ **Scrolling:** The Scrolling menu provides three options:

> **Auto:** A scroll bar shows only if the page scrolls off the top or side. Otherwise, no scroll bar appears.
>
> **No:** A scroll bar never appears regardless of whether the page scrolls off the side. Use this option when you don't want scroll bars to interfere with design. (It's also a lesson to those who try to look at Web pages on Palm organizers!) Use this option only when even the smallest monitor can view all pertinent elements of a page.
>
> **Yes:** Scroll bars appears whether they're needed or not. This option makes sense when you want a consistent design at all times on all monitor sizes.

✔ **Resize Frame:** If a check mark is in the box, the frame can be resized (changed in size), but if it is not checked, the frame cannot be resized. Because a frame design generally does not include changing frame sizes, this attribute is left unchecked. If some frames can be resized and others not, a greater possibility exists of warping the appearance of the page.

✔ **Preview Frame:** Here's one of those great little buttons in the Frame Inspector that makes Web page development easier. While you're push-ing and pulling on the frame, you may want to remind yourself what the initial Web page in the frame looks like. Click Preview Frame in the Frame Inspector and — voilà! — you get to see the page without having to leave Frames Editor view of the document window. (This feature is available only on the Macintosh.)

Figure 9-3: The Inspector in Frame mode with a frame named banner and a preview of a page in the frame.

Tweaking the frame size and placement

The best visual method of getting the frames just right involves dragging the dividers between the frames left and right or up and down. You can drag columns only left and right, and you can drag rows only up and down. The most effective way of getting the frame just right requires that you preview the initial page while you're resizing it. Here's how to preview your page:

1. **From Frames Editor view of the document window, open the Inspector by choosing Window⇨Inspector from the menu bar.**

   The Frames Editor Inspector appears on the page.

2. **Click a file icon in one of the frames.**

   The frame is now selected. Note the changes in the Frame Inspector whenever you click different frames.

3. **Either double-click the file icon in the frame (in Windows or on the Macintosh) or, in the Frame Inspector, select Preview Frame (Macintosh only).**

   The Web page for the frame opens in the Layout mode of a new document window. (When you select the Preview Frame, the page has the same configuration as the frame.)

4. **Place the pointer on one of the dividers and move it until the page looks like you want it to within the frame.**

   You should preview your completed frame set on different combinations of platforms and browsers in Preview view of the document window before publishing the page on the Web. Frames have less tolerance for graphics and text being scrolled out of sight, and you probably need to resize your frames more than once to get the appearance of the page just right.

After you get your pages hooked up with all your frames, you may realize that a frame may look better somewhere else. For example, a column on the far left may look better on the far right, or a column at the top of the page may look better on the bottom. Here's an easy way to move your frames in the document window: From Frames Editor view, click below the file icon in the frame and drag the frame to a new location. Remember that columns can move only right and left and that rows can move only up and down.

Adjusting the Frame Set

You can start with the selection of adjustments that GoLive provides on the Frames tab of the Objects palette, but you may want to fine-tune the size of the frames in the frame set. The frame set orders the frames in terms of rows and columns using either pixels or percentages. Two rows or columns have to equal 100 percent of the frame set. Using percentages makes it easier to envision how much a row or column takes up proportionately on a page.

In some applications, a graphic may consume a certain number of pixels, and the frame dimensions may have to be based on the pixel unit rather than on percentages. In these cases, the other frames in the row or column need to be carefully balanced so as not to block the graphic.

The Frame Set Inspector is a great tool for handling such balancing chores. To transform an Inspector into the Frame Set Inspector, simply click on the border between two frames in a frame set. An open Inspector immediately becomes the Frame Set Inspector.

The Frame Set Inspector options can be a little confusing, so check out the following list for the lowdown on what the options mean:

- **Width/Height:** Generally, you don't need to change this option because you can drag the size to fit. However, you can make changes based on pixels, the percentage of the page, or scale (an object).

- **Orientation:** Here's another of those options that is not altogether clear. By selecting other than the default orientation, you arrange the frame dividers in a way that looks nothing like the frame set you dragged over from the Objects palette. Leave the orientation alone unless changing it is the only way you can get the set arrangement you want..

- **BorderSize:** Finally! Here's an option you can use. Generally, I prefer to minimize the border size to 1 or, more often, 0. Like table borders, wide borders in frame sets tend to create a rat-maze effect. Pay close attention to the border attribute and consider a seamless frame set where the borders are invisible.

When editing, you can edit with a big, fat border much more easily than with a skinny one. You have to click the divider to select the Frame Set Inspector, and with skinny dividers it's easy to miss and hit one of the frames instead. So, while you're editing, leave the border size wide. After you're done editing, you can reduce the border to a smaller size that's compatible with the design.

- **BorderColor:** You can use border color effectively. By using minimal-size borders and subtle color differences between the background color of the pages and the border, you can distinguish between the frames without a jarring separation. Click the BorderColor well in the Frame Set Inspector (which brings up the Color palette), select a border, and click the color you want on the Color palette.

- **BorderFrame:** The border frame is made up of narrow lines framing the border. If the border frame is turned off (set to No), only the border color shows in the width determined in the BorderSize window. Try different combinations to see what you get. Essentially, you can make the border itself larger or smaller, but the frame around the border is a Yes/No option.

Frame sets don't have cell *padding* — the distance between the object in the cell and the walls of the cell — that you find in tables. One way to mimic frame padding is to use the border size as the pad. Switch BorderFrame to No and use the same border color as the background color of the Web pages in the frame set. Increase and decrease the size of the border until you have the padding in the frames you want.

- **Preview Set/Stop Preview:** These two buttons may not seem like much, but in developing a Web page with frames, you'll love them. While in Frames Editor view, you frequently need to look at the frame set with the pages in the frames. Rather than leave Frames Editor view and click Preview view in the Frame Inspector (refer to Figure 9-3 for a page being previewed) and then return to Frames Editor view for more work on the frame set, you can just turn the preview on and off with these buttons. It's easy and has no calories. (This feature is only in the Macintosh version.) Figure 9-4 shows the Macintosh Frame Set Inspector about to be turned off.

Figure 9-4:
The
Frame Set
Inspector
on the
Macintosh.
The
Windows
version is
the same
except that
it has no
Preview Set
or Stop
Preview
options.

Navigating with Frames

Frames done well are a joy to design and develop. However, one area tangles up just about everyone at one time or another: navigating in frames. A link on a normal, nonframe page means that when the user selects a link, the linked page replaces the current page. With frames, you want the linked pages to appear in specific targets (frames) but not in others. For example, if you design one of your frames to be a navigation bar, you don't want it to be replaced by another page.

GoLive automatically includes the names of the frames in the link options on the Text Inspector's or Image Inspector's Link tab when a link is established. (That's why it's so important to name your frames as soon as you can.) A pull-down menu provides two sets of link targets. The bottom set lets you open up a new window to display the page you're linking to, and the top set lets you open the page you're linking to in one of the other (named) frames in the current window. First, consider the menu options for opening a new window to display the page you're linking to:

✔ **_blank:** Opens a new window and leaves the current window open also.

A new page outside the frame set opens. Usually, the page covers up a good portion of the frame set page, which isn't a good thing. However, sometimes the designer wants to open a page and leave at least part of the linking page visible as well. Users can compare the information on the linked page with the linking page. With external links, opening a new window guarantees that the linking frame set will not be lost. (The viewer may have to shift the pages around to get a clear view.)

✔ **_self:** Technically, _self doesn't open a new window, but rather opens the page in the frame with the link. (GoLive must think that consistency is the hobgoblin of little minds.) Essentially, with _self target, the linked page replaces the linking page.

Don't use _self with a frame housing your menu or navigation page. If you do, as soon as you link to another page, your menu goes "Adios" and in comes the linked page into the frame. (I hate it when that happens.)

✔ **_parent:** The linked page is loaded into the parent frame set. The current frame set is replaced by a new page or frame set. The whole frame set disappears and a page or new frame set takes its place.

✔ **_top:** The entire frame set is discarded and the new page is brought up in a new window. This option seems to work exactly like _parent except in cases where nested frame sets are employed. In a nested frame set, _parent replaces only one of the frame sets and leaves the others. (A *nested frame set* occurs when a page with its own frame set is opened inside a frame. See the last section of this chapter for a discussion of these frame set arrangements.) The _top option discards all frame sets and brings up a new window. For the most part, _parent and _top work the same if you don't use nested frame sets.

Linking to frames within a frame set

With frame sets in GoLive, you don't need to open a new window to display a page you're linking to; the top set of menu options in the Text or Image Inspector lets you open the new page in any of the named frames of the current frame set. When you name a frame, that name is immediately entered into the menu set, where it's always available for use. (The number of names listed obviously depends on the number of frames you have created and named in the frame set).

Figure 9-5 shows how the sample page menu options are displayed on a pulldown menu in the Text Inspector after a link is established. In this example, the frame set has three frames, named banner, menu, and news; the target for the link from the sample page is set for news, which means that when a viewer clicks the hot link in the sample page, the page you have set up as the target for the link appears in the frame named news.

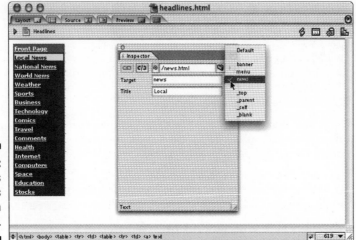

Figure 9-5:
Selections
for links
in an
Inspector.

Up to this point in my treatment of GoLive, I've made few references to the term *target* because the default target has been the option of choice. However, with frame sets, the default is almost *never* the right choice. It would be better to select _self as the target than to leave it at default (which is _self) just to stay on your toes. In pages without frame sets, the default just replaces the current page with the linked page. That works fine. If you want to keep your page in place in a frame, you had better choose a different target frame than the one the link is from or bring up a new window (_blank) for a target.

The procedure for establishing a link in one frame and showing the linked page in another frame uses the target menu extensively. Use the following steps:

1. **Begin in Frames Editor view of the document window.**

2. **Open the Inspector by choosing Window⇨Inspector from the menu bar.**

   The Frame Inspector appears. (If the Frame Set Inspector appears, it simply means that one of the borders is selected. Click in a frame to change it to the Frame Inspector.)

3. **Select a file icon in one of the frames on which you want to create a link.**

   A border appears around the inside of the selected frame.

4. **Either double-click the file icon (in Windows or on the Macintosh) or select Preview Frame in the Frame Inspector (only on the Macintosh).**

   The selected page appears.

5. **Select the text or graphic for the hot spot for the link.**

   Keep the text or graphic selected for the rest of the operation. The Inspector becomes either the Text Inspector or the Image Inspector.

6. **Click the Link icon in the Toolbar or Text (or Image) Inspector.**

   The Link icon's symbol is two chain links.

7. **In the Text (or Image) Inspector, fill in the URL window by using the Point-and-shoot Button or the Browse button or by typing the URL address.**

   Your link is established. The links can either be internally to a file in the site window or elsewhere on your computer or to an external source anywhere in the world.

8. **In the Text (or Image) Inspector, pull down the menu with the double arrows, to the right of the Target window.**

   Select from the top set of menu options the frame in which you want the linked page to appear. The frame replaces whatever page is in the selected frame. Usually, a menu page in a narrow, vertical frame is the source of the link and an adjacent, larger frame is where the linked page appears. You can choose any of the selections from the top or bottom portions of the pull-down menu (refer to Figure 9-5).

A frame menu

Many page designers want to keep all linked pages within the confines of a frame set. The links are all on a single page that remains in a frame and new pages are displayed in one or more frames. That page is called a menu because it has a list of all links. Follow these steps to make your own menu. (If you've used the sample site from previous examples in this chapter, most of the following will have been done already. Just to be sure that you don't miss anything, you still should take a look at these steps.)

1. **Choose File⇨New Site⇨ from the menu bar.**

   The GoLive Site Wizard appears. (Whoop-de-doo!)

2. **In the Site Wizard, choose Single User⇨Single User⇨Next⇨Blank Site⇨Next⇨Type a news-related name for the site in the Site Name⇨ Next⇨Browse to find the location where you want your site to go⇨ Finish.**

3. **When the Site window appears, click the File tab.**

   The File view of the Site window appears.

4. **Choose Window⇨Objects from the menu bar.**

   The Objects palette appears on the page.

5. **Choose Window⇨Inspector from the menu bar.**

   A generic Inspector appears.

6. **Click the Site tab on the Objects palette and then drag three Page icons (first icon on the left) from the Site tab to the Files tab of the site window.**

7. **Leave index.html as it is and then give each of the other files the following names:**

```
banner.html
headlines.html
front.html
news.html
```

   To rename files in the Site window, just click the names to select them (right-click in Windows) and type a new name.

8. **Open index.html from the Site window by double-clicking its file icon.**

   A blank page appears in Layout view of the document window.

9. **Click the Frames Editor tab in the document window.**

   A blank page appears, announcing "No Frames."

10. **From the Frame tab of the Objects palette, drag the tenth frame icon from the left to the document window.**

    The Inspector becomes the Frame Set Inspector.

11. **In the Frame Set Inspector, enter 0 for BorderSize and click the check box next to BorderColor. Then click the color well.**

    The Color palette appears.

12. **From the Web Color List, the third button from the right on the Color palette, select a white swatch.**

    The color well turns white, and so does the border. If you don't have a border, the border color really doesn't make much difference, although it's a good habit to consider border color — even if it's just to be sure that the background color and the border colors are the same. (It's double insurance when you're using invisible borders.)

13. **Set BorderFrame to No in the Frame Set Inspector.**

    You don't need no stinkin' border frame. Border frames sometimes get in the way.

14. **Select the lower-left column of the frame set by clicking in the left frame area. The Inspector becomes the Frame Inspector.**

15. **Type menu in the Name window of the Frame Inspector and choose No from the Scrolling pull-down menu.**

16. **Select the lower-right frame by clicking in the right frame area and, in the Frame Inspector, type news in the Name window; then choose Auto from the Scrolling pull-down menu.**

17. **Select the top frame. and, in the Frame Inspector, type** banner **in the Name window; then choose No from the Scrolling pull-down menu.**

    Steps 15–17 provide frame names that are used as target names when a link is made to bring up an HTML page in one of the frames.

18. **Drag the file headlines.html from the Site window into the menu frame , the file banner.html into the banner frame, and front.hml to the news frame.**

    Alternatively, you can click the Point-and-Shoot button to bring the files to the frames.

19. **Double-click the headlines.html file in the menu frame to open it in Layout view of the document window.**

    A new document window opens with the headlines.html page in Layout view. The original document window with the frame set remains on the screen. Any file in a frame set appears in Layout view when it is opened from an icon in a frame. Any open document windows stay where they are on the screen until you close them.

20. **From the Basic tab of the Objects palette, drag a Table icon into the headlines.html page.**

    Use the Inspector palette to change the dimensions from 3 rows and 3 columns to 17 rows and 1 column. I used the rows to closely but evenly space the link text that will go in there. You can add any links names you want, but name the top link Front Page and the second name Local News. See Figure 9-6 for examples.

Figure 9-6:
The left
frame holds
the menu.

21. **Select Local News in headlines.html.**

    The Inspector becomes the Text Inspector.

22. Click the Link icon on the toolbar or Inspector and drag the point-and-shoot line from the Link tab of the Text Inspector to connect to the news.html file in the Site window.

As you make the link, choose news from the Target pull-down menu of the Text Inspector. Be sure to correctly specify the target. Otherwise, the local news appears in the menu frame, effectively knocking out the menu. (A tornado got the menu!)

23. Repeat Step 22 for the Front Page text in the headlines.html page and make the link to front.html.

Now you have two links. If you feel like it, you can link up everything and have your own online publishing empire. Just remember to specify your target as the news frame. Or else!

24. Open banner.html by double-clicking it in the Site window and create a heading for your page.

I used some text to name it and then, to add a bit of tacky realism, I placed a fictitious little ad for a business that sells computers by the pound. See Figure 9-7 for an example.

Figure 9-7:
The single frame in the top row holds the banner name plus a bit of advertising copy.

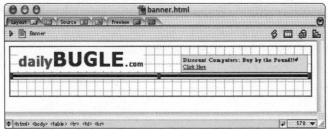

25. Open news.html by double-clicking it in the Site window and create a heading for your page.

Remember that you will have the banner above your and the menu off to the left. That means that you will not have as much room as you would if the whole browser area were available for the page. Check out Figure 9-8 for an example.

After you have completed everything, your site with frames allows the viewer to get lots of information in a small area. Moreover, you as a designer can integrate the different parts so that all the parts appear as a single page organized to make finding information easy and seamless. Figure 9-9 shows how the whole page comes together.

Figure 9-8:
Pages that will go into the news frame need to be sized to fit between the banner and the menu frames.

Figure 9-9:
All the parts orchestrated to create a dynamic and integrated page.

Adding Frames

Adding a single frame to a frame set is deceptively easy. In looking at the different arrangements of frame sets on the Frame tab of the Objects palette, you may not see the set you want. Suppose that you want a frame set with exactly four equal frames — two rows and two columns. No such animal can be seen in the frame set icons on the Frame tab. Fear not — it's easy to fix. Here's how:

1. **Open a new page in GoLive by choosing File⇨New or by pressing Ctrl+N (in Windows) or ⌘+N (on the Macintosh).**

   A new, untitled page appears in Layout view. Switch to Frames Editor view in the document window by clicking the Frames Editor tab (the second tab from the left).

2. **Choose Window⇨Objects to display the Objects palette.**

3. **Click the Frames tab of the Objects palette and drag the third (from the left) frame set icon to the page in Frames Editor view.**

   Two frames appear on the page, stacked vertically (see Figure 9-10).

4. **Choose Window⇨Inspector to display the Inspector.**

5. **Click in the top frame and the Inspector becomes the Frame Inspector.**

   Note the pop-up menu value next to the Height text window. The initial height should be 80 pixels.

6. **Change the pop-up menu from Pixels to** Percent **and change the Percent to** 50.

   The top and bottom frames now take up equal amounts of the page.

7. **Drag the single frame (the first one on the left) icon from the Frames tab of the Objects palette into the top frame of the Frames Editor.**

   Now the top row has two columns, or frames (see Figure 9-11).

8. **On the Width and Height pull-down menus of the Frame Inspector, choose Percent and type** 50 **in the Size window in the Frame Inspector.**

   Repeat this process with all four frames until you see four equal frames, as shown in Figure 9-12.

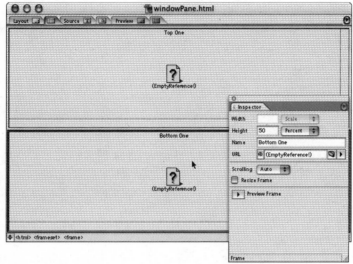

Figure 9-10:
A two-frame
frame set
on a page.

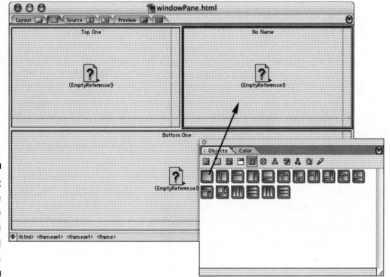

Figure 9-11:
A single
frame
added to an
existing
frame set.

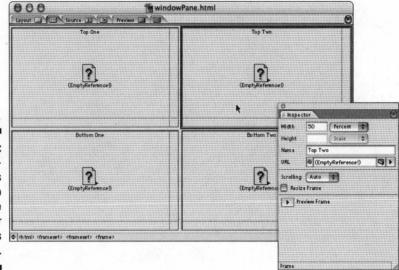

Figure 9-12:
Four equal-
size frames
set up
using the
Inspector
in Frames
mode.

By adding additional frames and changing the frame sizes, you can come up with virtually any frame set you want. When a frame set of more than a single frame is added to a frame set on a page, the set is treated as a nested frame set. You can arrange and rearrange nested frame sets by pressing the Alt key (in Windows) or the Option key (on the Macintosh) and then clicking and dragging a frame set to a different place on the page. As soon as the pointer turns into a fist with a + sign, it's ready to be moved. (***Remember:*** To move a single frame, just drag it to the page.) If your original frame set displeases you, just move the frames around until the frame set suits your tastes and purposes. Believe me, it's much easier than moving furniture.

If you Alt+drag (in Windows) or Option+drag (on the Macintosh) one of the frame separators, you can automatically add two frames. Try dragging the frame dividers up, down, left, and right to see the different combinations you can create. Also, you can generate a frame context menu by Ctrl+clicking the page icons.

Chapter 10

Cascading Style Sheets

· ·

· ·

Before Cascading Style Sheets (CSS), Web page designers pulled out their hair trying to get text to behave like it does on paper. In the whole history of page design, never was there a time that limited styles and layout like the original HTML did. However, with the introduction of CSS, a whole new set of possibilities opened up to designers — possibilities that GoLive makes easy to apply. At one time considered essentially to be a part of Dynamic HTML, Cascading Style Sheets are now seen as an essential formatting tool for everything from PHP to XML as well as HTML.

In the bad old days, Web designers had to rely on tables to do all the formatting on Web pages. CSS eliminated this dependence on tables, thus letting designers pick and choose whether (or when) they wanted to use tables for formatting. (The CSS features of GoLive, for example, don't prevent you from using tables or the grid — actually a variant on the table form.) Using CSS, you can define entire styles quickly and easily so that if you need a purple, 15-point font in Verdana with a yellow background, all you need to do is define it and then apply it to the text. Moreover, you can indent paragraphs (just like grown-up page designers), set margins, and pretty much make text behave the way you want.

This chapter examines not only CSS, but also the great tools GoLive 6 uses to make generating CSS very simple. With the help of familiar tools like the Inspector and the toolbar, you get a chance to create on your Web page the kind of text you thought only the pros could do.

Getting Control with CSS

Style sheets, like JavaScript, are defined in the head of an HTML page. A style container, <STYLE> </STYLE>, demarcates the area where you place CSS code, but with GoLive you define your style sheets in a cool CSS Style Inspector. Understanding a little about the way CSS works under the hood helps you with any tweaking you may want to do. (If you need a refresher course on HTML terminology — including words like heads, tags, and containers — check out Chapter 6.)

Before doing CSS the easy way, it helps to know what CSS looks like in Source view or on the Source Code palette, just for a little context. Remember that a *container* is a set of HTML tags with a beginning and an end. Anything between the tags is in the container and is affected by it. The STYLE container allows you to create as much CSS as you want with different definitions. All style definitions are put in the page's Head area. Choose Window⇨Source Code to open the Source Code palette, or in the document window click the Source tab to look at the code.

Redefining tags

In the <STYLE> container, you can do one of three things: Redefine a tag, create a class, or create an ID. When you redefine a tag, your definition replaces the original definition given in HTML. For example, you can use the <A> tag, the tag reserved for links, to redefine how your links will look:

```
<HTML>
<HEAD>
<STYLE TYPE ="text/css">
    a {
    color: olive;
    font-family: Arial;
    text-decoration: none
     }

</STYLE>
</HEAD>
```

The redefinition of the <A> tag makes all link fonts the color olive , in the Arial font, and with no underline. So, whenever you make a link on a page with that style definition using GoLive, you no longer see the blue underline in the current font face. For example, if you select a default-colored Times font and use the Text Inspector to link it to another page, your link automatically turns the color olive and converts the font to Arial, and you see no sign of the underline usually associated with linked text.

After you redefine a tag, all you need to do to apply the tag's style is put text into the tag's container. Suppose that you redefine <H3> to be a purple-colored font with a green background. The following line creates the purple text on a green background:

```
<H3> I look like a grape on the grass. </H3>
```

(The style code looks like this in the Head-area STYLE container: — H3 { color : purple; background color: green } —.)

When a background color is applied with CSS, it applies to only the text in the container and not to the whole page. If the <BODY> tag is redefined in CSS, the background color applies to the entire page.

Creating classes

CSS provides a way for you to better control what your text looks like. In changing a tag, you're limited to the structures HTML provides. However, CSS offers more. So, besides redefining existing tags, you can create your own defining words, called classes. *Classes* are used to define the font, colors, and structure of the text you put on your Web page. In defining classes, words beginning with a period (.) signal that the word will be a class — a "dot definition." Classes are something like new style tags, but there is no need to replace an existing tag's definition. My favorite CSS class defines the text with a yellow background. In a paragraph, it makes the text stand out just like highlighted text in a book. I use it in the following demonstration of making a class:

```
<HTML>
<HEAD>
<STYLE TYPE ="text/css">
    .highlight {background-color : yellow}
</STYLE>
</HEAD>
```

Applying classes is a little trickier in HTML. The dot-defined classes need to be embedded in other tags, like <P>, or put into a <SPAN> or <DIV> container. (This role is a new one for <P> that until now just created a new paragraph.)

When you apply classes, the period or dot is dropped. As a general rule, use `<P>` or one of the `<H>` tags when you want to apply the class to the whole paragraph. Use `<SPAN>` when you want to apply it to a little part of the paragraph. For example, you would use `<SPAN>` when you want to apply CSS to a sentence in a paragraph but not to the whole paragraph. The `<DIV>` tag is used to apply the CSS to more than a single paragraph. The following script uses both `<P>` and `<SPAN>` containers:

```
<HTML>
<HEAD>
<STYLE TYPE ="text/css">
    .backlight {background-color : black; color : white}
    .bigugly {color : purple; size : 24 pt; background-color
             : lime }
</STYLE>
</HEAD>
<Body bgcolor="white">
<P class=bigugly> This is big and ugly.</P>
Only part of this line is <SPAN CLASS=backlight> important.
         </SPAN> The rest is not.
</BODY>
</HTML>
```

Had I used `<P>` or `<H>` rather than `<SPAN>`, a paragraph jump would break the line. Obviously, doing all this work in HTML may take a while, but with GoLive it's pretty easy. However, you have many options, and you'll see what they are.

Making an ID

An ID is much like a class definition. The essential difference is that ID attributes must be unique — no two ID attributes can be the same. Thus, an ID can be used to uniquely identify its element. Here's a simple example:

```
<HTML>
<HEAD>
<STYLE TYPE ="text/css">
    #banana { color : yellow; background-color : black}
</STYLE>
</HEAD>
<Body>
<span id=banana> I need a boat for these.</span>
</BODY>
</HTML>
```

Now that you have a little background in CSS and how it works under the hood, the next section should be a relief. GoLive 6 makes it easy to create style sheets without having to enter source code. (Rats! And I wanted to enter code until I'm blue in the face.)

Making Your First Style Sheet the Easy Way

Getting a simple style sheet made in GoLive helps to see how easy it is. Follow these steps for a simple change of tags:

1. **Open a page by choosing File⇨New from the menu bar or by pressing Ctrl+N (in Windows) or ⌘+N (on the Mac).**

   An untitled page appears in Layout view of the document window. (If the page is untitled, why does it have the title Untitled.html? The answer is so that it is reminded to give it a proper name.)

2. **Choose Window⇨Inspector from the menu bar.**

   The Text Inspector appears.

3. **Type** "This is not a test. It's the real thing!" **on the page.**

   Leave the default settings for the text, changing nothing. (I'll be looking. . . .)

4. **In the right corner of the page, click the CSS button on the upper-right side of the document window — it looks like a staircase.**

   The CSS Editor opens. Along the bottom edge, you see (if you look) a new toolbar. The CSS Toolbar is easy to overlook in this operation, but it's crucial to getting started with CSS in GoLive.

5. **Click the Tag icon (< >, called the New Element Style) on the toolbar.**

   The Inspector changes into the CSS Style Inspector and a new Tag icon appears in the CSS Editor, labeled element.

6. **Click the Basics tab (a pencil icon) of the CSS Style Inspector and in the Name field replace** element **by typing** H4.

   You can put any tag you want. H4 frequently gets ignored, so I chose it.

7. **Select the Font tab (second tab from the left) in the CSS Style Inspector.**

   The tab is marked F for Font. Not surprisingly, the CSS Style Inspector provides several font options. Read on!

8. **Pull down the menu next to the Color window of the Font tab and select** maroon.

   You see 16 named colors. Maroon is a nice color for this demonstration. (Okay, pick fuchsia, if you must!)

9. **Pull down the menu next to the Size window of the Font tab and select** xx-large.

   You are presented with 20 different font-measuring units. Use any one you want. I chose xx-large because I want you to see that the H4 size is not what it was before you used CSS to change it. That's it. You've completed the process of transforming a tag. If you click the Basic tab (the pencil icon) of the CSS Style Inspector now, you see the code generated for the new tag. The CSS Editor goes to the back automatically when you go on to some other task — just click the page.

10. **Select the text you typed on your original page and choose Header 4 from the Paragraph Format pull-down menu on the left side of the toolbar.**

   A large maroon message appears on the page.

You've only scratched the proverbial surface of CSS, but you can see how powerful it is.

The CSS Style Inspector and CSS Toolbar appear and disappear between visits to the page. Whenever you select text on which to try out your new CSS, the Inspector turns into the Text Inspector. To get the CSS Style Inspector back, you need to click the CSS button — the little staircase in the upper-right corner of the document window. (The CSS Style Inspector can be an elusive little bugger, hiding out behind other pages.)

Working with the CSS Editor

Getting the CSS button to perform a few simple tricks for you is relatively easy, but if you really want to unleash the true power of CSS, you may want to familiarize yourself with all the options available for CSS in GoLive. To do that, you need to take a closer look at the CSS Style Inspector as well as the CSS Editor and CSS Toolbar.

The CSS Editor and the CSS Toolbar on the editor are fairly simple, but you do need to keep an eye on them and know how to use them if you want them to work effectively with CSS. At this point, you need to concern yourself only with classes and tags on the CSS Editor and their corresponding icons on the toolbar. IDs, the other option in the CSS Editor and on the toolbar, are similar to both tags and classes in setup and applications, but they require a little coding. (See the section "ID, Please" to find out how to use them.)

To get CSS going in GoLive, click the CSS button to open the CSS Editor and then add new classes and tag definitions by selecting the Tag (< >), Class ({}, or ID (#) icons on the CSS Toolbar. Classes and tags are named in the Name window of the CSS Style Inspector. Figure 10-1 shows how a new class is created as soon as you click the Class icon on the CSS Toolbar. The new class shows up on the CSS Editor and the CSS Style Inspector.

As soon as the designer using the CSS Style Inspector has defined the tag or class, those changes are echoed in the CSS palette used to apply styles to text. (The CSS palette is new in GoLive 6 and is introduced later in this book.)

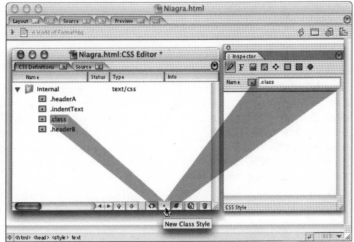

Figure 10-1:
The CSS
tools work
together
to create
Cascading
Style
Sheets.

Remember that your selection on the CSS Toolbar sets the sequence in motion. Once defined, by selecting text and using the Style tab of the Text Inspector, you can use the new class or tag to apply the style.

After you're comfortable with the idea that the CSS development sequence begins with the CSS Toolbar, much of the rest is pretty straightforward. The next step is to look at all the options available on the CSS Style Inspector.

Modifying Your Fonts

The Font tab, the second tab from the left on the CSS Style Inspector, automatically generates CSS code for the many combinations of options GoLive makes available for fonts. The following list focuses on each option:

- ✔ **Color:** The 16 choices of color on the pop-up menu echo those of the W3C (World Wide Web Consortium), but you need not limit yourself to those. Click the color well on the Fonts tab to open the Color palette and choose any color you want from the Color palette (see Figure 10-2).

- ✔ **Size:** Font size is a bit tricky because you have so many options. Unlike standard HTML, where a few sizes fit all, Cascading Style Sheets provide font measurements in picas and points as well as other units of measurement. Use any of the units you want or a combination in your sheets.

- ✔ **Line height:** This dimension is something like leading in traditional line-distance measurement. *Leading* refers to the amount of space between lines. Only new lines receive the values in line height, though. Wrap-around lines are automatically determined by the font size, but when a new line is created by a carriage return, CSS applies the line height. (In the old days, before computers, they added extra lead between lines to control the vertical line spacing of type; hence the word *leading*.) However, on the Web it's useful to select a percentage so that the line differences look good on different sizes of browser windows and monitors.

✔ **Font window:** Directly below the Font Family window is a Font window. Click the New button, and then you can type the name of the font or click the pull-down menu (the up- and down-arrow icon above the New button) to choose the font you want from the menu. Below the Font window is another pull-down menu that shows the existing font families you defined. Whichever combination you select becomes part of the CSS font family for the current definition.

✔ **Style:** The font's style options are limited to unchanged, italic, oblique, and normal. Italic and oblique are similar in their appearance on the Web.

✔ **Weight:** The weight of a font pretty much refers to how bold it is. In the old days, if more ink were applied to a font, it weighed more. No color or tint change makes it "heavier." This option thickens the appearance of a font. In addition to the normal and bold weights is a range from 100 to 900 and relative weights of lighter and bolder. Some variations of weights may not show up on your browser, so you have to check to make sure how the weights show up on the different browsers.

✔ **Decoration:** The decoration options include none (my favorite), underline (usually used for links), strike, overline, and blink. Blink, thankfully, has been purged from browser versions 6.0 and later. (Blink was shot by a firing squad made up of designers.)

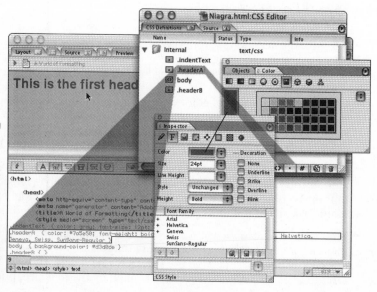

Figure 10-2:
Working on a font using the CSS Style Inspector, CSS Editor, and Color palette.

After you name your class or tag, put some text on your page and select it. Apply the class or tag to the text by selecting the Style tab of the Text Inspector and then clicking the style you want. Open the CSS Editor to initiate the CSS Style Inspector again and continue making changes. As you add and make changes to the class or tag, you can see them taking place in the selected text on the page. This technique enables you to get a better idea of what your CSS definitions look like and reduces development time.

Styling Your Text

After you create a new class by clicking the class icon on the Style Sheet toolbar, you can do some interesting things with the text. Select the Text tab (the third one from the left) of the CSS Style Inspector and prepare to make your blocks of text do your bidding. These options are available:

- **Text indent:** Rather than use block text (unindented paragraphs) or   (code used to create a blank space in HTML), you can simply and cleanly indent text. I generally use one em space for an indent, but you can choose from point, pica, pixel, ex, millimeter, centimeter, inch, percentage, or normal. (For HTML, normal means "do nothing.") In building text blocks, the indent is a wonderful addition to HTML page design because it's automatic for the whole paragraph. In pages with lots of text, the paragraph indent sure beats block upon block of text.

- **Word spacing:** As with a text indent, you have several measures from which to choose, but I leave it unchanged or normal. If a problem occurs with the spaces between words, select your favorite measure and make the necessary changes. Word spacing can come in handy when you're designing interesting headers.

- **Letter spacing:** For headers and special effects, putting spaces between letters can make your page look great. For those who insist on using ALL CAPS to decrease communication, readability, and good sense, there's hope. Try dropping some extra letter spacing between ALL CAP (if you must) and some word spacing as well. Figure 10-2 shows a line of text in all caps (the top line) and one with 1ex space (the width of the letter *x* in a font) between letters and words.

- **Vertical alignment:** Vertical alignment sets the selected text higher or lower relative to the paragraph. Several options are available here, but be sure to try them out in different browsers to see what you get. For example, the sub (subscript) and sup (superscript) often don't appear in a browser; if you use them, try to do it so that words like *1st* and *H2O* are clear enough to understand even if the subscript or superscript formatting doesn't make it through a viewer's browser.

- ✔ **Font variant:** Only three variants exist: unchanged, small caps, and normal. Normal is the default font, and unchanged makes no changes in the current font's variant, if it has one. All this selection does is provide small caps as a variant for adding interest to a font. Small caps require Internet Explorer 5 (IE5) or Netscape Navigator 6 (NN6) or later.

- ✔ **Transformation:** The transformation option changes any text into one of three types: initial capitals (good for headers), all uppercase, or all lowercase.

- ✔ **Alignment:** CSS provides four alignments: left, center, right, and justified. Most browsers don't yet support justified text, but if CSS standards are met, they soon should.

The GoLive Preview mode may be overly generous when it comes to displaying some CSS features. In testing what shows in Preview mode against what the browser shows, I find that the preview in GoLive shows both spacing and vertical alignment differently in Preview mode than in the browser window. However, the preview doesn't display small caps even though Internet Explorer 5 and later and Netscape Navigator 6 and later do. Test it in the browsers before you put it on the Web!

Adjusting Blocks

The Block tab, the fourth tab from the left on the CSS Style Inspector, works *something* like the <BLOCKQUOTE> tag, but as with everything else in CSS, you have far more control. The tag indents a block of text in the <BLOCKQUOTE> container, and each nested container indents the text block one more tab. The <BLOCKQUOTE> groups text into blocks with a common indent. In HTML, each instance of the <BLOCKQUOTE> tab indents the block one more tab.

- ✔ **Margin:** The first four cells of the margin column set the text a specified number of units, or percentage of the page, from each of the four sides of a box. A left margin of 10 pixels, for example, sets the text 10 pixels in from the side. The fifth window sets all four margins to either multiple units or a specified number of units inside an invisible margin box.

- ✔ **Padding:** The padding sets the text in the specified number of units from the border set up by the margin. Imagine a box with a specified margin around it. Inside the margin is a visible border. The inset inside the border is the padding.

- ✔ **Block:** The block elements set the outside boundaries and elements as a floating box. The Float setting from the pull-down menu gives options for wrapping text left and right, unchanged, or none. Practice with all the block elements to get your text groupings looking the way you want on the page. (Floating boxes are independent blocks of text and graphics that can be moved on a page — they "float" to different positions. Chapter 16 describes how to work with these dynamic features.)

Stating Your Position

The parameters of the Position tab (the fifth tab from the left on the CSS Style Inspector) apply to floating elements, primarily floating boxes. Floating boxes are like little acetate overlays that float over the main page. (The term *layers* is used also.) Select text in an existing style sheet and fill in the positioning properties, and the text is gathered into a floating box. Imagine all the position properties in terms of a smaller window superimposed on the document window. The position of the box is relative to the top and left sides of the window. For example, a position of 200 (left) and 500 (top) places the floating box 500 pixels from the top of the window and 200 pixels from the left side. The clipping properties refer to how the text and other objects in the floating box are to be cropped, scrolled, or wrapped. Chapter 16 fully covers floating boxes and their properties. (Older browsers do not display layers or CSS.)

Picking a Border

Borders are visual boxes of color surrounding text. As with using the <BLINK> tag, you can ruin a good page easily by using the wrong border with CSS. However, used judiciously, text borders can make your page stand out just right. The Border tab (the sixth tab from the left on the CSS Style Inspector) contains the following three columns:

- **Border width:** You can specify the width of the four borders individually by typing the first four fields or for the whole border by entering changes in the fifth field. Measure borders in point, pica, pixel, em (same as em dash), ex (the width of the letter *x*), mm, cm, or inch. Or, you can just select thin, medium, or thick.

- **Color:** The center column determines color. Drag and drop colors from the Color palette or choose one of the colors from the pop-up menu. Just for the fun of it, try using a different color for each side of the border.

- **Line style:** Choose from dotted, dash, solid, double, groove, ridge, inset, or outset style lines for your borders. Any box (well, *almost* any box) you can create by using a graphic tool, you can also create with the border.

Doing a Background Check

Background control in CSS far exceeds the background color or image available to define an entire page. When you select the Background tab (the seventh tab from the left in the CSS Style Inspector), you can decide not only which background image you want, but also which way you want it to tile! Chapter 7 shows how to add background color and images to your page as a whole. CSS, however, allows you to add a background image to any selected text on the page. So, if you want a single character on your page with a unique background image, you can do it! Here are the options:

- **Background image:** Add the background image as you would on a page by using the Page icon and Page Inspector. The image you choose shows up on only the portion of the page you defined with the CSS tag or class. Simply choose the background image in the CSS Style Inspector by either using the point-and-shoot line (as described in Chapter 1), clicking the Browse button, or simply dragging the file from the Site window to the Background Image window.

- **Color:** Either choose from the 16 colors on the pull-down menu or grab your favorite color from the Color palette and drop the color in the color box. Or, just click the Color well in the CSS Style Inspector to choose the color you want from the Color palette.

- **Repeat:** The Repeat window refers to repeating a background image. The Repeat selection treats the background image like a normal background image on the page. Select Repeat x to repeat the tile horizontally and Repeat y for a vertical tiling of your background image.

- **Attached:** The background image can either scroll or stay put (fixed).

- **Top:** This option indicates the number of units the background image is from the top of the text block.

- **Left:** This option indicates the distance the background image is from the left of the text block.

Loving Those Lists (And Other Stuff)

If you use lists in your HTML, you'll be delighted to find out that you can change both bullets and numbers — including ones you make yourself. The List and Other Properties tab, the last tab on the right of the CSS Style Inspector, lets you customize your lists and get ready for future browsers that implement new CSS properties. Look at everything you can do on this tab:

- **Bullet Image:** Make a little red heart GIF (one of the Web-safe graphic file formats), drop it into the Image window, and send a Valentine list to your sweetie! Those dots, circles, and squares get boring.

- **Style:** Change the boring dots to boring discs or squares! Choose your style based on your page design.

- **Position:** This option is cool. Put the bullet on the left or the right of the text in the list.

> ✔ **Other Property:** This option is the CSS wish list. Visit www.w3c.org to look at the options available for CSS that have not yet been implemented on the major browsers. For example, text-shadow promises to provide a shadow with colors. You just write it in, and if the feature is implemented in a browser, it shows up on the Web page in the browser. (Be realistic about using this feature. If a property has not been implemented, the chances of people seeing it on your page aren't so hot.)

Applying Style Sheets to Your Page

Applying CSS styles to your Web page is simple. In fact, I find it less difficult than wandering through all the formatting menus on the menu bar. After you've created your own style sheets, getting them on your Web pages is a snap. Follow these steps:

1. **Open a page by choosing File⇨New from the menu bar or pressing Ctrl+N (in Windows) or ⌘+N (on the Mac).**

   An untitled page appears in Layout view of the document window.

2. **Type the following sentence on the page:** This is the first head style and size.

   The text line is simply something to select and was used in Figure 10-3. You can write anything you want.

Selected text　　　　　　　　　CSS palette

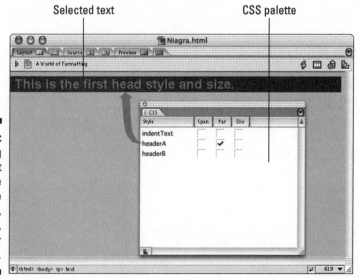

Figure 10-3:
Working on a font using the CSS Style Inspector, CSS Editor, and Color palette.

3. **Create some style sheets by following the steps in the section "Making Your First Style Sheet the Easy Way," earlier in this chapter.**

   Use as many options as you want. Start by creating something simple, such as a class that generates a big, colored font, or change a tag so that the text has a colored background.

4. **Close the CSS Editor but leave the Inspector on the stage.**

   You can dock or minimize the CSS Editor by pressing the minus (–) button on the Editor's window, if you prefer.

5. **Select the text on the screen.**

   The Inspector becomes the Text Inspector.

6. **Choose Window⇨CSS from the menu bar.**

   The CSS Palette appears. You see three columns — Span, Par, and Div — with check boxes under each column, as shown in Figure 10-3. Each of the styles you have created has a separate row.

7. **Check the Par box for one of the styles, as shown in Figure 10-3.**

   Kazaam! Your text changes to the style sheet you created. The Par is a substitute for the <p> tag container.

Span

When you need to apply CSS to a little part of your paragraph, a single word, or even a single letter, select Inline. The HTML tag <SPAN> provides the container.

Paragraph

You can paint an entire paragraph with CSS. Select text in the paragraph and check the Par column. In HTML, the <P> tag provides the parameters.

Division

Selecting the Div column provides CSS effects over all the text in the DIV block. Not surprisingly, the <DIV> tag provides the container in HTML for this selection. If you select the Div column, GoLive sets up the <DIV> tags in the HTML for the selected area automatically. When you select a block of text for CSS and select the Div column, GoLive effectively creates a Div container. However, if you select some of the text in the Div container and deselect the CSS style, only the selected text is removed from the Div container.

Varying Style Sheets

Suppose that you want to use two different style sheets on the same text. Is it possible? Yes! You can use not only more than a single style on selected text, but also more than a single Style column selection. Suppose you want to indent a line of text. Rather than have to recode an existing style, you can add an existing style that indents for you, as shown in Figure 10-4.

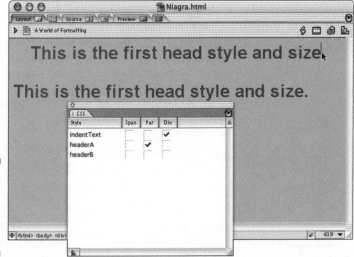

Figure 10-4: Select more than one style at the same time.

You can cause conflict if you use two styles with different properties. For example, if one style defines the text color as red and another style applied to the same text defines the text color as purple, you have a conflict. These types of conflicts are especially evident in cases where the different levels of the page (such as Inline or Paragraph) are selected to be styled. However, CSS wisely gives the smaller level precedence over the larger level. Therefore, Inline takes precedence over Paragraph, Paragraph over Division, and Division over Area.

Understanding External Style Sheets

After you go to the considerable work of creating the style sheet you want, you probably don't want to repeat the process for every page in your Web site. Fortunately, GoLive provides an easy way to store all the style sheets in files you can use on the page. Not only do external style sheets relieve your burden of redoing the work, but you can also use a single style sheet in as many pages as you want. Because you save external style sheets as .css files on your system, you can use them again on other sites.

When you create a style sheet in GoLive, CSS script is generated automatically and put into the HTML tags in the Head area of the page. With external style sheets, a single tag line calls up all the styles created on the external sheet. You can save a single style in one .css file or several files. A *.css file* is a text file with all the CSS information to format the material on your page, and you can use the file on any page in any site.

Creating external style sheets

The first step is to create an external .css file that you then fill with different styles. The process is exactly the same as discussed earlier in this chapter for creating style sheets, but you have a couple of extra steps to preserve the style sheet in a file. Here's how:

1. **Open the Site window and then open a page in Layout view of the document window.**

   The Layout view page should be on top of the Site window.

2. **Choose File⇨New Special⇨Cascading Style Sheet.**

   An untitled CSS Definitions palette appears. (It works much like the CSS Editor does.) Click it to activate the CSS Toolbar along the bottom of the palette. This step is crucial for creating external style sheets. Note that the CSS Definition palette arrives with body, p, and td tags already appearing on the page.

3. **Click the Class (.), Tag (<>), or ID (#) button on the toolbar to get started creating as few or as many tags, classes, and IDs as you want.**

   Use the same techniques for creating classes and tags, as discussed earlier in this chapter, beginning with the section "Working with the CSS Editor." See the section "ID, Please," later in this chapter, to find out how to create IDs in external style sheets. Figure 10-5 shows a class, .xmas (a big, green font with a red background), added to the default tags on the CSS Definitions palette.

4. **Choose File⇨Save or press Ctrl+S (in Windows) or ⌘+S (on the Macintosh).**

   A special Save CSS dialog box appears. Near the lower-left corner of the dialog box, you see Site Folder.

5. **Click the arrow next to the Site Folder to display a pull-down menu and select Root Folder.**

   The other selections on the pull-down menu are Stationeries, Components, and Templates. Ignore them.

6. **Click the Save button after making sure that you included the name of the file in the Save As window at the bottom of the dialog box.**

   Double-check to make sure that you leave the .css extension on the file-name you use (see Figure 10-6).

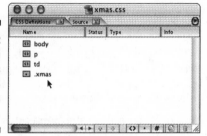

Figure 10-5: Adding definitions to the CSS Definitions palette.

Figure 10-6: Saving an external Cascading Style Sheet to the root folder.

Using external style sheets

After you save an external style sheet to the root folder of your site, you can use it whenever you want. (You must get the external file into the root folder of your site so that the file can appear on the Files tab of your Site window.) Follow these steps to get your text wearing the latest external style sheet — straight from Paris:

1. **Open the Site window and, on the Files tab, double-click a page icon to launch it into Layout view of the document window.**

   Layout view and the page should be on top of the Site window.

2. **Choose Window⇨Inspector from the menu bar.**

   The Text Inspector appears.

3. **Click the CSS button (it looks like a staircase) in the upper-right corner of Layout view of the document window.**

   The CSS Editor opens.

4. **Click the New Item icon (it's the one that looks like a staircase) on the CSS Toolbar.**

   A Page icon labeled (Empty Reference!), a Warning icon, and an External Folder icon appear in the external CSS Editor. The Inspector becomes the External Style Sheet Inspector, and (Empty Reference!) appears in the link box along with the Browse and Point-and-Shoot buttons.

5. **From the External Style Sheet Inspector, drag the point-and-shoot line to select the external style sheet file from the Site window, as shown in Figure 10-7.**

   Remember that the external style sheet file has a .css extension.

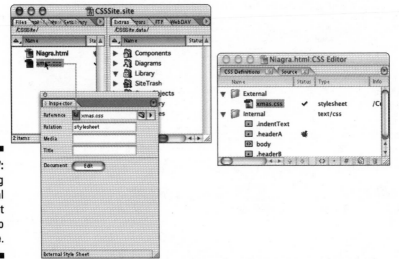

Figure 10-7:
Importing
an external
style sheet
file into
a page.

Voilà! You've done it. You now have an external style sheet in your page. Now you are ready to use your external style sheet. Just select the text, click the Style tab of your Text Inspector, and you see your external style listed. Figure 10-7 shows plain-vanilla text transformed into a reverse pattern (light text on a dark background) by an external Cascading Style Sheet.

ID, Please

IDs are a special type of CSS used for a limited and unique kind of style sheet. When you require special formatting for a dramatic effect on a small part of your page, IDs can produce the appropriate style. (There's no style you can produce with IDs that can't be done with classes, but IDs don't show up on the Text Inspector's Style tab because they are for very limited use.) Unlike tags and classes, you have to go into Source view and get your hands dirty in code! You create IDs just as you create classes, except that you start by selecting the ID (#) symbol, rather than the class icon (•), from the CSS Toolbar. IDs, though, are for limited use. For example, Figure 10-8 shows a background splitting a line of text using IDs.

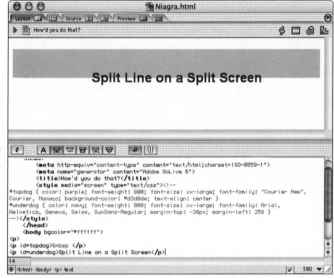

Figure 10-8: IDs inserted in the HTML in the split-screen source code.

Follow these steps to see how easy it is to create your own ID:

1. **Open a new page by choosing File⇨New from the menu bar.**

   Layout view and the page are on your screen.

2. **Choose Window⇨Inspector from the menu bar.**

   The Text Inspector appears.

3. **Click the CSS Button (it looks like a staircase) in the upper-right corner of Layout view of the document window.**

   The CSS Editor opens.

4. **Click the ID icon (the one that looks like a tic-tac-toe symbol — #) on the CSS Toolbar.**

A new #ID appears in the CSS Style Inspector. Give it a name, but leave the pound sign (#) where it is. You may name it #Henry or #Shift or whatever you want as long as you keep the pound sign in place.

5. **Create a Cascading Style Sheet using the techniques discussed earlier in this chapter.**

Use the same techniques for creating classes and tags, as discussed earlier in this chapter, beginning with the section "Working with the CSS Editor."

6. **Choose File⇨Save or press Ctrl+S (in Windows) or ⌘+S (on the Macintosh) to save your page to your disk drive.**

In the directory window, click the disk and directory in which you want to save your file and give it a name with the .html extension.

You have now created a Cascading Style Sheet ID. The next step is putting the ID to work on your page. The following section explains how to do so.

After you define and name an ID in the CSS Style Inspector, you can put it into your HTML. Doing that requires opening Source view of the document window or using the Source Code palette and typing the ID and its associated tags. The simple ⟨P⟩ tag is used in the following example. The following lines of HTML show how two IDs are used together to create a line of text split by a color block.

```
<P id="topdog">   </P>
<P id="underdog"> Split Line </P>
```

The CSS Editor has a list of all the IDs you created.

When GoLive generates the CSS code in an ID, it precedes the name of the ID with a pound (#) sign. However, when you place the ID in a paragraph, drop the pound sign, just like you drop the dot (.) in a class definition. Figure 10-8 shows what your IDs can do for you.

Previewing CSS

As time goes by, fewer and fewer people will use their Civil War–era browsers (for example, Version 3 and earlier), and previewing pages containing CSS will not be as critical. However, for now, what you see in GoLive may not be what you expect. To prepare for different views of your page using CSS, check out the page with different browsers *and* different versions of those browsers. Version 6 and later of Internet Explorer and Version 6 and later of Netscape Navigator handle CSS pretty well and similarly. However, check with *some* of the earlier versions of both major browsers and the Windows and Macintosh platforms.

Some designers are putting in messages on their Web pages, indicating that older browsers will not be able to see many of the features of the Web sites they create. (Come on, people! Browsers are free!) Using CSS is becoming less and less of a problem as users adopt the latest versions of browsers. Although designers are encouraged to keep in mind that older systems and browsers may not see the updated elements in newer browsers, there's a limit. If you try to appeal to the guy with a computer whose system runs on charcoal briquettes rather than on electricity, you may lose the rest of your audience who is expecting more interesting Web designs and sites.

If you experiment enough with CSS, you can create some great-looking headers, styles, backgrounds, and other effects without having to import graphics into a Web page. Nothing is wrong with graphics, but — compared to CSS — they're slower to load and can be more time-consuming in going from page to page.

Part III

A Site for Sore Eyes: Caring for, Feeding, and Organizing Web Sites

The 5th Wave   By Rich Tennant

"I can't really explain it, but every time I animate someone swinging a golf club, a little divot of code comes up missing on the home page."

In this part . . .

Part III shows you how to rule the world and then clone it! Taming a Web site used to be about as easy as herding cats, but you will soon have those sites as docile as a flock of sheep. In this part, the World Wide Web is at your beck and call because you'll find out how to use the considerable GoLive 6 power to organize pages in a site and keep them that way on your desktop and on a server. What's more, you can see how to clone your work so that when you develop a great site component or template, you can stash it where you can bring it out and use it again and again. Find out how to put up your Web site on a server and then make changes to it. GoLive 6 makes it all behave!

With the new GoLive 6 Design window, you can style your sites with all different types of arrangements. After you get the one you want, GoLive 6 automatically turns a set of pending icons into a set of pages ready and organized for content, sitting right in front of you in the Site window. With the Navigation window, you can globally change pages and images so that daily, weekly, or monthly updates of your site are a piece of cake rather than a tangle of Web pages.

Ever create a really great page and wish that you could do other pages in your site almost the same way without having to start over? Using the GoLive 6 stationeries and components, you can have little icons stored in your site totally re-create an entire page or an essential component (like your graphical navigation system) just by using the drag-and-drop feature.

Finally, Part III tells you everything you need to know about using the great GoLive 6 File Transfer Protocol (FTP), built right into the Site window. When you're ready to post your site on the Web, you just give GoLive your host's URL and your ID and password, and GoLive does the rest. You can send your entire site with a single click of the mouse. When it comes time to update your site, GoLive knows which pages have been changed and which haven't, and it just sends those pages with changes. I'll bet that you're thinking "Cool beans," but you know that there's more! That's right. Chapter 13 shows you how to work with WebDAV to coordinate work with others. Without leaving GoLive, you can work with others to create and change files in GoLive. Go, team!

Chapter 11

Diagramming the Whole Site

● ●

In This Chapter

▶ Diagramming sites with diagrams

▶ Creating a table of contents

▶ Changing elements globally

▶ Changing the organization of existing sites

▶ Putting external links in order

▶ Controlling site colors and inspection

▶ Getting your fonts in order

▶ Bringing site elements together

▶ Generating site statistics

● ●

Chapter 4 introduces the many and varied ways to deal with links in GoLive and how to use the Site window to help with your links. This chapter extends your understanding of the Site window and tells you how to get total control of your site.

For a site to look like a site and not an odd collection of pages, you need to think in terms of common design features. This chapter shows you how using the Site window can help you coordinate many common design elements that go into your Web site. For example, a color scheme and choice of fonts tell the viewer whether your page is serious, playful, businesslike, or even bizarre. If you try to gather up design elements page by page, you are not only in for more work, you're also less likely to have a consistent design. So, let's get lazy and deal with the site the easy way with GoLive 6.

Diagramming Your Site

In Chapter 3, I suggest that you get some graph paper and outline your site, including all the links and pages, as a first step in designing your site. Now, however, I introduce you to a GoLive 6 feature that may make the paper step unnecessary and further increase your ability to create great Web sites. The new feature resides on the Diagrams tab and menu bar of the Site window. Here's how it works:

1. **Create a new site by choosing File⇨New Site⇨Blank or by pressing Alt+Ctrl+N (in Windows) or Option-⌘+N (on the Macintosh) and use the GoLive Site Wizard to open a new site.**

   In the Site Wizard, use the defaults and put your new site on your desktop. You don't need to do anything in the document window or Layout view to create several Web pages and a site outline.

2. **Choose Window⇨View Palette or undock the View palette by clicking the View palette tab at the side of the screen.**

   The View palette (along with its roommate, the Inspector) appears on the screen.

   By dragging the tabs of your palettes to the side of the screen, you can "dock" them. To undock them, just drag them from the side. Docking helps to keep the palettes out of the way when you don't need them.

3. **Click the Diagrams tab of the Site window.**

   An empty Diagrams tab appears.

4. **Choose Diagram⇨New Design Diagram from the menu bar.**

   An Untitled Diagram icon appears on the Diagrams tab of the Site window.

5. **Click the file to select it and then rename it (on the Macintosh) or right-click the icon and choose Rename (in Windows).**

   The name of the design need not be the same name as the site. In fact, using different names is a good idea so that you can try out several different designs and not confuse them.

6. **Double-click the Diagram icon on the Diagrams tab of the Site window.**

   An empty diagram window appears.

7. **Click the Files tab of the Site window and drag the file index.html to the diagram window.**

   A Diagram icon appears in the diagram window with an anchor next to it and a Point-and-Shoot button on or below the icon. (Depending on what kind of design icon you use, the Point-and-Shoot button is either on or below the icon.) To change the icon's appearance, select the radio buttons on the Display tab of the View palette. I prefer the oval shape in the diagram window to distinguish it from the Navigation and Links view windows (see Figure 11-1).

The first page the viewer sees is the *anchor page.* In the context of designing a site, the anchor page establishes a point in the site hierarchy. With either the entire site or a portion of the site, the anchor page typically sits at the

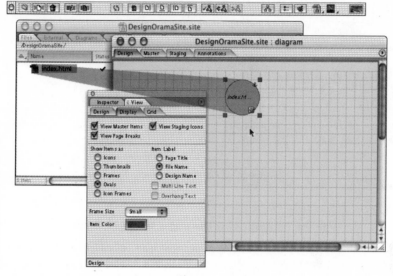

Figure 11-1:
The diagram
window
after
dragging the
index.html
page into it.

top of the hierarchy. It can be an entry page into the site, a home page, a core page, or some key page in a section of the site. However, you *do* need an anchor page in the design for later transition into live pages, as I discuss in the section "Submitting a site," later in this chapter.

Adding pages to the design

Okay, now that you've got your anchor page, it's time to add new pages. Adding new pages to a diagram window is a little different from adding pages to the Site window from the Files tab. The pages you add are planning pages. They are not real pages that are part of your site yet, but rather *pending* pages that you work with, adding and deleting, until you get the site organization you want. You can see what your pages look like and get a look and feel for how the site will flow before adding new pages and links. The process is something like sketching a design on paper before you put the pages and links in place. They're not real pages — just a mock-up of what you *may* want to put into your site. Later, you find out how to turn the mock-ups into actual Web pages. (Try that with graph paper!) Here's how to add pages, picking up from the seven steps in the preceding section.

1. **Choose Diagram➪New Pages from the menu bar.**

   The New Pages dialog box appears (see Figure 11-2).

2. **Type the number of new pages you want in the Number of Pages to Create text window.**

   In the example shown in Figure 11-2, five new pages are added.

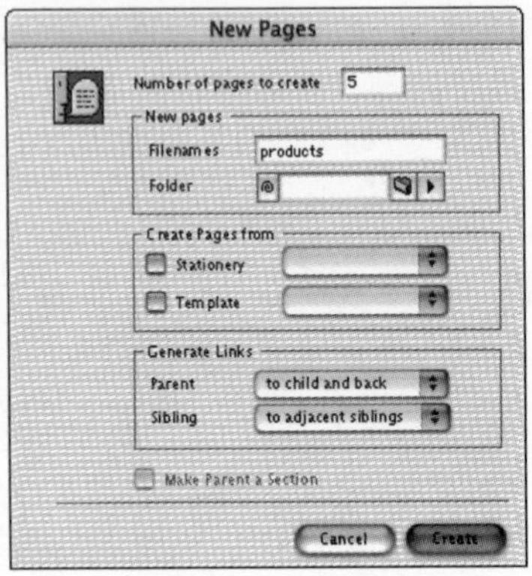

Figure 11-2:
Add pages
and pending
links to
design in
the New
Pages
dialog box.

3. Type the filenames for the pages in the Filenames window.

The Filenames window generates a series of names beginning with the name you put in the window. For example, if you enter the name products, GoLive 6 generates Products.html, Products1.html, Products2.html, and so on, up to the number of pages you want to create (see Figure 11-3).

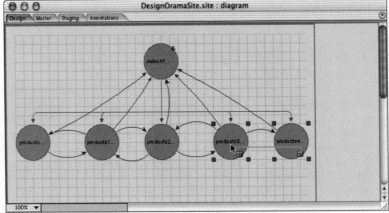

Figure 11-3:
Pages
added to the
Design tab
of the
diagram
window.

4. In the Generate Links section of the New Pages dialog box, select the type of link arrangements you want from the pull-down menus and then click the Create button.

First, on the Parent menu (refer to Figure 11-2), select to link to either each child, each child and back, the first child only, or none. Next, from the Sibling menu, choose the pending links to be either to the adjacent sibling or to none. You also have the option of using stationery or *templates* (premade page designs you have stored as stationery or template pages) or making the parent a section. A *child* refers to a page directly below the current page in the hierarchy, a *sibling* refers to a page on the same level in the hierarchy, and a *parent* is a page above the current page in the hierarchy. The *hierarchy* is a sequence of pages with the top page the first page that is viewed. When pages are on the same level of a hierarchy (siblings), they can be selected in no special order by the page or pages before them in the hierarchy because they reside in the same level. A parent page precedes the current page.

After you add new pages, each gets a name and Point-and-Shoot button. Figure 11-3 shows the pages you created by using the options in the New Pages dialog box.

You can add pages to your design easily by clicking one of the Add Page icons on the Diagram toolbar. An untitled page appears. However, I like choosing Diagram⇨New Pages from the menu bar, even if I'm adding a single page. As soon as you add a single page or multiple pages, name them. Naming a page right away helps you see what the page does. More importantly, there's no need to waste time later in finding the page and renaming it. Choosing Diagram⇨New Pages (not New Page) is the only way to name your page or pages immediately. By doing so, later on, when you are attempting to remember what a page is supposed to do in relationship to other pages in the site, you won't be lost.

Adding pending links and annotations

The Point-and-Shoot buttons on the Page icons in the diagram window exist to help you make any additional pending links you may want. For example, in Figure 11-3, if you want to create a link between Products4.html and Products1.html, you pull a point-and-shoot line from Jean4.html over to Products1.html.

A more interesting feature of the diagram window is its annotations. While building a design, you may have a special comment for a page or a link. Use the annotations feature to remind yourself why a particular link or page is important or unique or just to insert a comment. (See the sections "Diagramming Your Site" and "Adding pages to the design," earlier in this chapter.) Follow these steps to use annotations:

1. **Choose Window⇨Objects or undock the Objects palette by clicking the Objects tab at the side of the screen.**

   The Objects palette appears on the screen.

2. **Select the Site tab in the Objects palette and drag a Diagram Annotation icon to a link or page in the diagram window.**

   When the Diagram Annotation icon is properly positioned over the page or link, you see the "halo effect." The pages get an outer ring around them, and the link arrows get fuzzy and wide. A yellow icon appears. Keep it selected.

3. **Choose Window⊏⊃Inspector or undock the Inspector palette by clicking the Inspector tab at the side of the screen.**

   The Inspector appears as the Annotation Inspector.

4. **Type the subject and text of the annotation you want to make and click the Display Subject and Display Text check boxes at the bottom of the Inspector.**

   Your annotation now appears on the link or file you selected in the diagram window. If you want to reposition the text and subject, use the Position pull-down menu at the bottom of the Annotation Inspector (see Figure 11-4). You also find that your annotations are now stored on the Annotations tab of the diagram window.

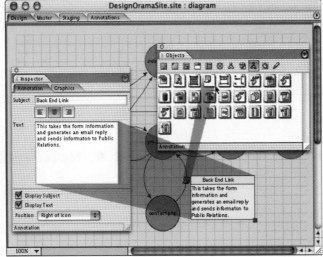

Figure 11-4:
Annotations
added in the
diagram
window.

If you want to remove any of the pending links or pages, just select the Page icon or Link Arrow line and click the Trash Can icon on the toolbar. Notice that when you select an arrow link, a little box appears in the middle of the line. You can drag the link to bow the link arrow to more clearly see the pending links between the pages.

Master Items

GoLive 6 has a new feature in design development, called the Master tab, on the diagram window. Sometimes, you have features you want on all pages of your diagram. Logos and legends often have to be a part of every page in one's design, and by placing the object on the master page, you can forget about not including it in your design. It will be there for you. You can effectively brand your diagrams by placing your logo on the master page of the diagram window.

Submitting a site

Suppose that you complete your design, your pending links are dandy, and the annotations make everything clear, and now you want to apply your design to the Site window. Remember that you're not dealing with real pages yet; you're just examining some designs. If you click the Staging tab of the diagram window, you see all the pages in the Diagram Pages folder, as shown in the left window of Figure 11-5.

Diagram pages are like blueprints: The concept exists, but nothing is concrete yet. When you submit a design, you turn your design pages into live pages. All the live pages are shifted into the Live Pages folder on the Staging tab of the diagram window. More importantly, the pages now appear on the Files tab of the Site window. That means that they're all set for you to work with. Follow these next steps in creating a site design to turn your design into a set of pages you can begin filling with content and links:

1. **With the diagram window on the screen, click the Check Diagram icon on the toolbar or choose Diagram⇨Staging⇨Check Staging from the menu bar.**

    GoLive checks to make sure that all the pages are linked to an anchor page and no problems exist with files or folders when the design is submitted.

2. **Click the Staging tab of the diagram window.**

    The contents of the Staging tab are displayed, as shown on the left side of Figure 11-5. If your page has no problems, you see check marks next to each of the pages in the Status column. Error or warning icons appear next to pages with problems or pages that have no content or links. Other than the index.html page, most have warning icons. Warning icons are removed as soon as you add content to the pages. If an error icon appears (a green bug), open the page and see whether the links conform to the design. If not, change either the links in the diagram or the page so that they are the same.

3. **If no errors exist, click the Submit All button on the Diagram toolbar or choose Diagram⇨Staging⇨Submit All from the menu bar.**

    All the pages in the diagram window have been moved from the Design Pages folder to the Live Pages folder on the Staging tab of the diagram window (see the right diagram window in Figure 11-5). The new pages also are on the File tab of the Site window now. However, you need to put all the links in the individual pages by following the design recommendations.

Figure 11-5:
The Diagram pages before (left) and after (right) being submitted. All the live pages, including the anchor page, appear on the Site tab of the Site window as well.

Generating a Table of Contents

When you create a site in GoLive 6, it generates a *root folder* automatically. Everything in your site should go in this folder or in a subfolder within the root folder. (Using the diagram window to create a site puts all the files submitted into the root folder automatically.) By the time you've created a bunch of pages, added graphics, added maybe a little JavaScript, made external links, and put in a kitchen sink, your site may be a little confusing — even to you. To make life much easier on yourself, you need to generate a table of contents or, as the pros say, a TOC. Use the following steps to get a grip on your site:

1. **Open your site by first choosing File⇨Open from the menu bar or pressing Ctrl+O (in Windows) or ⌘+O (on the Macintosh) and then opening a completed site from the directory dialog box.**

   Your site opens in Files view of the Site window.

2. **Choose Diagram⇨Navigation from the menu bar.**

   The Navigation window opens, and you see icons of your site pages and link arrows. You can open the Navigation window from any tab in the Site window.

3. **Choose Diagram⇨Create Table of Contents from the menu bar.**

Sit back and wait while GoLive generates a TOC page, as shown in Figure 11-6.

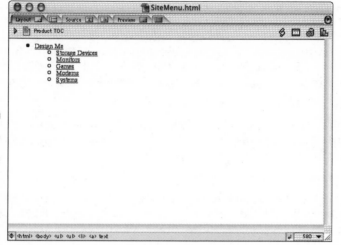

Figure 11-6:
Generate a
Table of
Contents
page auto-
matically
in GoLive 6.

The TOC page shows all the pages in the root folder. They're organized in the hierarchy of links. The *hierarchy* simply refers to each page in relationship to other pages. A *parent* page is higher in the hierarchy than a child page (the page it links to downward), and a *sibling* page is on the same level in the hierarchy. To some extent, the concept of hierarchy doesn't make much sense in a fully hypertext environment when everything is linked to everything else. It makes sense only when a site is designed in a sequence. A parent page precedes a child page, but a sibling can be selected in any order from a parent. Sibling pages on the same level may link to one another in any order. As a sequence, the hierarchy makes sense, but not as a wide-open, hyperlinked site where any one page is linked to any other one. (The hierarchy also makes sense to bureaucrats.)

Limiting the TOC page to those pages found in the root folder is both a good and bad feature. On one hand, if you have a page sitting on your computer's desktop that you linked but didn't place in the root folder, it doesn't show up in the TOC or on the Site tab of the Site window. The good feature is that you can see that the page is missing from the TOC and get busy and put it into the root folder. The bad feature is that if you forget all about the page, it isn't placed in the root folder. When you publish your page, the link goes "Huh?" and doesn't have a clue where the page on your desktop is located. That's why you want to be sure that all your files are in the root folder. (At the end of this chapter, I show you how GoLive saves you from even this problem!)

Making Global Changes

When you have to replace an image or set of images in a Web site, GoLive makes it easy with global image replacement. Suppose that you have a ho-hum logo in the upper-left corner of your page, just like Jakob Nielsen (the author of *Web Usability*) tells us to do. After putting the logo into 215 pages in your site, you come up with a logo that rocks your socks. Rather than have to wade through all 215 pages, you can make one change and change all the images in one fell swoop. (Once, a swoop fell on me.) Here's how to perform a global image replacement:

1. **Open your site by choosing File⇨Open from the menu bar or pressing Ctrl+O (in Windows) or ⌘+O (on the Mac) and then open a completed site from the directory dialog box.**

   Your site opens in Files view of the Site window.

2. **Drag the new graphic file from where you have stored it on your computer to the Files tab of the Site window or choose File⇨Import⇨Files to Site to place the file in the root folder.**

   You should be able to see all your HTML files and your media files and their related folders in Files view of the Site window.

3. **Choose Window⇨In & Out Links Palette, click the In & Out Links button on the Site toolbar (the eighth button from the left), or undock the In & Out Links palette.**

   Unless you have a page or image selected, the In & Out Links palette is blank.

4. **On the Files tab of the Site window, select the image you want to replace.**

   Be sure to select the one you want to eliminate. It now appears on the In & Out Links palette with all the links to it. Notice how many pages are linked to the same image (see Figure 11-7).

5. **Pull the point-and-shoot line from the file to be eliminated on the In & Out Links palette to the new image file on the File tab of the Site window.**

   In Figure 11-7, you can see the file Logo.jpg being replaced by NewLogo.jpg. Notice that most Web pages in the site use Logo.jpg. NewLogo.jpg replaces all of them. As soon as you release the mouse button, the point-and-shoot operation is complete and the Change Reference dialog box appears (see Figure 11-8).

6. **Click the OK button in the Change Reference dialog box.**

   If you intend to replace the image in all pages in the site, just click OK. However, if you want to leave the original graphic in any of your Web pages, uncheck the boxes next to the pages where you want to keep the original graphic. Figure 11-8 shows all the boxes checked, indicating that the new one replaces all the original graphic files.

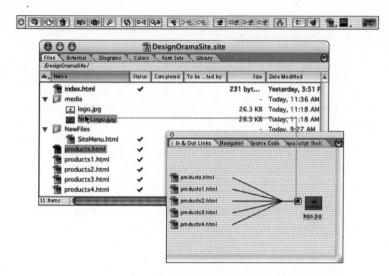

Figure 11-7:
Global
replace-
ment of an
image file.

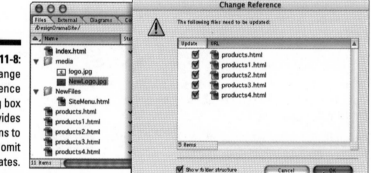

Figure 11-8:
The Change
Reference
dialog box
provides
options to
omit
updates.

When a new image replaces an old one, the *old* height and width are maintained. If the images have identical dimensions, you should have no problem. However, if the dimensions are different, the Resize Warning icon appears on the image in each of your pages in Layout view. If that happens, you need to select each image, call up the Inspector (it appears as the Image Inspector), and then click the Image Resize Restore button on the Image Inspector to fix it. (If you have to resize the replaced graphics page-by-page on your whole site after a whiz-bang global change, you may wonder, "What's the point of a global change if I have to fix it page by page?" That's reason enough to make sure that the old and new images have the same dimensions.)

Reorganizing Existing Sites

If you wish that you could fix up some of your existing sites using GoLive 6, but you don't want to start from scratch, there's hope. Because GoLive handles just about every aspect of Web sites better than other tools, it comes as no surprise that GoLive has a way to help you tweak to perfection an old site constructed using some other Web site program. If you have a site on your computer with major portions of it safely stored in one folder, you're in luck. However, even if your Web site is scattered all over your computer's folders, disks, and directories, you can still pull it together. Start by importing the folder with the site's root folder and index page:

1. **With GoLive 6 open, choose File➪New Site➪from the menu bar.**

   The New Site Wizard opens.

2. **In the New Site Wizard, choose Single User➪Next➪Import from Folder➪Next.**

   At this point, you find yourself in the section where you must first click the top Browse button to select your site folder and then click the bottom Browse button to select the home page for the site.

3. **After selecting the site folder and home page, click the Next button.**

   You're asked to choose a location for your new site.

4. **Click the Browse button, select the location for your new site, provide a name for it, and then check the Create Project Folder button. Press the Finish button.**

   Wait a little while GoLive generates a data folder. and saves your new site in a project folder.

That's it. Your old, messy site is at least partially enthroned in a GoLive 6 root folder. You should now have two folders and a file:

- ✔ **The root folder**
- ✔ **The data folder:** It has the same name as your root folder except that it has a .data extension.
- ✔ **The site file:** It has the same name as the root folder and has a .site extension.

Create another folder and put the two folders and the site file together. Otherwise, you soon have another mess on your hands because you have no single place for all these folders and files you just generated. After you have the Site window open, you can import into your new site all the files not included in the root folder you created and again (or for the first time) have control over your site.

Organizing External Links

Your Web site may have several external links (such as links to other Web sites) that you want to use in your site. GoLive has a unique way of dealing with external site links in the Site window. Rather than try to remember a long URL for an external link, GoLive can use your browser's own bookmarks. In fact, a good way to organize your Web site is to begin with your browser.

Bookmarks have long been a standard feature of Web browsers because they seem a natural and efficient way to store Web addresses for easy access. In Netscape Communicator, you bookmark a page by choosing Bookmarks⇨Add Bookmark from the menu bar. With Internet Explorer, bookmarks are called Favorites. In Internet Explorer, choose Favorites⇨Add to Favorites from the menu bar to bookmark a Web page. To put that efficiency to good use for handling the external links for your own Web site, start by bookmaking the Web addresses you need in one of your browsers. After you have all the bookmarks you need for your site, integrating them into the Site window is simple. Follow these steps:

1. **Open the Site window by clicking the Select Window button on the toolbar or choosing File⇨Open on the menu bar.**

   The Site window opens in the most recently used view.

2. **Click the External tab of the Site window.**

   External view of the Site window opens. You see four columns: Name, Used, Status, and URL.

3. **Open your browser.**

   Remember to open the browser that has the bookmarks or favorites you want in your site.

4. **In Netscape Communicator, choose Bookmarks⇨Edit Bookmarks from the menu bar to open the Bookmarks window; in Internet Explorer, choose Favorites⇨Organize Favorites to open a Favorites window.**

   In both browsers, the Bookmarks/Favorites window opens.

5. **Drag the URL icon (an @ symbol in Internet Explorer 5 on the Macintosh or a stylized E in the Windows version of Explorer or a bookmark ribbon in Netscape Communicator) from the browser to the Name column of the External tab of the Site window.**

   Voilà! You can now see all the external links you bookmarked in your browser on the External tab of the Site window. Figure 11-9 shows how the Site window's External view looks with installed links.

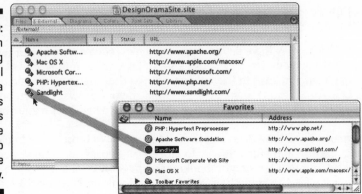

Figure 11-9:
You can drag external links from a browser's bookmarks to the External tab of the Site window.

You can even drag a URL directly from a Web page. Just find the link on the page you like and drag-and-drop it on the External tab of the Site window. That action may save a step or two, but it's usually easier to organize the external links in your Favorites or Bookmark folders first.

Changing links on the site

You can't create a link from the Site window, but you can replace an existing link using the In & Out Links palette. You use a similar technique for replacing links as you do for changing images on your site. Suppose that an external link has changed addresses or you find an external link that you simply like better than a previous one. Making the change requires some tab flipping, so note the steps carefully:

1. **Open your Site window by clicking the Select Window button on the toolbar or by choosing File⇨Open from the menu bar.**

   The Site window opens on the most recently used tab.

2. **Click the External tab of the Site window.**

   If no external icons exist on this page, follow the steps outlined in the preceding section and add some. Select the external site you want to change.

3. **Open the In & Out Links palette by clicking the In & Out Links Palette button (the eighth from the left) on the Site toolbar.**

   You can also open the In & Out Links palette by choosing Window⇨In & Out Links Palette from the menu bar or just undocking it.

4. **On the In & Out Links palette, select the page linked to the external site you selected.**

   If you selected the link you wanted to change, the page shows up on the In & Out Links palette. By clicking the link on the In & Out Links palette, it becomes the selected item.

5. **Pull the point-and-shoot line from the icon of the external link you want to replace to the External tab of the Site window.**

   Figure 11-10 shows the point-and-shoot line making a connection to an external site.

6. **After you have the point-and-shoot line over the new icon, release the mouse button.**

   Whew! The steps for this task are not that complex. Practice a few times and you'll find it to be a simple way to replace URLs on your site.

Organizing external links that you use throughout your site saves time and reduces typing errors if you key in your external URLs. Also, by using browser bookmarks, when you make the changes with the In & Out Palette, you're further assured that you didn't type an incorrect URL by mistake.

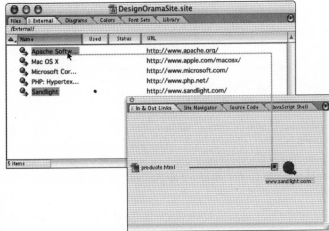

Figure 11-10:
Point-and-
shoot
change of
URL in
the Site
window.

Hold the phone! (Hold the e-mail!)

The External tab of the Site window is a great place to store URL addresses, but that's not the only kind of address you can store there; the External tab also lets you store any e-mail addresses you may want to use in your Web site. To make things even more convenient, e-mail addresses are stored on the External tab with the handy `mailto:` preface already attached so that when you drag and drop them into a Web page, they're all set to bring up an e-mail page for a quick bit of electronic correspondence. For a big Web site, making it easy for the viewer to contact the organization is important; it means that it's also important for the designer to have an easy way to place and change e-mail addresses in the site. The following steps show how easy it is:

1. **Open the Site window by choosing File⇨Open from the menu bar.**

   The Site window opens on the most recently used tab.

2. **Click the External tab of the Site window.**

   External view may have some icons from external URLs or be empty, depending on what you've been up to.

3. **Choose Window⇨Inspector or undock the Inspector by clicking the Inspector tab at the side of the screen.**

   The Inspector becomes the Reference Inspector.

4. **Click the In & Out Links Palette button (the eighth one from the left) on the Site toolbar.**

   Although the In & Out Links palette isn't used in this operation, it conveniently shows both the e-mail address and the Address icon (a picture of a face). Because you need to recognize the Address icon in future operations, you should have a peek at in the In & Out Links palette.

5. **Choose Window⇨Objects from the menu bar or undock the Objects palette.**

   The Objects palette opens to the most recently selected tab or the Basics tab.

6. **Click the Site tab on the Objects palette.**

   The Site tab is the seventh tab from the left. An organizational chart icon identifies the tab. (You'll be a bureaucrat in no time!)

7. **Drag the Address icon (the picture of a face) from the Site tab of the Objects palette to the Name column of the External tab of the Site window.**

   An untitled address icon appears with that happy-blockhead-guy of a face.

8. **With the Address icon on the External tab of the Site window selected, click the Edit button in the Reference Inspector.**

   The Edit URL window appears.

9. **In the Edit URL window, replace the untitled address with the full e-mail address.**

   Leave the `mailto:` part alone. Just type the e-mail address after `mailto:`.

10. **Click the Change button in the Edit URL window.**

    Now your new e-mail address should appear in the Reference Inspector.

11. **Put the cursor in the Name window of the Reference Inspector; type a name for the e-mail address and then click the OK button.**

    The In & Out Links palette, the External tab of the Site window, and the Reference Inspector all should show the correct e-mail address.

When you organize a site for a company composed of many people with different e-mail addresses, collecting the e-mails in External view of the Site window makes it easier to use and reuse e-mail addresses and make sure that they're consistent.

Site Color Control and Inspection

Chapter 7 introduces the Color tab of the Site window and shows how to create a color palette to give your site a cohesive and coherent color scheme. This chapter shows that you can do more with your site colors, both when you create a site and when you renew it. From the Color tab of the Site window, you can inspect the colors in the site and find what pages use different colors. Color inspection uses the In & Out Links palette in conjunction with the Color Inspector, the Color tab of the Site window, and the Color palette. (Image colors on media files, however, are not shown.)

If you have been using colors from the Web Name List on your pages, when they are transferred to the Color tab of the Site window they are listed as "untitled" in the Name column of the Color tab. However, they are named in the HTML Name column. If the colors are not from the Web Name List of the Color palette, the name given to the colors in the HTML Name column is the color's hexadecimal value. However, the Name column of the Colors tab *does* show a color swatch, to show what the color looks like. To see which pages on your site are sporting a lovely shade of chartreuse or Dodger blue, do the following:

1. **Click the Color tab of the Site window.**

   For a developed site that has been saved or imported, you should see a list of untitled colors in a New Colors folder unless you have given them a name. Select a color. (If no colors are there, choose Site⇨Get Colors Used to place them on the Colors tab of the Site window.)

2. **Click the In & Out Links button (the eighth button from the left) on the Site toolbar.**

   Select any of the colors used in your site. Sometimes, you will have created a color palette for your site but not used all your colors yet, so some colors may not show a connection with a page. Figure 11-11 shows the colors associated with the site.

3. **Choose Window⇨Inspector or undock the Inspector by clicking the Inspector tab at the side of the screen.**

   The Inspector becomes the Color Inspector, appearing with a color well showing the selected color from the Color tab of the Site window. If your color is untitled, you can change it to something a bit more useful if you

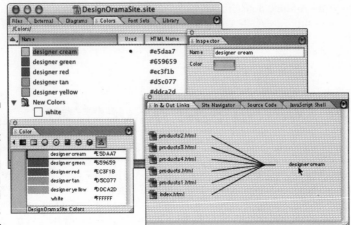

want. (I like to use a common site name to name all my colors so that I know the originating site. Of course, you can name them after your cat, if you want.)

4. **Choose Window⇨Color Palette or undock the Color palette.**

   The Color palette appears. Okay, it's getting a little crowded, but all the windows are working together (see Figure 11-11). With the color selected on the Color palette, you can now apply it to a page in Layout view, if you want.

Copying the site colors to another site is simple. (The technical term for this process is Not Reinventing the Wheel.)

1. **Open the Color tabs of the Site windows of both the site that gets the colors and the one that has the colors you want to export.**

   You see two Site windows. One should have all the colors you want to export in Colors view of the Site window.

2. **Drag some or all of the colors from one Site window to the next.**

   All the colors dragged from one site to the other now appear in the receiving site's Color view in the Site window.

Although you can make global changes in files, you can't make global color changes. In the global rearrangement of links, the old filenames are replaced with the new. In GoLive, that's not possible with color names. However, you can make global changes to background *images*. Remember that a background *color* is not an image and that although a background image can be swapped for another one, the same is not true with colors. The reason is that a background image, like all images, is an independent file and must be linked to your page. Because links can be changed, the background images can be changed as well by using the global tools.

If you want to make global changes with background colors in a site, you can use a solid block of color from a graphic. That is, you use a background image for your background color. Create all the background color-block images you want and make global changes all you want. (If this idea sounds loopy, consider it an easy way to routinely change a Web site to maintain user interest.)

Organizing Fonts for a Site

Rather than go stark-raving mad by fumbling through menus to find the font you want, organize them on the Font Sets tab of the Site window. Every single font you use in your site should be on the Font Sets tab of the Site window for easy access and design coordination. The first step is to get your fonts on the Font Sets tab of the Site window:

1. **Click the Font Sets tab of the Site window.**

   Unless you've imported the site, the page is blank. Otherwise, it shows the font sets used in the pages that make up your site.

2. **Choose Window⇨Inspector from the menu bar or undock the Inspector.**

   The Inspector becomes the Font Set Inspector and displays the fonts of any font set you select on the Site window.

3. **Choose Window⇨Objects from the menu bar or undock the Objects palette by clicking on the Objects tab at the side of the screen.**

   The Objects palette appears on the screen.

4. **Click the Site tab on the Objects palette.**

   The Site tab has the organizational chart icon on it, and when the tab is selected, ten icons appear. Look for the Font icon. It has an italicized *A* on it. This icon is different from the icon with the folder *and* the italicized *A*, so be careful. (Just select the fifth icon from the left.)

5. **Drag the Font icon from the Site tab of the Objects palette and drop it in the Name column on the Font Sets tab of the Site window.**

   An untitled new font appears on the Font Sets tab of the Site window. The Inspector is now the Font Inspector.

6. **Select the untitled font set named New Font and open the pull-down menu located in the lower-right corner of the Font Inspector.**

   All the fonts on your system appear.

7. **Scroll through the font list and select the font you want.**

   The font name appears in the Font Name column and in the Font window next to the pull-down menu.

8. **In the Name column on the Font Sets tab of the Site window, enter a name for the font.**

   Use the font's name that is in your system's font set.

You can follow these steps and substitute a font set for a single font. (Use the Font Set icon, rather than the Font icon, on the Site tab of the Objects palette.) A font set can include several fonts or just a single font. With fonts like Verdana, you probably should include Arial or Helvetica or both. That's because some (very few) computers may not have Verdana; to keep the font in a sans serif face, you need other fonts, such as Arial or Helvetica, that cover just about all computers.

Figure 11-12 shows a site with several fonts in the Site window. If you select a font with the In & Out Links palette open, all the pages in the site using the selected font are displayed, as shown in Figure 11-12. You also can add individual fonts by simply dragging them from a page in the document window and dropping them on the Font Sets tab of the Site window.

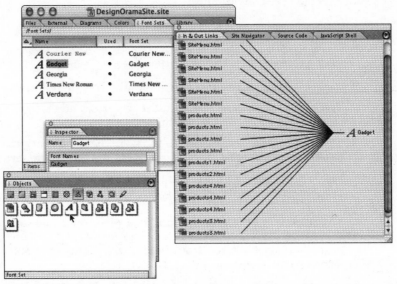

Figure 11-12: Place fonts on the Font Sets tab of the Site window.

Getting the fonts in the Font Sets view

If you open an existing site created with another program to create a GoLive site file, all the fonts in the imported site are placed on the Font Sets tab of the Site window. However, if you're working on a current GoLive site and haven't placed the fonts on the Font Sets tab, you can move all the fonts from all the pages with a single operation:

1. Click the Font Sets tab of the Site window.

The empty Font Sets view in the Site window opens. No fonts or sets are there yet.

2. Choose Site⇨Get Font Sets Used from the menu bar.

All the fonts used in the site appear on the Font Sets tab of the Site window. (That makes life easy.)

Using your site fonts

Applying fonts from the Font Sets tab of the Site window is much easier than using the menu bar. In Chapter 2, you find out how to select a font by rummaging through the menus. Using the fonts from the site, all you need to do is grab the font or font set you want and plunk it down on the selected text. Here's how:

1. Select the text you want for the font in Layout view of the document window.

The selected font is highlighted.

2. From the Font Sets tab of the Site window, drag the desired font or font set to the selected text and drop it.

Shazaam! You have transformed the font to the one selected from the Site window. If you select a font set, the top font is selected for the actual style. In cases where the font is not in your system, the browser automatically selects the next font in the set until it gets one on the viewer's system. If none of the fonts is there, a default font used by the viewer is substituted.

Cleaning Up Your Site

When everyone gets busy, site work gets messy. (Dust bunnies are everywhere.) Some internal-link HTML pages may not have been put into the root folder, or maybe you've created a new image that somehow didn't get placed where it belonged. Put all these oversights together, and your site looks about as organized as a pillow fight. Take heart, for GoLive knows how to de-slob your site in one simple, yet effective, operation:

1. Open the Site window to any tab.

This step is easy because any tab in the Site window works.

2. Choose Site⇨Clean Up Site.

The Clear Site dialog box appears, as shown in Figure 11-13. The check boxes allow you to select what you want to be moved and not.

3. Check those items you want moved into the Site window and root site and those you want removed and click OK.

That's it. You're all done!

Figure 11-13:
The Clear
Site dialog
box.

The Clean Up Site operation is equivalent to a site spring-cleaning. What's more, all the external links, colors, and fonts are placed under the appropriate tab in the Site window. (GoLive automatically cleans sites created from existing sites.)

If you check out the Preferences⇨Site⇨Clean Up Site command, you can set options to move to or remove from the root folder. Generally, the default Preferences work fine, but if you want to fine-tune any aspect of cleaning up your site, take a look at the available preferences.

Rather than add color, external links, and fonts to a site individually, use the Clean Up Site option. One operation takes care of all the tabs, and it takes no more time.

Getting Site Statistics

After slaving on your site, you don't want to find out that no one wants to look at it because your pages take far too long to download. Although the Document Statistics information in GoLive is not really a site operation, finding out how to put that information to work for you is a necessary part of good site management. Slow pages affect your site, so it makes sense to put your pages on the digital scale and weigh them as part of your site evaluation. Here's how:

1. **Open a page in the document window.**

   Any of the views works.

2. **Choose Special⇨Document Statistics from the menu bar.**

   The Document Statistics window appears with information about byte count, character count, and word count for the selected page.

Figure 11-14 shows a fairly light page, with a total byte count of 20.2 kilobytes. With the slowest modem (9600 bps), the page takes 21 seconds to load. (Pages in general should not take more than 10 seconds to load, but people with 9600 bps modems are used to waiting.) More typically, a 56k baud modem takes only 3 seconds, but with a T1 line or faster connection the page is up in a second. Notice that both the text and graphics are included in the calculation of weight.

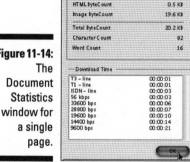

Figure 11-14:
The
Document
Statistics
window for
a single
page.

The times for the downloads are based on certain standardized times for optimal conditions. With more people spending more time on the Web, the Internet does get clogged up; during heavy-usage periods, such as the middle of the day, everything can slow down to a crawl. So, you have to take the time estimates with a grain of salt and realize that the times are relative estimates at best. Also the Document Statistics window doesn't measure movies and sound files; if your pages have these types of files, you had better get the old stopwatch out and time them yourself.

If your business depends in any significant way on your Web site, open your pages at different times of the day to find out how long they take to open. During peak hours, you may want to consider a very light *text-only* page to get the information to the viewer quickly.

Chapter 12

Design Once, Template Often: Stationery, Smart Objects, and Components

● ●

In This Chapter

▶ Repeating stationery items

▶ Making stationery objects work for you

▶ Importing stationery

▶ Putting reusable components to work

▶ Creating component pages

▶ Applying components to pages

▶ Getting smart with Smart Objects

▶ Identifying and fixing bugs

▶ Using and customizing the GoLive 6 spell-check feature

● ●

Stationeries and components are GoLive 6 tools for saving individual pages and page elements. If you spend all the time you need to get the right look and feel for a particular page, you then can use that page as a stationery that you can apply to all the other pages on your site. As a result, all the pages on your site consistently display the same look and feel. In GoLive 6, the steps for creating this type of template are pretty straightforward. If you're careful to get the process right the first couple of times, you end up with the results you want. (The voice of experience is speaking here.)

Likewise, a major element in your page can be useful for several pages. Rather than redo that element, you can make a component from it and reuse the component. Moreover, when you change the original component file, all the files with the component are changed too. Suppose that you have a set of graphic navigational tools that you spent lots of time creating. Rather than remake the same set of navigation tools for every page, turn them into components and use them throughout your site.

Cloning Stationery Items

The basic plan in devising a stationery is to create a page just the way you want it, including all the images, colors, fonts, forms, and you-name-its that go into a Web page. Then you store the page as a *stationery item* (a fancy word for a template) in the Stationery folder you find on the Extras tab of the Site window. After you place a page in the Stationery folder, the page automatically appears on the Site Extras tab of the Objects palette, where you can use it as a template whenever you need it. Follow these steps to get a page into the Stationery folder:

1. **Choose File⇨New Site.**

   The New Site Wizard appears. Click through the wizard to create a blank site.

2. **Double-click the index.html file in the Site window to open it.**

   The page opens into Layout view of the document window. This page is the one to use for creating a special stationery page. Remember that this page is a special page, so watch all the design features carefully. For example, make sure that the colors look good together. (Chapter 3 describes key page-design elements.)

3. **After you fully complete the page, choose Site⇨Clean Up Site from the menu bar.**

   Make sure that all the elements for your page are in the root-site folder — that's exactly what the Clean Up Site command does. Although such a move technically isn't necessary, you may easily regret not doing so later because you use the stationery item as a template. Remember that the Clean Up Site command doesn't throw out good stuff. It simply moves files to your root-site folder that aren't already there, as I discuss in Chapter 11.

4. **Save the page as a Stationery by choosing File⇨Save As from the menu bar, and in the Save As dialog box choose Stationery from the Site Folder drop down menu.**

   You then see a Stationery icon in the Stationery folder as well as your original file's Page icon still on the File tab of the Site window, as shown in Figure 12-1.

You did it! That's all you need to do to create a stationery item. Next, you need to know about some ways to use the item as a template, which I describe in the following sections.

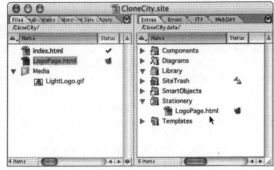

Figure 12-1:
The
Stationery
icon now
appears
in the
Stationery
folder.

Making Stationery Objects Work for You

Making and using stationery are really two separate operations, and so I treat them as such. You don't need to turn off your computer or close GoLive 6, but after you create stationery, putting it to use requires a different mindset. To appreciate and understand why a template is a useful tool in managing your Web site, consider the page shown in Figure 12-2. The page, an example of a page you can use as stationery, has a graphic logo set up as a Smart Photoshop Object, a bar menu, and CSS is used to provide the color combinations for the site.

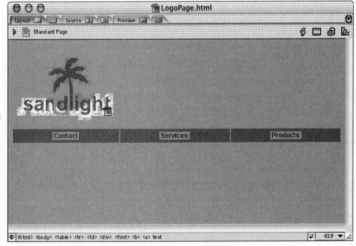

Figure 12-2:
A typical
Web page
you can
use as a
stationery
object.

The page shown in Figure 12-2 represents a page that contains key elements in a Web site you can use as a template for other pages in the site. Using stationery, however, you can store it in the Stationery pad on the Site Extras tab of the Objects palette, and you only have to drop it on a page for reproduction. Rather than have to re-create the main navigation elements and the logo each time a new page is added to the site, all you have to do is drag a stationery element to the File column of the Site window. By using stationery, you can quickly develop any other page containing the same components. To use stationeries as templates, just follow these simple steps:

1. **Begin on the Files tab of the Site window. Choose Window⇨Objects from the menu bar to open the Objects palette or undock the Objects palette by clicking the tab at the side of the screen.**

   The Objects palette appears on-screen.

2. **Click the Site Extras tab (the eighth tab from the left on the Objects palette).**

   After you select the Objects palette's Site Extras tab, you see the Stationery Item icon on that tab. (If you don't see it, click the drop-down menu button at the bottom of the Site Extras tab to toggle it to Stationery.)

3. **Drag the Stationery icon from the Site Extras tab of the Objects palette to the Name column in the left pane of the Site window (see Figure 12-3).**

Drag as many Stationery objects as you need from the Site Extras tab on the Objects palette to the site window.

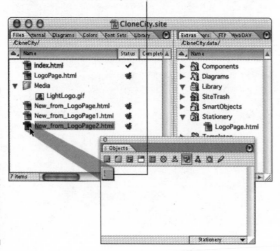

Figure 12-3: You can move the Stationery icon by dragging it from the Objects palette.

If you want the file to go into a folder or subfolder, you can drag the Stationery icon directly to the right pane of the Site window and to the icon of the folder in which you want to place it. The filename then reads `New from` plus the name of the original file from which the stationery was created.

4. **Change the filename to the one you want to use by clicking the icon and typing the new name to replace the current name.**

   The new name now appears on the Page icon.

5. **Click the Page icon to select it and choose File⇨Open from the menu bar (or just double-click the icon).**

   After the file opens, you see your template page. It looks identical to the page you saved as stationery.

After your page is open, you can make any changes you want and save the page. After you develop a template page for a site, the idea is to use that template to maintain the same design on your pages but to change certain key elements periodically. In Figure 12-4, for example, the page is now the Contact page, and a label and form elements have been placed on it (Figure 12-2 shows the original version), but the rest of the page remains the same.

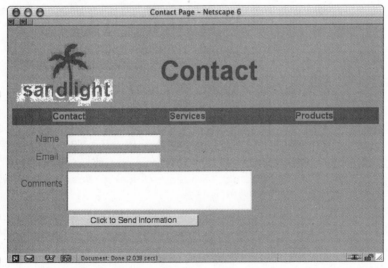

Figure 12-4: Changes in the page resulting from using stationery to update the page, as seen in a browser.

Importing Stationery

You may find that a page can serve — beyond one that works for just a single site — as a template for a number of different sites. You can use stationeries that you develop on a given site in a number of different ways, although the simplest way is to transfer the template page from the source site to the new site. To do so, follow these steps:

1. **Open a new site in the Site window and click the Files tab of the Site window.**

   The site is the one you want to receive a stationery item.

2. **If the right pane of your new Site window isn't open, click the double-arrow button in the lower-right corner of the Site window.**

   The right pane opens in the Site window. (Be careful to avoid clicking the left and right horizontal scroll arrows down there. The correct arrow set is the one *farthest to the right* — directly under the downward vertical scroll button.)

3. **Click the Extras tab of the right pane of the Site window.**

   You see the Stationery folder with the other folders in the right pane. You want your new stationery item to go in the Stationery folder.

4. **Click the Stationery folder to select it.**

   By selecting the Stationery folder, the imported stationery item goes directly to the correct folder.

5. **Choose Window⇨Objects to open the Objects palette or undock the Objects palette by clicking its tab at the side of the screen.**

   One way to check whether the import operation for the stationery item is successful is to check the Site Extras tab of the Objects palette. After you finish the import operation, you see the new Stationery icon waiting there for you. If you don't see it there, the import operation didn't succeed and you need to try again.

6. **Choose Files⇨Import⇨Files to Site from the menu bar to open the Add to Site dialog box. In the dialog box, find the Stationery folder from the original site and select the page you want to import.**

   You must first locate the Stationery folder in the source site with the stationery item you want.

7. **Select the Stationery Item file, click the Add button, and then click the Done button to close the Add Files dialog box.**

   A Copy dialog box appears.

8. **Click Ok in the Copy dialog box.**

   Because you selected the Stationery Item file in the import operation, you're all set. Check the Site Extras tab of the Objects palette, and you see your imported Stationery icon.

You can use an imported Stationery icon just as you use any other Stationery icon. The fact that you import it doesn't bear on its use.

Working with Reusable Components

In some sites, the pages don't share a general template, but they do include several components that you painstakingly construct and need to reuse again and again. One of the more common elements you see in use on several pages in a site, for example, is a navigation system. This system can consist of an image map, images with *rollovers* (images that change as the mouse pointer moves over them), a bar with CSS-defined links, or several icons indicating the different major sections in the Web site. You don't need to rebuild these components for each page, but as is the case with stationery items, you can place them in a special folder on the Extras tab of the Site window. This folder is known, curiously enough, as the *Components folder,* and after you place a component there, it also appears on the Site Extras tab of the Objects palette.

To best understand how to use *components,* think of the process in two parts. The first part involves creating a single page containing the elements you want to use on several different pages — for example, a navigation bar. You go ahead and create the page, but you put on the page only those objects (such as a graphic navigation system) that make up a component. The second part then involves creating the components for these selected objects.

You can't save background and text colors or text link colors as component elements *unless* they are created with CSS. You can, however, save more complex components, such as rollovers. Go figure.

Constructing your components

When a key feature, such as a menu bar, is used several times on different pages in a site, think about making that feature into a component. It may be a special logo, a rollover action to remind the viewer that your products or services are the best, or a set of buttons with rollovers run by a JavaScript script. You don't want to think in terms of creating entire pages to clone — that's the job of stationeries. You just want reusable parts. To construct the components for your page, follow these steps:

1. **Choose File⇨New Site⇨Single User⇨Next. Provide a name for the site in the New Site Name window and click Next. Click the Browser button to select where you want the site to go. Then, click Finish.**

   The Site window appears. Click the Files tab of the Site window to open Files view and note the single new file, index.html.

2. **Double-click the index.html file in the Site window to open it.**

3. **Create a page containing just those elements you want to place on several different pages, such as navigation bars (refer to Chapters 2 and 3).**

   In the example shown in Figure 12-5, I just used the same menu bar created in the preceding stationery example. The page contains a table, links, and CSS to color the links.

Figure 12-5: You save only the elements for the component as a page — in this case, the navigation bar composed of a table, underlying CSS, and links.

4. **Save the page by choosing File⇨Save or pressing Ctrl+S (in Windows) or ⌘+S (on the Mac). Then close your page by choosing File⇨Close or pressing Ctrl+W (in Windows) or ⌘+W (on the Mac).**

   Because you open the page from the Site window, the page automatically goes into the site's root folder after you save it.

Turning your page items into components

In the preceding section, I show you how to put together a little navigation bar to create a terrific component. You don't want to have to make the same navigation bar again. Because the navigation bar is in a component, you just grab the component and use it on your page. To turn your page items into components, follow these steps:

1. **Begin on the File tab of the Site window, where you saved the page you want to turn into a component.**

   See the steps in the preceding section for details on this procedure.

2. **If the right pane isn't open in your Site window, click the double-arrow button in the lower-right corner of the Site window.**

   The right pane opens in the Site window. (Be careful to avoid clicking the left and right horizontal scroll arrow down there. The correct arrow set is the one that's *farthest to the right* — right below the downward arrow on the vertical scroll bar.)

3. **Drag the page containing the component from the Name column of the Files tab to the Components folder on the Extras tab of the Site window.**

   Note that you drag the whole page, so be certain that only the elements you want in the component are on the page. GoLive 6 doesn't use background colors for your page, but it does preserve the background colors used in the table.

4. **Rename the page in the Components folder by clicking on it and typing a new name.**

   I renamed the component page FineParts.html to remind myself that this page contains only parts (components) and not the whole page (stationery). You don't have to rename the component, especially if the name of the page you dragged into the component folder has a name that fits your purpose.

5. **Choose Window⇨Objects to open the Objects palette or undock the Objects palette by clicking the tab at the edge of the screen.**

   The Objects palette appears, as shown in Figure 12-6. The file Fineparts.html now appears in the Components folder.

Figure 12-6:
Files in the
Components
folder of the
Extras tab
of the Site
window and
the Site
Extras tab of
the Objects
palette.

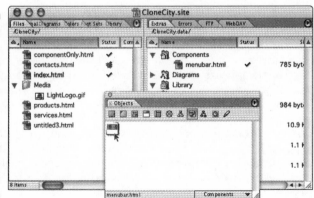

The process is now complete. You see a component element on the Site Extras tab of the Objects palette. Had you used graphic elements in the component, you would see them as well.

Putting Components to Work

Components are interesting little critters. You place a Web page in the Components folder, and then you put the component elements into another Web page from the Objects palette. It sounds strange, but the process works just fine and saves lots of time. Even if your components contain JavaScript, the component elements place what you need into your Web page correctly. Check it out for yourself by following these steps:

1. **Open an existing page by choosing File⇨Open from the menu bar or create a new page in Layout view of the document window by choosing File⇨New from the menu bar or typing Ctrl+N (in Windows) or ⌘+N (on the Macintosh).**

   Select a site with a component you've already stored away. Otherwise, see the preceding section for information about creating a component.

2. **Choose Window⇨Objects from the menu bar to open the Objects palette or undock the Objects palette by clicking the tab at the side of the screen.**

   The Objects palette appears on-screen.

3. **Click the Site Extras tab of the Objects palette (the eighth tab from the left).**

   You see your component on the Site Extras tab. If you don't, toggle the little Stationeries/Components button at the bottom of the Site Extras tab until the button appears.

4. **Drag the Component icon from the Objects palette to the page in Layout view of the document window.**

   If you have more than one component, select the one you want, and the component name appears at the bottom of the Extras tab. You can drag a component onto a grid, into a window, or anyplace else where you can put a Web-page object, as shown in Figure 12-7.

If you look closely at a component in Layout view, you can see a tiny green corner in the upper-left area of the box surrounding the component on the Web page. (That corner isn't visible in browsers.) The green corner tells you that what you're seeing is a component. That information is handy if you're editing the page later.

Drag component to the page.

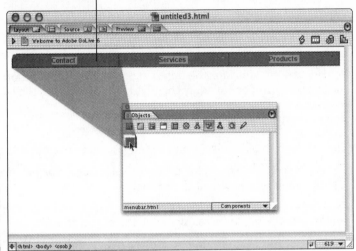

Figure 12-7:
Placing a
component
on a Web
page.

Getting Smart with Smart Objects

If you look closely at Figure 12-2, you may notice a little icon in the lower-right corner of the logo. The icon indicates that the image is a Photoshop Smart Object. On the Smart tab of the Objects palette, the first three objects can be linked to other applications that automatically update the object in the Web page when the Smart Object is changed. For example, if you have the company logo on all 567 pages of your site and your boss says that she wants to change the logo (again!) and wants all the changes implemented on all the pages of the site immediately, you can do it quickly using Smart Objects. All you have to do is to make the changes to the original object (like the logo) and — presto, change-o! — all the logos are now the new ones.

I show you how to use the Photoshop Smart Object in the following steps because it was used in the example shown in Figure 12-2. The Smart Illustrator object works with Adobe Illustrator, and the Smart Generic works with other applications (like Macromedia Fireworks), where changes made in the original graphic show up in GoLive as soon as the changes occur. In other words, Smart Generic is the Smart Object for any other application used to create Web media.

1. **Open a new page in GoLive by choosing File⇨New Page or pressing Ctrl+N (in Windows) or ⌘+N (on the Macintosh).**

   A new, pristine page appears, welcoming you to GoLive 6 in Layout view.

2. **Choose Windows⇨Objects or undock the Objects palette by clicking on its tab at the side of the screen.**

   The Objects palette pops up on your page.

3. **Click the Smart icon to reveal the Smart Objects on the Objects palette. (The Smart icon is the second one from the left.)**

   You see the ten icons for the different Smart Object operations. For your purposes in this section, only the first three icons from the left are relevant.

4. **Drag the Smart Photoshop object onto the page.**

   The Photoshop object icon (an eye) appears on your page.

5. **Choose Windows⇨Inspector or undock the Inspector palette by clicking on its tab at the side of the screen.**

   As soon as you select the Smart Photoshop icon in the document window, the Inspector is ready to link the object to a file.

6. **Use the point-and-shoot line or the browse option to link a Photoshop file to the Smart Photoshop object.**

   As soon as you make the link to the Photoshop file, the image appears on your screen. You can tell that it was done in Photoshop if you see the little Adobe Photoshop icon in the lower-right corner, as shown earlier in this chapter, in Figure 12-2.

If you don't have Photoshop, try using the Smart Generic object. In limited experiments with Macromedia Fireworks, the Smart Generic object worked just like the Smart Photoshop one. Using Smart Objects saves you a good deal of time.

Getting the Bug Out

In addition to the Extras tab, with its Stationeries and Components folders, the set of tabs in the Site window includes an Errors tab. The Errors tab is the gateway to the many different ways in which GoLive 6 helps you make sure that your site is clear of flaws. The Status column of the Site window Files tab contains different icons representing degrees of problems, and GoLive 6 provides mechanisms to help you fix the problems these Bug (Error) icons indicate.

To understand all the errors that can show up on the Errors tab and in the Status column of the left pane of the Site window, Figure 12-8 shows a "wounded site" suffering from all the bugs that a willful designer can apply. The example serves as a reference point to different bugs and how to fix them in GoLive 6.

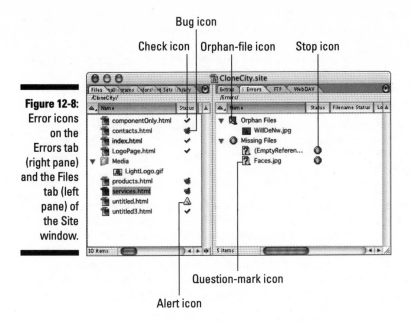

Bug icon

Check icon Orphan-file icon Stop icon

Question-mark icon

Alert icon

Figure 12-8:
Error icons
on the
Errors tab
(right pane)
and the Files
tab (left
pane) of
the Site
window.

A rogues' gallery of trouble

First, you need to know that getting into trouble in GoLive 6 isn't an easy task.
Making the errors that appear in Figure 12-8 is very difficult because GoLive 6
keeps opening up helpful windows to update files and perform other good
deeds to keep the site bugfree automatically. Bugs *can* creep in, however,
and you need to know how to recognize them and rid yourself of them. The
following list describes the various Error icons, shown in the figure, that
GoLive 6 uses to identify problems on your site:

- **Check:** The check mark you may see in the Status column in the left
  pane of the Site window means that everything is okay with a file. "Let
  sleeping dogs lie," in this case. You need to do nothing to the file. That
  doesn't mean, however, that the connection *to that file* is working.
  Elsewhere in the site may lurk a bug connecting to the file because of an
  incorrect link name.

- **Bug:** A Bug icon appearing in the Status column tells you that some kind
  of error is in the file, but it doesn't elaborate on what kind of error.
  Clicking the Errors tab provides more information about the bug.

- **Alert:** Nothing is wrong if an Alert icon (the yellow triangle) shows up in
  the Status column. It simply means that a page is a new one with nothing
  on it. If a closed folder contains a page with nothing on it, you see the
  yellow-triangle icon next to the folder. If the folder itself is empty, however, no Alert icon appears.

✔ **Stop:** A Stop icon in the Errors pane of the Site window means that a link has lost its connection with the file. Usually, this icon means that the file was formerly in the root folder and that you deleted it or used an incorrectly written external URL in the original link. For example, if you typed the URL for the external link without the `http://`, the page would be expected to be in the root directory. Because it would not be there, the Stop icon indicates that fact.

✔ **Question Mark:** An icon associated with the Stop icon is the Question Mark icon. If GoLive 6 simply can't find a file, both the Question Mark icon and the Stop icon appear in the Errors pane of the Site window. Usually, that combination means that you wrote the wrong URL in the URL window of the Link Inspector as you were defining a link.

✔ **Orphan File:** If a file lies outside the root folder, the Orphan File icon (a folder with an *X* on it) appears in the Errors pane of the Site window. Don't overlook this warning! As you publish your site on a server, you want all the files associated with the site in the root folder. When you test your page, the link may work fine because it resides on your computer and your browser just follows the path. If you don't make the necessary changes, however, no one can find the file after the site is on the server.

To catch spelling and grammar errors, you must use the spell-checking feature of GoLive 6. The bug-catching feature of GoLive 6 doesn't extend to spelling or other inaccuracies in your page. (See the section "Spell checking," later in this chapter.)

Elementary bug-squashing

Getting rid of bugs usually depends on what the bug is. A generic procedure, however, works for most bugs you're likely to encounter. Virtually all bugs you encounter involve a link to another page or a graphic image file with a poor link. (More advanced users employing more complex dynamic links will find that they get more interesting bugs!) Following are a few basic steps to take if you want to play bad-link exterminator:

1. **Begin on the Files tab of the Site window and click the Errors tab (if it's not already selected), as described in the preceding section.**

   If you don't have a site with lots of bugs, open one of the pages in the site and put in a bad link. Just follow the instructions for creating a link in Chapter 2 and use xyz or some other name not in the site's root folder. You get a bug as soon as you save the page. All the site's errors appear on-screen.

2. **Choose Window⇨Inspector from the menu bar to open the Inspector or undock the Inspector by clicking its tab at the side of the screen.**

   If none of the files is selected, you see the generic Inspector.

3. **On the Errors tab of the Site window, click the Stop icon for one of your problem files.**

Each Stop icon is associated with a particular file. The Inspector becomes the Error Inspector. In the Error Inspector, you see a single URL text box for entering a corrected URL for the target of your file's link.

4. **In the URL text box in the Inspector, type the correct URL name, pull the point-and-shoot line from the Point-and-Shoot button (the one with the spiral to the left of the text box) to the correct file on the File tab of the Site window.**

Or, you can click the Browse button (the one displaying a folder to the right of the text box) to search for the missing file by selecting different directories that appear in the directory window until you see the file you want.

Entering URLs is not a good place to have typos. If you place an incorrect name in the URL text box, the link never works right. So, make sure that you verify that the URL name corresponds to the name of the target file for your link.

If a URL consists of a long name, GoLive 6 offers a trick that enables you to expand the URL text box in the Error Inspector. Press and hold Ctrl+Alt (in Windows) or ⌘+Option (on the Mac) until you see a Pencil icon replace the Folder icon on the Browse button next to the URL text box. Click the Pencil icon and an Edit URL window opens so that you can enter a very long URL, browse, make the link relative or absolute, add and delete parameters, and generally live it up!

Orphans in the storm

If the Orphan icon appears, the procedure is a little different, but you can fix all orphans with a single operation. Just follow these steps:

1. **Begin on the Files tab of the Site window with the Errors tab selected in the right pane, as described at the beginning of the preceding section.**

You see the Orphan File warning icon (the one with an *X* over a folder icon) on the Errors tab pane. If you don't have an orphan, you can easily make one by opening any page and establishing a link with a file outside the root folder. If you don't see the file on the Files tab of the Site window, it's outside the root folder. (See Chapter 2 for information about creating links that *are not* orphans.)

2. **Choose Site⇨Clean Up Site from the menu bar.**

GoLive 6 gathers all the linked files into the root folder. If you're not sure exactly where you put the orphan file on your computer, using the Clean Up Site command is the easiest course for GoLive 6 to go after all of them.

3. **After GoLive 6 prompts you to update all the file links, click the OK button.**

   Generally, I just click the OK button. If problems exist in your orphan file (like it has a bad link), you find out when it's in the Site window.

4. **After GoLive 6 prompts you to copy files to the root folder with the Clear Site dialog box, click the OK button.**

   GoLive 6 brings the orphan file into the root folder. That procedure usually does the trick. Magically, all orphan icons disappear.

Remember that GoLive 6 is on your side. If something isn't quite right, GoLive 6 tries to make it right. Probably the most important items to keep in mind to avoid bugs on your Web site are as follows:

✔ Keep all the files in the root folder so that you can see them in the Site window.

✔ Use the point-and-shoot or browse-and select-methods of making all your links. That way, you avoid typos when keying in URLs or filenames.

Spell checking

A final kind of troubleshooting that GoLive 6 helps out with is spell checking. As is typical of GoLive 6, the spell checker works by checking an entire site. You may, however, spell-check individual pages or even selected text. GoLive 6 provides several options for checking your spelling as well. Just follow these steps:

1. **Begin on the Files tab of the Site window for the site you want to spell-check.**

   You need to see all your files. The spell checker *doesn't* check for misspellings in graphics. (That's where I like to make all mine.)

2. **Choose Edit⇨Check Spelling from the menu bar or press Alt+Ctrl+U (in Windows) or Option+⌘+U (on the Macintosh).**

   The Check Spelling window appears. (I call it a spell checker to keep all the windows straight.)

3. **Open both the More Options menu and the Check in Files menu at the bottom of the spell checker by clicking the little downward-pointing arrows.**

   You see seven options from which to choose in the More Options section and a check box next to the Check in Files portion of the spell checker.

4. **Open the Files From drop-down menu, select the current site, and then click the Check in Files check box. (Look to the right of the Files From menu for the drop-down menu buttons.)**

Now you can check the whole site with a single operation. Be sure that you have selected the Name column of the Site window when you attempt to select your site. You see the Start button light up, all set to check your spelling.

5. **Click the Start button to begin checking for errors.**

    Your first typing error appears, as shown in Figure 12-9, unless you have none, as is the case with my sites. (Yeah, right!)

The spell checker goes through your site page-by-page until it finds an error. After an error appears, the page opens on-screen with the potential misspelling highlighted, and the spell checker provides several options for dealing with the word, as shown in Figure 12-9.

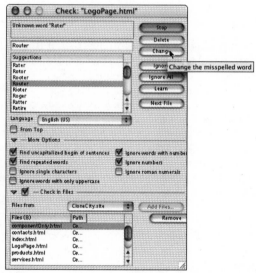

Figure 12-9:
The spell checker at work on a Web site in GoLive 6.

The following list explains each option in detail:

- ✔ **Delete:** This option is useful if you inadvertently put double words in the text next to one another, like like this this. Click Delete to get rid of one of the double words.

- ✔ **Change:** If the spell checker doesn't recognize a word, one or several words appear in the Suggestions list box. In Figure 12-9, the word *router* is misspelled *roter*. The suggested word appears in both the Suggestions list box and the text box directly below the misspelled word. Click the Change button to change the misspelled word to the one in the text box directly below where the misspelled word appears. You may also type the correct word in the text box directly below the misspelled word if the suggested one isn't correct.

✔ **Ignore and Ignore All:** The spell checker doesn't recognize proper names, such as Hinkelbump, or specialized terms, like *ethnomethodology,* so you can skip these "misspellings" by clicking the Ignore button. If you expect several such instances of a word you want to skip, just click Ignore All, and the spell checker no longer stops and asks if it encounters that particular word.

✔ **Learn:** Clicking Learn adds the word to your dictionary. Your site may use words such as *eBusiness,* for example, and you plan to use the term often. Also, you can include in your "learn list" the use of intercase spelling, like *JavaScript.* Just click the Learn button to add to the spell checker's dictionary. The spell checker never stops on that word again.

✔ **Stop:** In the middle of checking your words, you can stop the checking process, go do something else on your page, and then come back and resume checking the spelling. As soon as you click the Stop button, the Start button replaces it. When you're ready to resume your spell checking, click the Start button, which changes to the Stop button again.

✔ **Next File:** If you're checking a site and you don't want to continue spell-checking the current page, just click Next File to close the current page and open the next one that contains a spelling error.

I found one rattling feature in the spell checker. If multiple occurrences of the same word are encountered back to back, the spell checker gives you the option of deleting one. So, if one page ends with *Aloha* and the next page begins with *Aloha,* the spell checker asks whether you want to delete one instance of the word. It is not unusual for sites to begin and end each page with a common word, such as a company's name. So be careful when checking for multiple occurrences using the *site* spell checker.

In addition to the button options, the spell checker in GoLive 6 offers seven options in the lower part of the Check Spelling dialog box. You can select these options by clicking a check box next to the one you want. These options, such as Find Repeated Words and Ignore Numbers, are self-explanatory and provide more flexibility to your spell-checking chores — and do a bit of grammar checking as well (refer to Figure 12-9).

Chapter 13

Servers with a Smile: Moving Files to and from Servers

*A*fter your site is complete, it's time to put your work on a Web server. It helps to think of the server as a computer that mirrors your own. A Web server shows the rest of the world exactly what you see when you open your site and use all the pages on your PC. If copies of all the folders and files are transported together to the server, all the relative links are maintained.

To get to a server, you need a Web hosting service. Such a service may exist at your place of business, educational institution, or government office. If you're starting up your own e-business, you need a Web host service. You can locate a host service through your ISP (Internet Service Provider) or by using a search engine in your browser. For example, if you type the words *Web hosting* in a search engine such as Google, Yahoo!, StarMedia, Lycos, or one of the other sites that provide ways to locate services on the Web, you find competitive deals for getting online for some serious e-commerce.

While you're thinking about getting on the Web, you should also think about getting a domain name. A server has an address (made up of unique sets of numbers, such as 24.3.129.174) that's about as easy to remember as a combination to a safe. A domain name replaces the server name with something like www.adobe.com, which is easy to remember and associate with a product. A surprising number of free hosting services exist, but they usually restrict what your page can look like and put ads on your page. However, you can get inexpensive Web hosting services without any restrictions if you shop around on the Web. (Search the Web with the words *Web hosting* and you'll find plenty.) Start off with an inexpensive Web hosting service and then upgrade as your needs increase.

Using FTP to Transfer Files to a Web Server

Before heading for the Web with your pages, you need to know a little about *File Transfer Protocol, or FTP.* Using FTP to put pages on the Web is like copying files from your hard disk to a floppy or high-capacity disk. All you're doing is moving your Web pages and associated files from your computer's disk storage to another computer's disk storage. If all the connections are established correctly, it's a piece of cake to transfer files. GoLive has two different built-in FTP programs you can use. The FTP Browser on the File menu works pretty much like regular FTP, and the Site FTP connects directly to your site for uploading and downloading site files.

If you think of FTP as putting files on another disk that just happens to be in another room, the prospect of loading your pages on a Web server isn't so daunting.

 People bandy about the term *server* without distinguishing between types of servers. Actually, any computer with server software can be a server. However, some servers specialize in certain functions. A file server stores files, a Web server delivers Web pages, and an e-mail server sorts and sends e-mail. An enterprise server is usually just a big computer that has different server software so that it can be all different kinds of servers. Remember that all the servers and the computer on your desktop are close relatives; what you put on your computer is just being placed on another computer when you publish your pages on the Web.

Initial FTP Setup

The first step in GoLive 6 to get your pages from your computer to a Web server is to set up your FTP addresses in the Available Servers window. Setting up one or more FTP addresses is simple. Follow these steps:

1. **Start GoLive 6 by launching it from your computer and Clicking New Page or New Site.**

   Use the Site or Page Wizard to create a new page or site. (You can use an existing page or site.) Just start that darn thing!

2. **Choose File⇨FTP Browser from the menu bar.**

   The FTP Browser appears. If you haven't set any FTP addresses yet, you don't see any listed on the Server drop-down menu.

3. **Click the Server drop-down menu and choose Edit Server.**

   The Available Servers window opens, showing all servers you have set up, if any.

4. **Click the New Item button (right next to the Trash icon).**

   A generic nickname and server name appear in their respective text boxes.

5. **Type the nickname, server URL, directory (see the following Warning paragraph), username, and password in the text boxes.**

   To enter the password, click the Save check box next on the Password row. See Figure 13-1 for some examples. The username and password are like those used in e-mail. In fact, in some sites you use the same username and password for e-mail as for FTP. It all depends on how the Web host administrator has the site organized. With several FTP sites, you may have more than one username and password.

6. **(Optional) Click the Advanced button to bring up the FTP Options dialog box.**

   The FTP Options dialog box opens. Of the four options, the Use ISO 8859-1 Translation and Resolve Links options are checked. Usually, you don't want to keep your connections alive, but you may want to select the check box for *passive mode* because certain firewall conditions require it. Check with the system administrator to see whether passive mode is required.

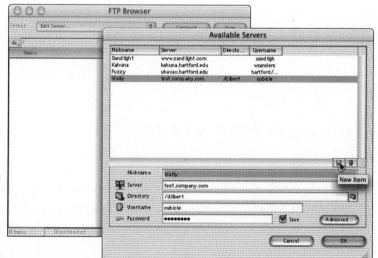

Figure 13-1:
Setting up
FTP servers
in GoLive 6.

7. Click OK.

Your FTP server is established, and all you need to do is to connect it to establish a link between your computer and your server.

In setting up your FTP connection, the Directory option is an important one if you're going to use the Incremental Upload option. If you decide that the easiest way to upload your files to your server is by using the toolbar's Incremental Upload button, you *must* establish the directory (folder) in which your site resides on your server. The easiest way to do that is to select the Browse folder in the Directory row of the Available Servers window and find the directory on your server. GoLive then automatically fills in the correct directory path for you. If you leave the directory information blank, the root folder automatically becomes the selected directory where all your files are sent using Incremental Upload. If you decide to do that, you have to open the directory folder after you have made FTP contact and drag the files from the left to the right pane in the Site window. Even if you open the directory folder you want by using the site FTP, the files are not transferred to that folder using Incremental Upload unless the directory is the one defined in the Available Servers window.

Moving from Site to Server

You may be all set to put your beautiful pages on a server. GoLive has three different ways to use FTP for getting your site onto a server, and I explain each method separately. (If you can't stand the suspense, I'll let you know right now that the first method uses the Site toolbar, the second method involves your dragging files from the left pane of the site window to the right pane, and the third method makes use of the GoLive menu bar.)

Whichever method you use, you should choose Site⇨Clean Up Site from the menu bar to get everything into the root folder. (See Chapter 12 for more information on the Clean Up Site command.) The root folder is the source of the FTP process; if your files aren't in that folder, one of the methods I describe in this chapter gets the files and folders to the Web server.

FTPing from the Site toolbar

To get your site on a server by using the Site toolbar, follow these steps:

1. Open in the Site window the site you want to mount on a Web server.

The Site window appears on the screen. Generally, you don't need the document window open when you're moving files from your computer to a Web server.

2. **Click the Files tab in the Site window.**

   All the files and folders for your site appear.

3. **If the right pane isn't open in your Site window, click the double arrows in the lower-right corner of the Site window.**

   The right pane opens in the Site window. (Avoid clicking the left and right horizontal scroll arrows down there. The correct arrow set is farthest to the right.)

4. **Click the FTP tab in the right pane of the Site window.**

   The tab should be blank. When you connect to an FTP site, you see the files on the Web server in this window.

5. **Choose Site⇨Settings or press Ctrl+Alt+Y (in Windows) or Option-⌘+Y (on the Macintosh).**

   The Settings dialog box opens. This is where you enter your server settings.

6. **In the Settings dialog box, click the FTP & WebDAV Server icon in the left column.**

   The FTP Server pane appears in the upper half of the right side of the Settings dialog box, as shown in Figure 13-2. (Later in this chapter, you find out how to use the bottom half of the dialog box to set up connections to a WebDAV server.)

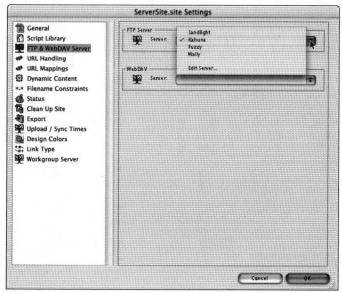

Figure 13-2:
Selecting an
FTP server.

7. **From the pop-up menu, choose your server.**

The name or names of the server (or servers) for which you have provided connection information are on the menu. If no servers are listed, choose Edit Servers from the pop-up menu and follow the instructions in the section "Initial FTP Setup," a little earlier in this chapter.

8. **Choose Window⇨Toolbar from the menu bar.**

The toolbar appears as the Site toolbar. Usually, the toolbar is on the screen, but just in case it was taking a nap, I wanted to remind you.

9. **Click the FTP Server connect/disconnect button (the tenth one from the left) on the Site toolbar.**

At the bottom of the FTP pane in the Site window, the word *Connected* appears. However, if a problem occurs, a warning window comes into view to inform you that the connection has not been established. Check your settings and try again.

10. **Click the Incremental Upload button (the 11th one from the left) on the Site toolbar.**

The Upload Options dialog box appears.

11. **Leave the default check boxes selected and click OK.**

Leaving Files and Folders checked is a good idea to ensure that the folders and files arrive at the Web server in the order arranged in GoLive 6 (see Figure 13-3).

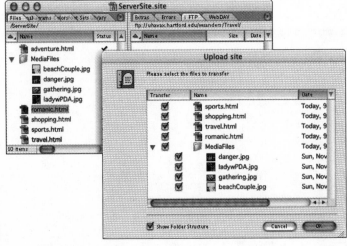

Figure 13-3:
The Site window during FTP transfer.

12. Click the OK button.

The Upload Site window appears. Make sure that all the pages you want uploaded are in the window and that the check boxes next to them are checked. If you have in the batch a page that you don't want uploaded, just deselect the box next to it.

13. Click the OK button in the Upload Site window.

If no errors are detected, your files are successfully uploaded and put on your server. In other words: You're on the Web!

After your files have been transferred to the target server, they appear in the FTP pane of the Site window. Figures 13-3 and 13-4 show the During and After views of an FTP operation. If you make changes to a file or two and upload the site again, only those files that have been changed are transferred. That saves lots of time. GoLive makes sure that all links are updated before you send in the changes.

Figure 13-4:
The Site
window
after FTP
transfer.

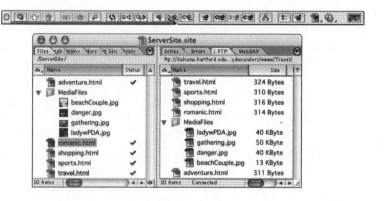

Dragging and dropping in the Site window

A second way to load your pages with GoLive 6 is by dragging the files from the left pane to the right pane in the Site window. Up to a point, this task is similar to uploading by using the Upload Site window. After you follow Steps 1–12 in the preceding section to connect to the FTP server, drag files or folders from the left pane (the Files tab) to the right pane (the FTP tab) of the Site window.

A loading window appears, showing the progress (or lack of) in loading the pages dragged into the FTP pane of the Site window. This method is more visual, but when you're loading an entire site, it may be easier to go through the steps using the Site toolbar's Incremental Upload button. Using the drag-and-drop method is a little easier for picking and adding or replacing individual folders and files.

FTPing from the menu bar

The final method for getting a site, a file, or a folder from your desktop to the server involves using the FTP Browser command on the menu bar. You don't need to open the Site window to put a site or a couple of pages or files on the server quickly; this method can be a simple solution:

1. **Open GoLive if it isn't already open.**

2. **Close any open pages as well as the Site window.**

3. **Choose Window⇨Inspector from the menu bar.**

   The Inspector appears on the screen. You use the Inspector to inspect the files and folders on the remote site as well as those on your own computer. If you have CGI files, such as ones written in Perl, you can use the Inspector to perform CHMOD, as shown in Figure 13-5.

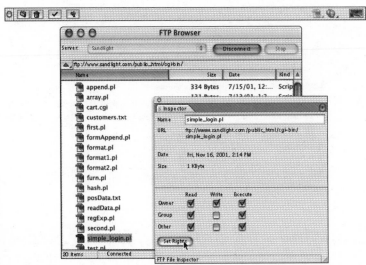

Figure 13-5:
The FTP
Browser
window.

4. **Choose File⇨FTP Browser from the menu bar.**

   The FTP Browser window opens, as shown in Figure 13-5.

5. **Select the server you want to use from the Server pop-up menu.**

   Your Web host provides a name for your site's major domain. You can select a server from the pull-down menu only if you have established the server in the FTP preferences. (See the section "Initial FTP Setup," earlier in this chapter, if you have no server.)

6. **In the Directory text field, type the name of the directory, if any, to which your site will be uploaded.**

   Either leave the directory window blank or enter the name of the directory in which you want to put your files. Click the folder icon to browse the folders at your site on the server.

7. **In the Username text field, type your user ID.**

   If you set up your pages with a Web hosting service, your user ID is the one the service provides. At an organization with its own server, get your user ID and password from technical support.

8. **In the Password text field, click the Save check box and type your password.**

   Use the password provided by the hosting service or your Web administrator.

9. **Click the Connect button.**

   If all your settings are correct and everything on the server end is working, you see `Connected` appear in the status window and the Disconnect button come to life. Be patient as all the files and folders on your server site appear in the lower portion of the window, as shown in Figure 13-5. (If you have no files or folder on the Web site yet, you see a blank pane where files are displayed.)

10. **Drag the files and folders you want to add to your Web server from the desktop or folder into the FTP Browser's main window.**

    The files and folders are sorted automatically and are added to the FTP Browser window when they are successfully uploaded. Select a file or folder and you can see information about it in the Inspector that now appears as the FTP Folder Inspector.

You can place nonviewable files on the Web server. *Nonviewable* files can't be viewed by a Web browser and are placed on the server for users to download from your Web site. How do you download a file? Just establish a link to the file from any Web page, and it is downloaded to the client computer when he clicks the link.

If you plan to put files on your site for others to download from their browsers, condense the files first. Use programs such as ZipIt or Stuffit to reduce the size of the file. That action saves not only file space on the server, but also the amount of time it takes to download the file.

In the example shown in Figure 13-5, the file selected in the window is a Perl file in the CGI-BIN. For the file to work with CGI, it must go through a *CHMOD* process. The CHMOD process applies only to CGI files, and, unless you're using CGI, you need not worry about it. (You've got enough to worry about.)

Making the AppleShare Connection

If your server is set up with an AppleShare connection to your computer, you can bring the server to your desktop. After it's on your desktop, you can treat the server just like another disk on your computer. From GoLive 6, you save your site directly to the server, just as you would save it to your own computer by using the Save command. (No need to even bother with FTP!) Here's how it's done:

1. **Choose Apple Menu⇨Chooser from the Macintosh desktop.**

   The Chooser appears on the screen with different icons.

2. **Click the AppleShare icon.**

   The AppleShare icon has a globe and files on a platter and is labeled AppleShare.

3. **In the AppleShare window, select the server you want to use.**

   Depending on the setup, enter the required username and passwords. Some connections are set up to remember your password like GoLive does, and it may be only a matter of selecting the server in AppleShare.

4. **Note the server's name (on an icon) when it appears on your desktop.**

   The server icon resembles the AppleShare icon.

5. **Create a GoLive site and save it to a folder on your computer by choosing File⇨Save.**

6. **After you save the site, choose File⇨Save As from the menu bar.**

   Locate and select the server name in the Save As window and then select the folder in which you want to save your site. This step is just like locating any other folder or drive on your computer.

7. **Click OK.**

   That's it. It's the easiest way to upload files to a server because the process is identical to saving your site to your PC from GoLive.

8. **When you finish using the server, throw the server icon into the trash.**

   This step breaks the connection between your computer and the server. Sometimes, when more than one computer has the server open on its desktop at the same time, conflicts arise; so, be sure to dump the server connection when you're finished using it.

Bringing 'Em Home: Downloading from GoLive

Generally, you don't want to download your files from the Web. To update your site, all you need to do is replace the existing files with the new ones. That way, you know that the files on your computer are the same as those on the server. Downloading an old file, fixing it up, and then putting it back on the server is a waste of time. Besides, you run the risk of mixing up your files. The old ones downloaded from the server duplicate the ones on your disk. Usually, the need to download a file occurs when you lose the files on your computer ("You mean, the drive I just formatted erased all my files?") or you download someone else's files in a cooperative effort. (To find out more, see the section "Working with WebDAV," later in this chapter.)

Bringing files and folders to your computer

If disaster strikes and you do need to download a few files from your site, the FTP Browser command from the GoLive menu bar can save the day. Getting a few files from your site to your computer is the reverse of uploading by using the FTP Browser. All you have to do is follow the steps in the section "FTPing from the menu bar," earlier in this chapter, and when the server site appears, just drag the files and folders you want from the FTP Browser to your desktop.

Creating a GoLive site from an existing site

If you want to pull sites from the Web into GoLive for editing and you don't have copies of the files on your PC, you need to create a GoLive site on your computer to store the downloaded site materials. For example, if you have clients with old sites that need fixing up, you have to download them. Fortunately, GoLive has a great way of creating a GoLive site from an existing site on the Web: It downloads the site into a GoLive 6 site right on your computer. Follow these steps to create a GoLive site from an existing site:

1. **Launch GoLive and choose New Site.**

   The Site Wizard appears. (Hiya, Wiz!)

2. **Click Single User⇨Next⇨Import from Server⇨Next⇨FTP⇨Next.**

   You arrive at the page where you enter the information for the server (see Figure 13-6).

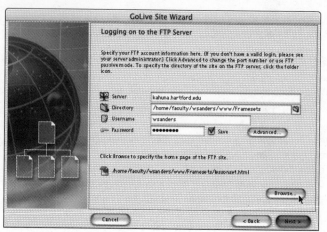

Figure 13-6:
The Site
Wizard
getting
information
to create a
GoLive site
from an
existing site.

3. **Fill in the Server (its URL), User Name, and Password text boxes.**

   Fill in all the text boxes except for Directory. Use the same process I describe in the section "Initial FTP Setup," earlier in this chapter.

4. **Click Browse to find the home page for the site.**

   The Select home page dialog box appears on the screen, displaying all file items stored on the connected server. Usually, an existing site has a home page, but if you don't know what it is, go back and look at the site through a browser. Note the name of the home page and then enter it by clicking the Browse button so that you can find the page in the correct folder. A home page may have a name like index.html. However, in a given site, several pages named index.html may exist, in separate subfolders. Using the Browse button allows you to locate the correct one. (Figure 13-6 shows what your screen looks like when you click the Browse button.)

5. **After the home page is selected, click OK and then click Next.**

   You're asked to provide a site name. Think of a noble and good name for your site.

6. **Type a site name and click Next.**

   You're now on a page that asks for the location on the computer where you want your site placed.

7. **Click the Browse button and select a location on your computer where you want your site to be stored. After you select a location, click Choose and then click Finish after you're back in the main part of the GoLive Site Wizard.**

After this operation is complete, you have a full site with all pages integrated into a root site. When you load the site by choosing File⇨Open from the menu bar and supplying the site name, all the files you just imported appear in Files view of the Site window. From that point on, just use all the GoLive 6 tools to edit and update the site. Later, you can export the site again by using the FTP tools in GoLive.

Working with WebDAV

Web site development is often a collaborative activity, with artists, designers, content suppliers, marketers, programmers, and a whole host of others working together to get a Web site up and going. What's more, these people are often in different places. By using WebDAV, people from all over can work on the same Web site collaboratively. You need to be connected to a server with WebDAV working, but, otherwise, the process for connecting to WebDAV is much like making connections through FTP.

Setting up WebDAV in GoLive

The first step in working with WebDAV is to set up the preferences so that your computer knows where to make a connection. Passwords and user-names are involved, just like e-mail or FTP, as described earlier in this chapter. To set up WebDAV in GoLive, follow these steps:

1. **Open an existing site or create a new site in the GoLive Site Wizard.**

   A new Site window appears on the screen.

2. **Choose File⇨WebDAV Browser from the menu bar.**

   An empty WebDAV browser window opens.

3. **Click the Server drop-down menu and choose Edit Server.**

   The Available Servers window opens, showing all servers you have set up, if any.

4. **Click the New Item button (right next to the Trash icon).**

   A generic nickname and server name appear in their respective text boxes.

5. **Type the nickname, server URL, directory, username, and password in the text boxes.**

   To enter the password, click the Save check box in the Password row. The username and password are like those used in setting up FTP.

6. **Click OK.**

   Your WebDAV server is established, and all you need to do is to connect it to establish a link between your computer and your server.

Setting up the WebDAV connection for your site

After you establish your basic connection information for WebDAV, you need to make a similar setting in your site settings. Figure 13-2 shows. earlier in this chapter, FTP settings that are configured. In the lower portion of the window, you can see the area where WebDAV settings go. Follow these steps to establish your WebDAV site settings:

1. **Open an existing site or create a new site in the GoLive Site Wizard.**

   A new Site window appears on the screen.

2. **Choose Site⇨Settings.**

   The Settings window appears. A column of icons for determining the settings is in the left pane, and, depending which icon you select, different options are in the right pane.

3. **Click the icon for the FTP & WebDAV server in the left pane.**

   The FTP & WebDAV pop-up menus appear in the right pane.

4. **Click the arrow to open the pull-down menu and select the WebDAV server you want to use.**

   Unless you put more than one WebDAV address in your setup, only one appears on the menu.

5. **After you make your selections, click OK.**

   Your settings are complete and the dialog box disappears.

6. **Click the Files tab of the Site window.**

   On newly created sites, you see only the single file named index.html.

7. **If the right pane isn't open in your Site window, click the double arrows in the lower-right corner of the site window.**

   The right pane opens in the Site window. (Avoid clicking the left and right horizontal scroll arrow down there. The correct arrow set is the farthest to the right.)

8. **Click the WebDAV tab in the right pane of the Site window.**

   Until you're connected, all you see is a blank pane. (That will change!)

9. **Choose Site⇨WebDAV Server⇨Connect from the menu bar or click the WebDAV Server Connect/Disconnect icon (thirteenth from the left) on the toolbar.**

The files on the WebDAV server appear on the WebDAV tab of the Site window. Some file icons may have pencil or faces and pencil icons next to them. The faces and pencils icon means that only certain users can open the files, and the pencil means that *only* you can edit the files. (The others who are using WebDAV do *not* see the pencil icons because they cannot edit the files.) In effect, the files are locked except for you or anyone specified by you. You can unlock your files so that other people can work on them by selecting the file and right-clicking (in Windows) or pressing Ctrl+click (on the Macintosh) and choosing Unlock from the context menu that appears. Later, you can reverse the process by choosing Lock from the same context menu (see Figure 13-7).

Figure 13-7:
WebDAV and some root folder files in the Site window with the Lock tab in the Inspector open.

Synchronizing your sites

After you make the connection with the WebDAV server, you're all set to upload and download files. In addition, you can *synchronize* your files, or make all the files on both your site and the WebDAV server the same. When you perform synchronization, GoLive 6 automatically uploads and downloads files so that the WebDAV pane and the Files pane are identical. With your

Web site open and your connection to the WebDAV server made (see the preceding section), you're ready to work with a team on WebDAV. All this takes place in the site window. Here's how to synchronize all your files or upload and download individual files:

1. **With the WebDAV and Files tabs selected in the Site window, click the WebDAV Synchronize All icon on the toolbar or choose Site⇨WebDAV⇨Synchronize.**

   The Synchronize window appears, as shown in Figure 13-8. Four buttons below the main pane provide options for (from top to bottom) Skip, Upload, Download, and Delete. In the unlabeled column between the Site and Server columns are boxes where the chosen options are displayed. Full synchronization automatically inserts those files that have been changed and that need to be uploaded or downloaded. (That's how to get *everybody* on the same page!)

Figure 13-8:
The
WebDAV
Synchronize
window.

2. **Make any changes by selecting individual files and clicking an option button. Then click the Synchronize button at the bottom of the window.**

   The Synchronize window disappears and all the files are either uploaded or downloaded. Now, everyone on the development team is synchronized!

Upload and download individual files

To upload and download individual files or modified files, you need not synchronize everything. (With great-big sites, synchronization can take a while because all the files have to be uploaded and downloaded.) Here's how to upload and download files:

1. **With the WebDAV tab and the Files tab selected in the Site window, select the individual file or files you want to upload or download by clicking the files in either the WebDAV pane or the Files pane.**

   When you want to select more than one file simultaneously, press Shift+click and select all the files you want.

2. **Choose Site⇨WebDAV Server⇨Upload Selection from the menu bar to send files from your site to the WebDAV server or choose Site⇨ WebDAV Server⇨Download Selection to send the file or files from the WebDAV server to your site.**

   GoLive sends your files to the server from your computer, and they appear in the WebDAV pane or Files pane of the Site window.

For group work on a project, especially when people doing the work are scattered all over the world, the WebDAV connection through GoLive 6 is great. Using the synchronize option is a powerful way to keep everyone working on the same page and coordinating efforts without wasting time. Keep WebDAV in mind when you have a project where several designers, developers, and programmers may need to coordinate their efforts.

When you have a big site, you can save lots of time for everyone involved using WebDAV by uploading or downloading only those elements that have been modified by choosing Upload Modified Items or Download Modified Items from the toolbar or by choosing Site⇨WebDAVServer⇨Upload/ Download Modified Items from the menu bar.

Part IV

Swinging Pages: Tapping the Power within GoLive 6

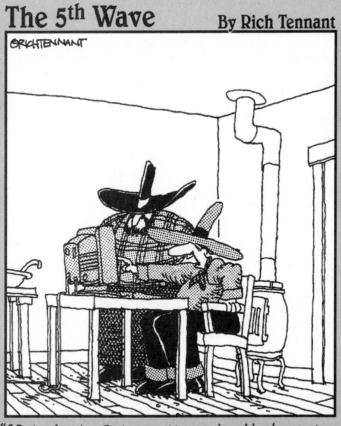

The 5th Wave
By Rich Tennant

"Well, shoot – I know the animation's moving a mite fast, but dang if I can find a 'mosey' function anywhere in the toolbox!"

In this part . . .

You'll have so much fun in Part IV that it should be illegal! Find out in this part how to use GoLive 6 to do everything from making buttons jump on-screen to hiding floating boxes. When you want your site to get eye-popping attention from weary Web surfers who have seen too many flat, motionless sites, you're ready for Part IV. You'll see how to make buttons that come alive by the surfer's simply passing a mouse over them. You'll have messages popping up to give a greeting or announce a special promotion. If that doesn't wake up an indifferent eye, have a herd of floating boxes fly around the screen with text, graphics, or both by using Dynamic HTML. GoLive makes both the creation of the floating boxes and their motion as easy as dragging an object around the screen while GoLive records the path and then re-creates it on a Web page.

One of the best-kept secrets of GoLive 6 is the availability of extensions. You can add to GoLive 6 all kinds of cool stuff (lots of it free) that extends its power. (Of course, after you read the section on extensions, you'll have to burn the pages. It has to be kept secret!)

What you've *really* been waiting for is the new GoLive 6 workgroup server. That's right — you're eyes aren't going blurry from too much Jolt cola! GoLive 6 has a server that allows you to set up and work with remote GoLive developers and designers from all over the world! (Finally, the design team from Outer Slobovia can work with you!) You'll see how to set up a server right on your computer whether you have a Windows PC or a Mac. You'll even learn to be a system administrator — a lifetime dream come true.

Chapter 14

Rollover Your Assets

• •

In This Chapter

▶ Image swapping

▶ Movement on Web pages

▶ Adding actions to Web pages

▶ Triggering action on Web pages

▶ Achieving actions with a mouse click

• •

*W*eb page designers use *actions* to make Web pages more interesting and take advantage of the computer's power to make rapid changes. An *action* is a change that happens on a Web page when the viewer makes certain moves. So, an action on a Web page is a reaction to what the user does. One of the most popular actions is the rollover. As the Web surfer moves her mouse over the page, changes occur depending on where she moves the mouse. A *rollover* occurs when the mouse passes over those parts of the page where the designer placed an action. (I use the term *hot spot* elsewhere in this book to indicate a spot that responds to a mouse click used as a link. An action is one type of hot spot.)

To make an action, GoLive 6 provides special palettes that create JavaScript code. Rather than have to spend a good deal of time writing JavaScript code, the designer (that's you) can now concentrate on where he wants the actions to be placed and on the overall look and feel of the Web page.

Swapping Images with a Rollover

A Web page is fundamentally different from a paper page in several ways. Images on a Web page can change when you place your mouse over them. For example, to get a viewer's attention to a text selection, many designers use a rollover. A *rollover* occurs as images swap when you place your mouse pointer over their areas on the page. Often, rollovers are buttons that initiate linking, but at other times they can be images that swap for other purposes, such as comparing views or making a point dynamically. After you do some preliminary work, GoLive makes creating rollovers simple.

GoLive 6 provides two different ways to create a rollover. One method involves selecting an image and then selecting the Rollover tab in the Image Inspector; the other method uses the Rollover object on the Smart Objects palette. Start by using the Rollover tab in the Image Inspector.

To get ready for a rollover, you need some images. First, create at least two graphics (JPEG, GIF, or PNG files) with identical dimensions. For this first example, I used Photoshop to fade one of the characters in a graphic and used Save As to save the file with a different name. Then I had two graphic files, both JPEG images with identical dimensions. When you're using rollovers, you *must* use objects with the same dimensions, even though the contents can be very different. (See Chapter 2 for details about graphic file types that may safely be used on the Web.) You can add a third image, but this first example uses only two. The third image, the "click" image, appears when you click the mouse button. This image must have the identical dimensions of the first two.

Working with the Rollover tab method

You begin by placing a graphic image on the page and then working with the Image Inspector. Before starting your Web page, use Photoshop or some other graphic application and create two images of identical size that look different. After you have created the two images, you're all set to make your first rollover with the following steps:

1. **Create two graphic images of exactly the same size. Then, open a new site and import the two images into the Site window by choosing File⇨Import⇨Files to Site.**

   If you want, you can put your media files into a separate folder for organizational purposes, but you don't have to. In the example, you see the files in a folder named Pix.

2. **Open the Objects palette by undocking it or choosing Window⇨Objects from the menu bar.**

   The Objects palette appears on your screen.

3. **Open the Index.html page from the Site window, select the Basic icon (the first icon on the left) from the Objects palette, and drag the Layout Grid icon to the page.**

   After you have the layout grid on the page, you can pull the side and corner pull-tabs to resize it to fit on the Layout page.

4. **Select the Smart icon (second from the left) on the Objects palette and drag the Rollover icon (from the left) to the page.**

With the Layout grid on the page, you can put it anywhere you want on the grid.

5. **Drag from the Site window the image file you want to appear first, and place it on top of the Image placeholder icon on the page.**

   The first image is the one the viewer sees when the page loads. She doesn't see the second image until she rolls over it with the mouse pointer. At this point, you should see the image on the page, and the Image icon placeholder will have disappeared.

6. **Open the Inspector by undocking it or choosing Window⇨Inspector from the menu bar.**

   When the Inspector appears, select the image and you see four tabs in the Image Inspector — Basic, More, Link, and Rollover. (You'll never guess which one you'll be using.)

7. **Click on the Rollover tab on the Image Inspector.**

   The Rollover tab appears and you see a thumbnail image in the top image box, labeled Normal, on the Inspector. Below the image, you see two more image placeholders, named Over and Down. You use the Over placeholder. Also notice a check box for Preload and a message window for use in the next step.

8. **Click the Preload and Message check boxes and then add a message to the message box.**

   By checking the Preload check box, you load the image with the page. In that way, when the viewer rolls over the image, he doesn't have to wait until the image loads because it's already loaded and waiting for him

   Preloading images in GoLive 6 is easy when you're creating rollovers. (All you have to do is check the Preload check box!) Even though setting up your rollovers is easy by checking the Preload option, you must not forget to do so. When you preload the images, they sit in memory and are immediately available. The effect is that as soon as the user moves the mouse over the rollover or clicks one, the images are swapped immediately. Otherwise, when the user moves his mouse over a rollover hotspot, nothing happens until the rollover image is loaded. That's not good for impatient Web surfers!

9. **Pull the point-and-shoot line from the Over placeholder to the image in the Site window you want to appear when the mouse is over the first image (see Figure 14-1).**

   As soon as you link the Over image in the Image Inspector, you're all done. You can test the image in Preview mode or in a browser. If you see it change, you've been successful. Congratulations!

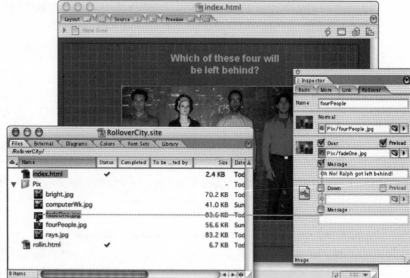

Figure 14-1:
Placing the
Over image
in the Image
Inspector.

As with all things Web, you want to test out your creation. Fortunately,
GoLive is designed so that you can test rollovers in Preview mode. When you
roll over the image, you should see it change from the original to the one you
placed in the Over placeholder in the Inspector. See Figure 14-2 to see which
of the foursome got left behind.

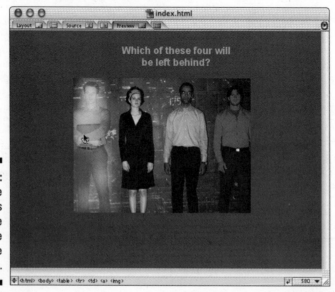

Figure 14-2:
When the
mouse rolls
over the
graphic, the
Over image
appears.

Using a Smart Object to make a rollover

A second way you can make rollovers with GoLive 6 is by using the Rollover smart object and the Rollover Inspector. Although the workflow is slightly different from using the Image Inspector, you should find the process similar. To prepare for this second way to create rollovers, you need three graphic images with the same dimensions. I took a photo of a man working at a computer and, using Save As in Photoshop, added a bright background segment to a second image. Then, for a third image, I added "rays" being emitted from the monitor. The effect is that the viewer sees a man working on a computer. When the mouse rolls over the image, a background is lighted up with a yellow background splash; when the mouse is clicked, red rays come out from the computer's monitor.

A group of objects, called *smart objects,* on the Objects palette constitute a special group of icons familiar to users of earlier versions of GoLive. The objects on the Smart tab of the Objects palette are a mixed bag of HTML tags and JavaScript functions that can be placed in the head or body of your Web page in Layout view of the document window. A class of smart objects in GoLive 6 act as placeholders for non-Web graphics, such as Photoshop-formatted ones. When the Photoshop file is dragged and dropped on top of the placeholder, a *smart link* is established between the Photoshop image and a new Web-safe file generated by the smart object. They play an important role in simplifying the work on your Web site.

After you create images, you're ready to impress your friends and dumbfound your critics. Here's how:

1. **Open a site and import into the Site window the three graphic images you created using File⇨Import⇨Files to Site.**

   In this example, I used the same Pix folder I use in the example in the preceding section. (I use recycled silicon.) You can open a new site, if you want.

2. **Choose Window⇨Inspector or undock the Inspector by clicking the Inspector tab at the side of the screen.**

   The Inspector appears on the screen.

3. **Choose Window⇨Objects or undock the Objects palette by clicking the Objects tab at the side of the screen.**

   The Objects palette appears.

4. **Click the Smart tab of the Objects palette.**

   The Smart tab is the second one from the left.

5. **Click and drag the Rollover icon (fifth one from the left) from the Smart tab of the Objects palette and place it on the page.**

The Rollover placeholder appears on the page with a question mark on the icon, and the Inspector becomes the Rollover Inspector. You see three windows in the Rollover Inspector with image icons on them. Beneath the icons is a check box, a Point-and-Shoot button, a window, and a Browse folder.

6. **With the Rollover placeholder selected on your page, click on the image icon labeled Normal in the Rollover Inspector.**

The Point-and-Shoot button is focused and ready to use in the Rollover Inspector.

7. **Place your first (Normal) image on the Web page either by dragging it from Files view of the Site window onto the Rollover placeholder or using the point-and-shoot line of the Rollover Inspector to select the image from the Site window.**

The image you select appears both in the Rollover placeholder and as a thumbnail image in the Normal window of the Rollover Inspector. The "normal" image is the default image — the one you see when you're not pausing over the image area. Any image can be the top one. Because this is just a practice run, use any image you like (see Figure 14-3).

When you use the point-and-shoot line, you can bring up the Site window by pulling the line to the Select Window toggle icon on the toolbar. The icon is the third one from the right on the toolbar.

Figure 14-3: Placing the Normal image.

8. **Type a name for the button in the Name window of the Rollover Inspector and add a short title for the graphic in the Alt text box.**

   Use any name you want or leave it as the default name *button.* If you add another Button image, GoLive gives it another name, like Button2. If you plan to have several rollovers on a page, you should name the buttons in relation to how you'll use them. For example, you may want to name them relative to the link they're connected to.

9. **In the Rollover Inspector, select the Over image placeholder and click the check box beneath the image placeholders.**

   If you don't click the check box, the Point-and-Shoot button doesn't become active. The Over figure is the one you want to appear when the mouse pointer is *over* the image. (That's why it's called *over.*) Refer to Figure 14-3.

10. **Use the Point-and-Shoot button to select the second image from the Site window.**

    A thumbnail of the second image now appears in the Over placeholder.

11. **Add a short title for the graphic in the Alt text box and add a message, if desired, for the browser's status bar in the Message box.**

    By adding a message, whenever the viewer passes the mouse over the image in a browser, the status bar displays the message.

12. **Repeat Steps 9–11 for the Down image.**

    The Down image should be called the "click" image because when the user clicks the image (the mouse goes down *and* up), the Down image appears (see Figure 14-4).

Figure 14-4:
All three images are placed.

Figure 14-5:
A click of the button displays the final image.

Your rollover should make swaps between three images. Initially, the viewer sees the man working on his computer in the example. The mouse pointer is moved over the image, and the background brightens up. (Is inspiration in the making?) Then the viewer clicks the image and — Shazaam! — rays stream from the computer's monitor to enliven (or electrocute?) the man working on the computer (see Figure 14-5).

Making Things Move on Your Web Pages

Actions *can* be events triggered by the Web surfer moving or clicking the mouse, but mouse movement isn't the only thing that can get your Web page jumping and jiving. Actions such as the appearance of a prompt or alert box can also be set off automatically when you load or unload a page. (Alert: "Are you sure you want to exit?") Other actions can be fired by key presses (press B for Boom!), and still other actions can be orchestrated sequentially with the help of the TimeLine editor.

I discuss the intricacies of the TimeLine editor in Chapter 16, so if you're interested in time-controlled actions for your page, you may want to skip a couple of chapters ahead. The next sections in this chapter concentrate on setting off actions automatically on loading or unloading a page and on triggering actions with the help of various mouse and key actions supplied by the viewer.

It's all in your head

Actions can be set off when a page opens or closes. For example, you may want to load a sound to play or a welcoming message to pop up when the page opens. Perhaps your domain name has changed and you want your old domain to forward your page to your new domain automatically.

To trigger an event that sets off an action, GoLive provides Head Action items, which work in ways similar to rollover actions. GoLive targets the head area because the head area of an HTML page always loads first, making available the JavaScript functions, CSS definitions, and other information your page can use as soon as the body of the program is loaded. For example, if you want all your rollover images preloaded before the rest of the page, you can have that done in the head. Then, when the user first encounters a rollover, she doesn't need to wait while the images for the Over and Click functions load. I find that calling up pop-up message windows is helpful when a page loads as well. Here's how to set up one for your page:

1. **Begin in Layout view of the document window.**

2. **Choose Window⇨Inspector or undock the Inspector by clicking the Inspector tab at the side of the screen.**

   The Inspector appears on your page.

3. **Choose Window⇨Objects or undock the Objects palette.**

   The Objects palette appears on the page.

4. **Click the Smart tab on the Objects palette.**

   The Smart tab is the second tab on the palette. Ten icons appear on the Smart tab.

5. **Open the Head window in Layout view by clicking the down arrow to the left of the Page icon, right below the Layout tab.**

   The Head window opens and you see tag icons for code in the Head area of the page.

6. **Click and drag the Head Action icon (the ninth icon from the left) from the Smart tab of the Objects palette to the Head window.**

   Figure 14-6 shows where the Head Action icon should be placed on the page.

Drag the Head Action icon to the Head window.

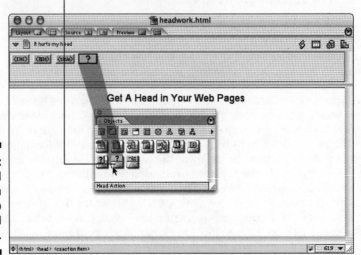

Figure 14-6:
The Head
Action icon
moves to
the Head
window.

7. **Click the Head Action icon in the Head window.**

   The Inspector becomes the Head Action Inspector, as shown in Figure 14-7. You see an Exec pull-down menu near the top of the Inspector and an Action button and pull-down menu beneath the Exec menu.

8. **OnLoad is the default option on the Exec pull-down menu in the Head Action Inspector, so you need not open the menu by clicking it.**

   You can optionally add a name in the Name text box.

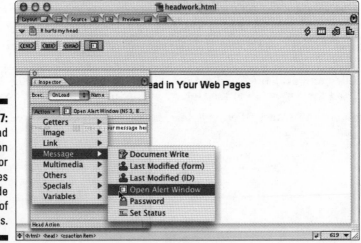

Figure 14-7:
The Head
Action
Inspector
provides
a wide
selection of
actions.

9. **Open the Action pull-down menu and choose Message⇨Open Alert Window from the Action pull-down menu, as shown in Figure 14-7.**

   The Head Action icon turns into a message icon, and the message window appears on the Head Action Inspector.

10. **Type a message in the message window.**

    The operation brings up an Alert box message as soon as the page opens. When the user encounters the pop-up message in the Alert box, he reads it and then clicks OK to make it disappear without affecting the page.

Because the message appears whenever a user opens the page, this is a good place to send out a welcome to the viewer. For eBusiness, the message could announce a special sale or new items available.

You can't get there from here: Automatic URL transfers

Sometimes when you create a new site, you place it in a new URL. However, many people still know the old URL, and it may even be linked from another site. Rather than force Web surfers to start at one page and click to another page, you can set up an automatic transfer to the new URL, and the Web surfer is none the wiser. The process is similar to forwarding mail to a new address. Follow these steps to set up an automatic transfer:

1. **Begin in Layout view of the document window.**

2. **Choose Window⇨Inspector or undock the Inspector by clicking the Inspector tab at the side of the screen.**

   The Inspector appears on your page.

3. **Choose Window⇨Objects or undock the Objects palette.**

   The Objects palette appears on the page.

4. **Click the Smart tab on the Objects palette.**

   The Smart tab is the second tab on the palette. Nine icons appear on the Smart tab.

5. **Click and drag the Head Action icon from the Smart tab on the Objects palette to the Head window arrow, right next to the Page icon in the Layout window.**

   The Head window drops down as soon as you drag the Head Action icon onto the Head window arrow. Drop the Head Action icon in the open Head window.

6. **Click the Head Action icon in the Head window.**

   The Inspector becomes the Head Action Inspector.

7. **Choose OnParse from the Exec pull-down menu in the Head Action Inspector.**

    The OnParse selection parses (interprets) the action from the Head area of the page. OnLoad waits for the page to load *first* before interpreting the action, which takes more time.

8. **Choose Link⇨Goto Link from the Action pull-down menu.**

    The Inspector provides a link to a URL and a Target window.

9. **Type the URL in the Link window for the new site address and a target for a specific frame or window if you want to specify one.**

    As soon as the page loads, it redirects the viewer to the new address. The visitor to your site doesn't even realize that she has been sent to another address.

Setting Up Actions with the Mouse

Actions set off by a mouse trigger are inherently interactive. The user directly initiates an action by doing something with the mouse, whether it's a click or a double-click or positioning the pointer somewhere on the page.

Adding a small window

A Web page has distinct advantages over a paper page in certain areas. One advantage is that a Web page is capable of showing a series of small images or a small bit of text and then letting the viewer open another window to show a larger view of an image or elaboration on the text. In that way, a single screen can reveal far more information than a paper page. The next action feature I describe shows how to superimpose a little information window on top of your main window.

You can put this space-saving feature (the small, added window) to work for you by doing the following:

1. **Choose File⇨New Site@ to open the GoLive Site Wizard, create a new single-user blank site, and click Finish when you've completed the wizard.**

    Your new Site window appears.

2. **When the Site window appears, click the Files tab just in case another tab has been selected.**

    Your new Site window appears with a single (lonely) page.

3. **Choose Window⇨Objects from the menu bar.**

   The Objects palette appears.

4. **Click the Site tab on the Objects palette and drag the Page icon (first one on the left) to Files view of the Site window.**

   An untitled page appears in the Site window. You can rename it by double-clicking it and typing a new name if you want or leave it untitled. (It's untitled, unloved, and neglected — for now, at least.)

5. **Double-click the index.html file in Files view of the Site window.**

   A blank page opens in Layout view of the document window.

6. **Choose Window⇨Inspector or undock the Inspector by clicking the Inspector tab at the side of the screen.**

   The Inspector appears on your page.

7. **Type some text in Layout view of the document window, select it, and then click the Link icon on the toolbar.**

   The Inspector becomes the Text Inspector and the text is underlined.

8. **On the Link tab of the Text Inspector, type a pound sign (#) in the URL window.**

   The pound sign is a false link, but it creates a hot spot in the selected text.

9. **Choose Window⇨Action.**

   The Action palette appears.

10. **Select Mouse Click in the Events column.**

11. **Click the New Action button (see Figure 14-8).**

   An Action pull-down menu appears below the Events column.

12. **Click and hold the Action menu to open it and choose Link⇨Open Window.**

   The Actions palette now shows several options for opening the new window, as shown in Figure 14-8. Options include whether the window scrolls and has a URL window and how big you want it to be on the screen. (The context-sensitive Actions palette has more secret windows than a castle.)

13. **In the Link window on the Actions palette, enter the name of the file you want to open in the new window.**

   You can enter the file by either clicking the Browse button or using the Point-and-Shoot button. Just drag the point-and-shoot line to the Select Window icon on the toolbar to bring up the Site window. Then select the file from Files view of the Site window.

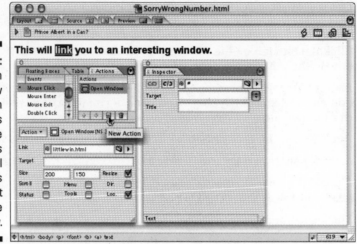

Figure 14-8:
The Open
Window
action on
the Actions
palette
provides
several
parameters
you can set
to open the
window.

14. **In the two Size windows on the Actions palette, enter the horizontal and vertical dimensions of the window you want to open.**

Pick a size that provides just enough room for the content of the window (Figure 14-9 shows the results).

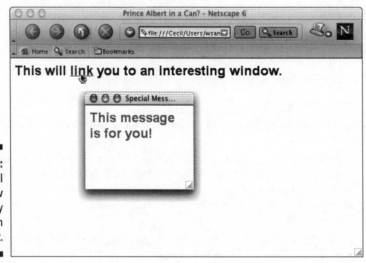

Figure 14-9:
A small
window
opens by
the action in
the link text.

15. **Check the boxes for Scroll, Menu, Dir, and other features you want to appear in the window; leave unchecked those features you do not want; and type the horizontal and vertical dimensions.**

   Because the window is supposed to take up a minimal amount of space, the fewer boxes you check, the better. Notice in Figure 14-9 that boxes are checked. All the check boxes represent options for the browser. I leave Resize checked in case the user wants to make the window larger or smaller and leave the location window open so that she can see where she is, but, other than that, the window options are not needed. These added windows can be used for showing the full size of a thumbnail image or for creating a floating menu, among many other uses in the designer's imagination. Figure 14-9 shows the page opened in a browser.

Working with user-controlled color

In addition to triggering actions using linked text, you can use linked images to create actions. To change the background color, follow these steps:

1. **Follow steps 1–9 in the preceding section, and rather than select text, select an image.**

   You should begin with the Actions palette open and a graphic image selected in Layout view.

2. **Scroll down the Events column of the Action palette until you find Mouse Up and then select it.**

   You must first press down the mouse button and then release it before the action launches when using the Mouse Up event handler.

   An Action pull-down menu appears below the Events column.

3. **Pull down the Action menu by clicking and holding the pull-down menu arrow and choose Others➪Set BackColor.**

   A color well appears on the Actions palette.

4. **Click the color well on the Actions palette to bring up the Color palette.**

   The Color palette appears.

5. **Select a background color from the Color palette.**

   When you select a color from the Color palette, the color appears in the color well on the Actions palette. As soon as you see the color you want in the color well, you're all finished. Save your page, give it a test drive in a browser, and see whether you like it.

If you want to surprise a viewer, use a text color the same shade as the background color. Then do a background color switch, and the text hidden in the background suddenly appears on the screen.

Chapter 15

Adding the Workgroup Server and GoLive Extensions

*T*his chapter examines the powerful Workgroup Server that comes with Adobe GoLive 6. With it, you turn your own computer into a server allowing you and others to work collaboratively on a Web site. Working right from GoLive, you set up your site as a workgroup site and then when you work on part of the site, others can see what you've done. After you're finished, they can add to it, change it, and make it into a collaboratively created site.

Another well-kept secret about GoLive 6 is that you can add extension modules that provide a whole new set of tools for doing different things with GoLive. These tools add functionality to GoLive and make your life as a designer or developer not only easier but also far more complete. Suppose that you have a client who wants a shopping cart module on her site so that customers can make online purchases. If you've made online purchases at places like Amazon.com or eBay.com, you've used a shopping cart. The problem is that a shopping cart module is fairly sophisticated and you don't have a clue how to set up the back end, the database, and a secure (encrypted) credit card transaction script. By adding a module, GoLive does all that for you, and all you have to do is drag and drop elements from a special palette added to the GoLive ensemble.

If the idea of turning your computer into a server seems like a daunting task, especially because your little iMac or portable Windows PC doesn't *look like* a server, I've got news for you: A *server* is nothing more than a computer with server software connected to the Internet. Some computers are made with the intention of supplying them solely with server software. You may have heard of an IBM server running Linux or Microsoft NT Server. With the right software, they would just be big word processors; because they are running server software, however, they're called servers.

Setting Up Your Workgroup Server

The first thing you must do to set up your Workgroup Server is to check your connection to the Internet. You need a high-speed connection, such as a DSL (Digital Service Line), cable modem, or T1 or T3 connection. In addition, you need a *static* IP address. Connections to the Internet on your computer are made using either Dynamic Host Configuration Protocol (DHCP) or a static IP address. The good thing about DHCP is that the network administrator doesn't have to hassle with a new IP address every time a user is added to the system. However, with DHCP, every time you start your computer you can get a differ-ent IP address. And, if your computer will be used as a server, it needs a static address. The following steps show how to determine the nature of your connection, first on a Windows computer and then on a Macintosh.

Checking your Internet Connection in Windows (XP)

1. **From the bottom menu, choose Start⇨Control Panel⇨Network and Internet Connections⇨Network Connections.**

   You see an icon noting *Local Area Connection Enabled* or some other connection.

2. **Right-click your mouse on the icon and then choose Status. When the Local Area Connection Status window opens, click the Support tab.**

   You see the words Internet Protocol (TCP/IP) and, below that, Address Type. If the address type shows Assigned by DHCP, you do not have the right connection and cannot have only limited use with the Workgroup Server. Try contacting your ISP (Internet Service Provider) and tell someone there to set you up with a static IP address. (If you have trouble finding your connection, check out the Help and Support Center by clicking the Help and Support button in the Start menu.)

Checking your Internet Connection on the Macintosh (OS X)

1. **From the Apple menu in the upper-left corner, choose System Preferences⇨Network.**

   The Network window opens.

2. **On the Show pop-up menu, choose Built-in Ethernet.**

   You see the settings for your Ethernet card. If the Configure pop-up menu shows Manually, you have a static IP address and may proceed. If the menu shows Using DHCP, you can make only limited use of the Workgroup Server. Contact your ISP (Internet Service Provider) and tell someone there to set you up with a static IP address.

If you absolutely have to use a DHCP connection, go ahead and install the server; to keep the same IP address, though, just don't turn your computer off! This advice doesn't guarantee that your ISP won't switch your IP address, but, if nothing else, you can learn how to work with the Workgroup Server. By reinstalling your Workgroup Server each time you want to use it, you can maintain a workgroup connection using DHCP — at least until the ISP automatically changes it. (You can also start looking for an ISP that will give you a static IP address.)

Installing your Workgroup Server

Installing your Workgroup Server is a piece of cake if your connection is right. Follow this set of steps:

1. **Find the WGS_Installer application on your GoLive 6 CD and launch it by giving it a double-click.**

   The Setup Wizard appears. Just follow the steps in the wizard and click Next or Continue until you're finished. About the only thing you can do besides click the Next button is to provide a name for your server. Be patient after the last step because it automatically opens your server monitor, as shown in Figure 15-1 and in the default browser. You do most of your setup for your sites in the browser.

2. **When the server monitor appears, click the Minimize button to get the monitor out of the way.**

   All the monitor does is to tell you whether it is running. Be sure that it is running, and then get it out of the way by sending it to the bar (or Dock on Mac OS X) at the bottom of the screen.

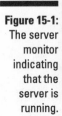

Figure 15-1:
The server
monitor
indicating
that the
server is
running.

3. **When the Easy Setup Assistant appears, click the Next button.**

   Use the Easy Setup Assistant. It makes setting up your server, um, ah, well, easy.

4. **In the System Account dialog box, enter the new password for the system administrator in both the Password and Verify Password windows.**

   If you're wondering who the system administrator is, it's you. Now that you have a server up and running, you're the boss and get to be a system administrator. As the system administrator, you have full privileges.

5. **Click Next to open the Creating New Users Accounts page.**

6. **Enter the name of the first user who will be working on the site besides you, along with her username and password.**

   Figure 15-2 shows what you see in the Setup Wizard. You must fill in the fields with an asterisk next to them (name, login name, and password), *and* you *must* also fill in the Repeat the Password window. The others are optional, but I like to fill in the e-mail window too. Sometimes, in working on a project, you have to e-mail one of the people working with you.

7. **To finish up, choose Next⇨Finish⇨Finish⇨OK.**

   You find yourself in the Abode Web Workgroup Server Administration Web page in your browser. If you're going on to the next section, keep this page displayed on your browser.

You can do much more with the Setup Wizard, but that's all you need for now. You will find creating new workgroup sites easier using GoLive 6's own Site Wizard. Adding users to the site is easily done using the Web Workgroup Server Administration page, as I explain next.

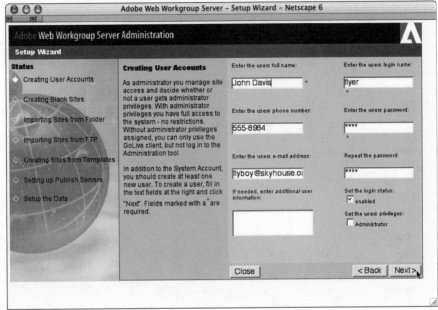

Figure 15-2:
Creating
a user
account in
the Setup
Wizard.

Using Adobe Web Workgroup Server Administration

Other than getting yourself established as the system administrator and maybe adding a user or two on the Setup Wizard, the Workgroup Server Administration software is where you do most of your server administration. Use the following steps to launch the Web page with the administration tools:

1. **Make sure that your Workgroup Server is running by double-clicking the Workgroup Server Monitor icon.**

   When your monitor is up and running, you see the monitor window, as shown in Figure 15-1. Click the Minimize button to get it out of the way.

2. **Open your favorite browser and go to the URL address** `http://localhost:1102`. **Enter your administrative username and password and click the Log In button.**

   You see a log-in section in the lower-right corner of your browser window. Be sure that you give the username you are using that has administrative privileges. When you log in successfully, you see a menu along the left side and a set of important information resources in the right window (see Figure 15-3). The key element in that information is the GoLive URL, which is given in IP address values, such as `http://12.243.69.91:1102`. (If the port you use is other than 1102, just substitute that port number for 1102.)

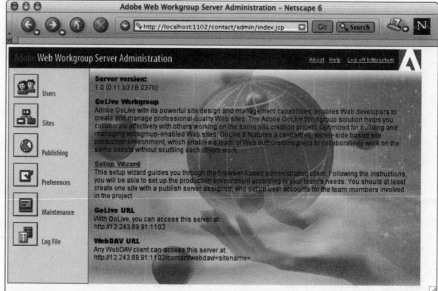

Figure 15-3:
The home
page for
the Web
Workgroup
Server
Administra-
tion.

3. **Write down the GoLive and WebDAV URL addresses for your server.**

When you set up your workgroup sites, you need these addresses. The value 1102 at the end of the address represents a port number, and your port number may be different. However, if your server is up and running, you need not worry about the IP address and port number because all that information is provided for you.

After you have your workgroup administration site up, you're all set to add and delete users, check your sites, and perform a number of administrative tasks. The tasks on the menu show six different administrative functions:

✔ **Users:** The Users page of the administrative pages allows you to add, delete, and change the status of any user you want. I found it just as easy and a bit more convenient to use than the Setup Wizard. An important feature of this page is the Assigned Sites section at the bottom on the window. You can assign and de-assign users to different sites. After a user is finished with her work on a site, you should de-assign her so that she doesn't inadvertently add something to a page that has been completed.

✔ **Sites:** The Sites page shows the sites connected to the Workgroup Server. You can add sites from here, but I found it easier to do with the GoLive 6 Site Wizard. However, to find out which sites are assigned to

the server, this is an important page. You select to edit, clean up, duplicate, or back up a site from this page. When you edit the site, you just
assign or de-assign users.

✔ **Publishing:** From a drop-down menu, you select a site and then click a
Publish Report hot spot to obtain a publishing report on a site.

✔ **Preferences:** Unless you're a bit more advanced, you can leave the preferences as they are. However, you can examine and change the server
and control ports, the log level to "error" (every error is logged), warning
or info, and set the FTP proxy host and port.

✔ **Maintenance:** You can perform three tasks on this page. First, synchronize
the Web Workgroup Server (WGS) with the server's file systems. Second,
clear up file revisions depending on the creation date and maximum
number of revisions. Finally, reset to their original lock state all files
locked by a user.

✔ **Log File:** The *log file* is a listing of all transactions that have occurred on
the server.

For the most part, you find that the main use you have for the Web Workgroup
Server Administration page is for finding out what sites are set up and assigning users to different sites. Much of the maintenance, publication, and other
tasks are performed from GoLive 6.

Creating a Workgroup Site

After you have your server set up and running, you're all set to create a workgroup site. You may have wondered in the Site Wizard what a workgroup site
is, and now you'll find out!

1. **Make sure that your Workgroup Server is running by double-clicking
   the Workgroup Server Monitor icon.**

   When your monitor is up and running, you see the monitor window, as
   shown in Figure 15-1. Click the Minimize button to get it out of the way.

2. **Open GoLive 6 and choose either Open Site from the initial menu or
   New Site from the menu bar.**

   The Site Wizard appears, offering two choices: Single User or Workgroup.

3. **Click Workgroup and then click the Next button.**

   You're at the page where you're asked to choose how you want to set up
   your new site.

 4. Select Blank and then click the Next button.

As soon as you click the Next button, you arrive at the crucial page where you enter the WGS URL. (You probably wrote down the URL when you were looking at Administration pages.) If you forgot to write down your URL, go to the URL `http://localhost:1102` on your browser to find it.

 5. Enter your server's URL and your username and password, and click Next when you're done.

Also, you see a window for a port number that should be filled in with your port. If not, check your port number on the administrative pages (see the preceding section.) Figure 15-4 shows how the completed page should appear before you click the Next button.

Figure 15-4:
Specify-
ing the
Workgroup
Server URL
and
logging in.

 6. Type the name for your site and click the Next button.

You arrive at the page for specifying your mounting location.

 7. Click the Browse button, find or create the directory where you want your site to be saved, and then click the Finish button.

When you click the Browse button, you see the familiar file menus and buttons to navigate to the place where you want to save the site on your computer. After you click the Finish button, your site comes up and you and the others using the Workgroup Server are all set to begin working on the site.

Assigning users to an existing site

After a site and a set of users is associated with a Workgroup Server, you can mount the site whether the server is on your computer or on another user's in Kankakee or Katmandu. To associate a set of users with your site, follow these steps and look at Figure 15-5:

1. **Open your Workgroup Server Administration page on your browser by going to the opening URL —** `http://localhost:1102`**. (Substitute 1102 for the port you're using.) Log in using your administrative username and password.**

   You see the home page of the Workgroup Server Administration. The menu is along the left side of the page.

2. **Click on the Sites button on the menu and then double-click the site name in the upper-left corner of the main page.**

   The page loads all the users the server administrator has added for the server, as shown in Figure 15-5.

3. **Use the mouse to click on the check boxes under the Assigned Users option.**

   In Figure 15-5, four users are assigned to the site. From their computers, using GoLive 6, they can all access the site.

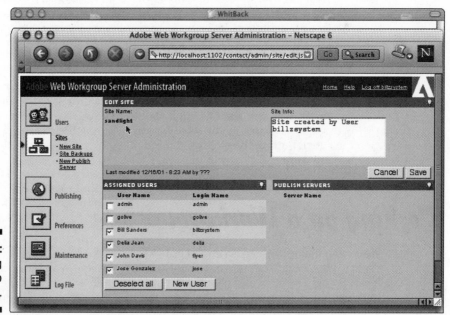

Figure 15-5: Assigning users to a site.

Mounting an existing site

The real group processing with a Workgroup Server begins when the different members of the team all mount an existing site. Only one of the users runs the server, and everyone can use it to mount a site created as a Workgroup Server. With GoLive open and no sites or pages loaded, use the following steps to mount a site:

1. **Choose File⇨Mount Workgroup Site from the menu bar.**

   The Logging On to the Workgroup Server page appears. It looks familiar because it's part of the GoLive Site Wizard that helped you create a workgroup site initially.

2. **Enter the server's URL and your username and password, and click Next when complete.**

   The URL is the one you set up or it's from someone else who set up the Workgroup Server. Figure 15-4 shows how the completed page should appear before you click the Next button. After you click the Next button, you see a page labeled Mounting a Workgroup Site. A window shows the sites you have been assigned to mount. Be patient — it may take a few seconds for the site names to appear.

3. **Click on the site you want to mount on your computer and work on, and then click the Next button.**

   The final page for mounting a site appears and asks you to specify the mounting location. Think of it as the server downloading the workgroup site to your computer (even if the server is running on your computer).

4. **Click the Browse button and find or create the directory where you want your site to be saved. Then click the Finish button.**

   When you click the Browse button, you see your familiar file menus and buttons to navigate to the place where you want to save the site on your computer. You may want to think about creating a folder (directory) with your username as the location for mounting the site. After you click the Finish button, the site is mounted on your computer and the Site window appears. Now you're cookin' with the team!

Working on a Workgroup Site

When you begin working on a workgroup site, think of it as working with a library. When you want to work on any site component, you must first check it out — just as you would check out a library book. When you have the book checked out, no one else can check it out and use it; when you're finished, you have to remember to check it back in.

During the workgroup process, you can see what others are doing with the various site elements. If a user has a Web page checked out, you see a lock symbol, indicating that it is being used, and you cannot check out the page until it has been checked back in. If you're working on a component, you see a "checked out" symbol on the Site window. Figure 15-6 shows a site where one user has a file named services.html checked out. In the lower-left corner on the bottom bar, you can see the name John Davis, indicating the identity of the user who is working on the file. If one of the other users attempts to open services.html, an Alert window tells him that John Davis is using the file. Likewise, if the user named John Davis attempts to open the file named index.html, he is told that another user has it checked out and will have to wait until it is checked in again. The names next to the files indicate who is assigned to edit the file, but any user assigned to the site may edit any of the files that are not checked out by another user.

Figure 15-6:
Site view
of a
Workgroup
Server
project.

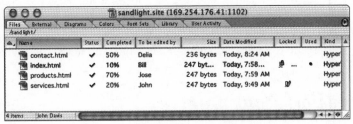

	Name	Status	Completed	To be edited by	Size	Date Modified	Locked	Used	Kind	
	contact.html	✔	50%	Delia	236 bytes	Today, 8:24 AM			Hyper	
	index.html	✔	10%	Bill	247 byt...	Today, 7:58...	🔒	...	•	Hyper
	products.html	✔	70%	Jose	247 bytes	Today, 7:59 AM			Hyper	
	services.html	✔	20%	John	247 bytes	Today, 9:49 AM	📝		Hyper	

4 items   John Davis

Using the Workgroup toolbar

When you create or mount a workgroup site, the Workgroup toolbar comes alive. The tool has only five buttons on it, and most everything you do on a Workgroup Server site, you can do with the Workgroup toolbar. Otherwise, you work on a site element using the regular GoLive tools. Figure 15-7 shows the Workgroup toolbar and what each of its buttons does.

Check Out

Undo Check Out

Revision List

Figure 15-7:
The
Workgroup
toolbar.

Compare
to Server

Check In   User Activity

The following list summarizes each button's use:

- **Check Out:** When you first want to work on a page, you select the page on the Files tab of Site view and click the Check Out button on the Workgroup toolbar. The Check Out icon appears in the Locked column of the Site window (refer to Figure 15-6), indicating that you're working on it and that others will see the lock icon.

- **Check In:** After you have finished with an element, you click the Check In button to make it available to other users.

- **Undo Check Out:** This button is used to return the page to the state it was in when you checked in. The option is most useful in cases where you accidentally check out the wrong page and don't want to indicate to the others in the workgroup that you altered it in any way.

- **Compare to Server:** This button opens a window showing the source code for the file you're working on and what the server version looks like.

- **Revision List:** This button opens a window and shows when revisions were made to indicated site elements and who made the revisions.

The Workflow palette

Workgroup sites have a special palette, the Workflow palette. Although this definite administrative tool has no effect on the site itself, it helps coordinate what everyone is doing. Each user is assigned one or more site elements to work on established on the Workflow palette. It is also used to record the percent of the element that has been completed. Use the following steps to assign editing tasks and record progress:

1. **In a Workgroup site, choose Window⇨Workflow.**

   The Workflow palette appears on the page. The Active Site line shows the name of the Workgroup site; the Name line indicates the selected element in the Site window; the To be Edited By window is either blank or contains the name of the assigned user who will work on the site; and the Completed pop-up menu shows the percentage of the work that has been completed on the element (see Figure 15-8).

2. **Select an element in the Site window to assign and enter the name of the user who will edit the element.**

   After you assign a username on the Workflow palette, the name appears next to the selected file in the Site window.

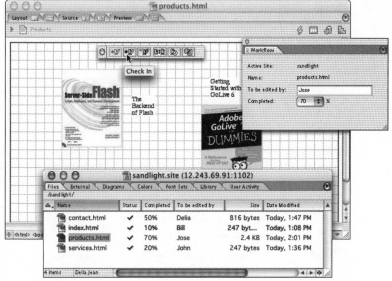

3. **The user assigned to the site element opens the pop-up window on the Workflow palette and selects the percentage of the element that has been completed.**

   All the users in the workgroup can see how much of a site element has been completed. More than a single user can be assigned to site element, such as a content developer and a graphic artist, and as each one completes the task, she enters the percentage of the complete element that has been completed.

Check Out

To check out and work on a site element, each user must go through the check-out process. If a user attempts to check out and use a page that another user has checked out, an alert message informs the user that the element is checked out and cannot be used. Apply one of the following check-out options:

- ✔ **Automatic:** Open a site element and begin working on it. As soon as work has begun, an Alert prompt asks whether you want to check it out; by clicking Yes, you check out the element. When the Check Out icon appears in the Locked column of the Site window, you can begin working on the element.

- ✔ **Workgroup Toolbar:** Select the element you want to work on in the Site window or open the element. Click on the Check Out button on the Workgroup toolbar and wait until the Check Out icon appears in the Locked column of the site window (refer to Figure 15-8).

Check In

After a user is finished working on a Workgroup file, she should check it in so that other users can either work on it or look at it. Checking in a file is simple, but before you do that, be sure to save it:

1. **Click on the element you want to check in, either on the page itself or the filename in the Site window, and then click on the Check In button on the Workgroup toolbar.**

   A Workgroup File Check In dialog box appears (see Figure 15-9). You can optionally add comments to explain to other people what you have done in the site element.

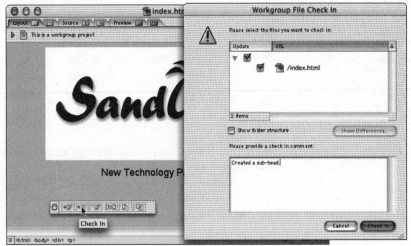

Figure 15-9:
Checking in
a file.

2. **Add any comments you want and click the Check In button.**

   After clicking the Check In button, wait a while as the server files are updated. As soon as the Check Out icon disappears from the Site window, the changes have been saved to the Workgroup Server file and the file is available to other users.

Undo Check Out

As just noted, the Undo Check Out button negates checking out a file. It returns it to workgroup use without logging any changes and is best employed as an Oops button when the wrong file has been checked out. It can also be used to return a page to its state when originally checked out when the user decides that the changes made should not be used after all.

Compare to Server

After working on a file, the user may want to check to see what changes he has made compared to the file on the server. By clicking the Compare to Server button on the Workgroup toolbar (refer to Figure 15-7), the user opens a dialog box with the local file in the upper-left window and the server's file in the upper-right window (see Figure 15-10). In the lower portion of the dialog box on the left is a window listing the lines where changes have been made, and buttons that skip sequentially jump to the next or preceding difference. All comparisons are in Source mode.

Revision List

When a user working on a site wants to see the revisions made in a file by members of the workgroup, she clicks the Revision List button on the Workgroup toolbar. When the Revision List window appears, the changes, comments, date of change, and usernames appear. You can compare different versions by holding down the Shift key and selecting the versions you want to compare and then press the Compare Revisions button to see the differences. You can compare the revisions to what you have on your local site and update any changes. Figure 15-11 shows a typical set of revisions made by different users.

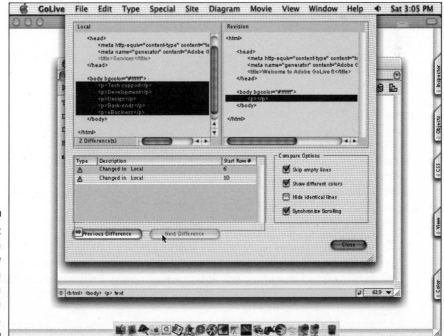

Figure 15-10:
The Workflow palette reflected in the Site window.

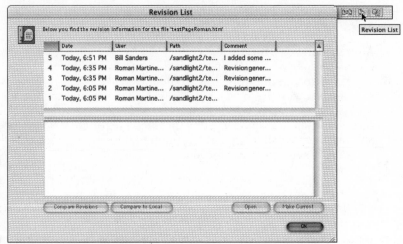

Figure 15-11:
The
Revision List
window.

User Activity

The User Activity button appears only when users are actively working on site elements they have checked out. By clicking the User Activity button on the Workgroup toolbar, the User Activity tab of the Site window appears. (You can also click the User Activity tab directly from the Site window to get the same results.) Figure 15-12 shows a workgroup site with two users working on files at the same time. Using this feature, you can monitor what others in the group are doing at any given time.

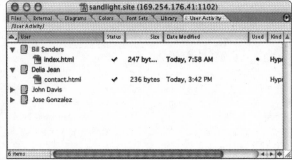

Figure 15-12:
The User
Activity tab
of the Site
window.

As more and more work is processed by teams, either on a LAN in the same building or at dispersed sites throughout the world, tools like the Workgroup Server (WGS) become more important. Professionally created Web sites have teams made up of designers, code developers, content providers, and project managers. The idea of a centralized and coordinated design-and-development effort is not dependent on the physical co-presence of the parties involved because the work they do can be shared in a collective effort through a Workgroup Server. The value of coordinated, cooperative, and collaborative work is preserved while the inconvenience and cost of mutual space are not.

Adding Extensions to GoLive 6

Adobe has opened up GoLive 6 to developers who want to provide extension modules to increase the utility of GoLive as a powerful Web-site development tool. With all the features in GoLive 6, some of which I haven't even covered yet, you may wonder "What more could be added?" The answer is "Lots of stuff that makes developing even very sophisticated Web sites simple for relative novices."

First, to see what extensions are available, check out the following sites:

  ✔ www.actionxchange.com
  ✔ www.actionext.com
  ✔ www.bigbang.net.au/golive

Some extensions include shopping carts for online eBusiness, enhanced Dynamic HTML development, and conversion of French francs or Italian lira to euros. You may need some, all, or none of the extensions, but you should see how to get them and use them in case you do. I use a shopping-cart extension in this section to run through the process of getting, installing, and using extensions in GoLive 6.

Getting your extensions

Probably the best place to start looking at extensions is the Xchange site, at www.actionxchange.com. This site is sponsored by Adobe Systems, Inc., and after you register, you can download any extensions you want. Some are free, some are shareware, and others are trial versions you purchase after you've tried them out for a while. The NetStores extension I examine is a 30-day trial version and can be downloaded for either Windows or Macintosh computers from either www.actionxchange.com or www.netstores.com. Follow these steps:

  1. **Open your browser and go to** www.netstores.com.

     The NetStores site opens and you see Adobe GoLive 6 in the left column.

2. **Click on the Adobe GoLive 6 link. When you come to the Download the Latest E-commerce Extensions for Adobe GoLive, click either the Macintosh or Windows download button.**

    You see a zip file on your hard disk: NetStores-GoLive-1.0.zip.

3. **Unzip the file to create a folder named NetStores-GoLive-1.0 containing the Extension folder named NetStores.**

    The NetStores folder contains all the files you need. You also find a ReadMe file in the NetStores-GoLive-1.0 folder with further information for installing the NetStores extension.

4. **Be sure that GoLive is *not* open and then drag the NetStores folder into the Extend Scripts folder, inside the Modules folder inside the Adobe GoLive 6.0folder.**

    As soon as the NetStores folder is in the Extend Scripts folder, you're all set. When you next open GoLive, you will have a different menu and a new palette.

Using extensions

After you have added an extension to GoLive, the next time you start the application, you see the effects of the extension. First, on the menu bar, you see a NetStores selection between the View and Menu options (see Figure 15-13). When you open the Objects palette, you see a new NetStores tab.

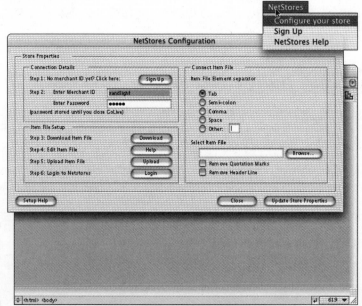

Figure 15-13: Configuration of an extension.

Because NetStores is a pretty powerful extension, and because it uses data stored on a NetStores server, the configuration process takes several steps. Figure 15-13 shows the six-step process. All along the way, the user is prompted. The downloaded item file is a database that can be edited in programs like Microsoft Excel, making it very easy to work with. You then upload it to the NetStores server and use it as your database.

Using extension tools

The extension tools you use with GoLive work just like the other tools that come with GoLive. With the NetStores extension, a new NetStores tab is added to the Objects palette. When you drag and drop one of the palette icons, it establishes the necessary connections to provide different functions. For example, Figure 15-14 shows a shopping cart icon being dragged and dropped into a layout page.

Drag and drop shopping cart in Layout view just as you would do with any other GoLive object.

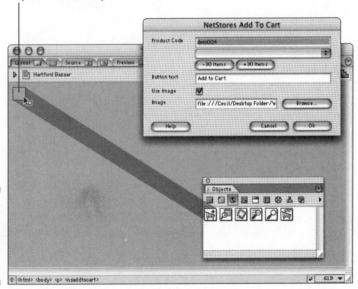

Figure 15-14: Drag and drop an extension object.

A dialog box appears. By filling in the product code number, you can easily either set up an Add to Cart button or substitute a graphic image to be clicked as a button that adds the item to the shopping cart.

Chapter 16

Dynamic GoLive 6

● ●

In This Chapter

▶ Understanding floating boxes

▶ Putting floating boxes on a Web page

▶ Placing text in a floating box

▶ Adding graphics to a floating box

▶ Changing the visibility of a floating box

▶ Moving floating boxes

▶ Using the Timeline Editor

▶ Mixing actions and movement

● ●

Making a Web page more interesting requires both talent and tools. One of the most interesting tools in the Dynamic HTML bag of trick is the *floating box*. Static boxes, like tables and forms, can do some interesting tricks, but they cannot fly around the page, change position and depth, and make themselves invisible or visible. This chapter introduces you to the truly dynamic world of Dynamic HTML and shows how easily you can use GoLive 6 to put Dynamic HTML to work.

About Floating Boxes

Dynamic HTML (DHTML) gets its name in large part by helping Web designers add mobile features, such as floating boxes, to a page. In addition to Cascading Style Sheets and some JavaScript to move the floating boxes, DHTML provides the designer (that's you) with the power to make animated, viewer-activated pages. (Imagine that a Web surfer moves the mouse and causes a floating box to fly across your page.) Floating boxes are so named because they float on top of a Web page, appearing on top of other windows and even changing position, if they're set up for that option. You control several attributes of floating boxes by using JavaScript, and GoLive 6 has been nice enough to figure out how to write all the JavaScript you'll ever need for creating a DHTML page with floating boxes.

The following list gives you a needed look at some key characteristics of floating boxes:

- ✔ **Visibility:** Floating boxes and their contents can be made to appear or disappear.

- ✔ **Position:** Floating boxes can change position. The boxes' distance (measured in pixels) from the top and left side of a Web page defines their position.

- ✔ **Background color and graphic:** Floating boxes can have their own background color or graphic, just like a Web page or window.

- ✔ **Text and graphic containment:** Floating boxes can contain text and graphics. Whatever happens to the floating box also happens to the contents. That is, when the floating box moves or disappears, the contents of the box move or disappear right along with it.

- ✔ **Layer Level:** Floating boxes can appear on top of or underneath other boxes. The layer level is known as *depth*. When moved, a box can glide over or under another floating box.

Just in case you do not have *at least* Version 4.0 of either Netscape Navigator or Internet Explorer, update your browser now. Netscape Communicator is available at www.netscape.com, and Internet Explorer is available at www.microsoft.com. (Remember that the browsers are free, and at the time of this writing the available versions are Netscape Navigator 6.2 and Internet Explorer 6.)

GoLive generates a good deal of JavaScript code when you start moving around or doing other tricks with your floating boxes. The JavaScript code often makes up the majority of the script in Source view of your Web page in the document window or Source palette. The following steps show how to send all the JavaScript code from your Web page to a separate file.

1. **Choose Edit➪Preferences from the menu bar.**

    The Preferences dialog box appears.

2. **Click the Script Library icon.**

    A JavaScript preferences pane appears on the right side of the Preferences dialog box.

3. **In the Preferences dialog box, you can now click the Import the GoLive Script Library radio button.**

    It may already be clicked. If so, just leave it as it is. Note that the default folder name for the script library is GeneratedItems and the name of the script library is CSSriptlb.js.

4. **Click OK to save this setting.**

    You do not need a filename. The next time you load GoLive 6, the settings are retained.

After you redirect your JavaScript code to a file separate from your Web page, you can more clearly see what's going on in your page's Source view. And you'll find other benefits to having your JavaScript separate: When your code is saved in a separate file, it is placed in your root folder so that you don't lose it. Finally, if you have several Web pages that use the same operations — and therefore use the same JavaScript code — you can save space by keeping one code file for use with all pages.

Setting Your Boxes

When using floating boxes, the first order of business is getting a floating box on your Web page. You need not use the grid for this operation because the floating boxes can be placed and moved wherever you want:

1. **Create a new Web site and open the Index page (index.html) in Layout view of the document window.**

   This sample site has a single Web page, so you can use the automatically generated index.html file. Be sure to have your graphics available in the root folder; GoLive generates a CSSscriptLib.js file (also in the root folder) for your external JavaScript code.

2. **Choose Window⇨Inspector from the menu bar or undock the Inspector by clicking the Inspector tab at the side of the screen.**

   The Inspector palette appears on your screen.

3. **Choose Window⇨Floating Boxes from the menu bar or undock the Floating Boxes palette by clicking the Floating Boxes tab at the side of the screen.**

   The Floating Boxes palette appears on the screen.

4. **Choose Window⇨Objects from the menu bar or undock the Objects palette by clicking the Objects tab at the side of the screen.**

   The Objects palette appears.

5. **Click the Basic tab of the Objects palette.**

   Twenty icons appear on the Basic tab of the Objects palette.

6. **Drag the Floating Box icon (the third icon from the left) from the Objects palette to your Web page.**

   A square box appears on the page, and a yellow icon slips to the upper-left corner of the page. The Inspector becomes the Floating Box Inspector. On the Floating Box palette, the word *Layer* appears next to the eye and pencil icons. I suggest that you change the name *Layer* to something that better represents what the floating box will be used for. In Figure 16-1, the Floating Box Inspector and the Floating Boxes palette show that I changed the name from *Layer* to *FloatText*.

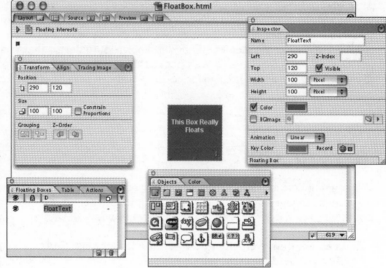

Figure 16-1:
The Floating
Boxes
palette, the
Inspector,
and a
floating box
on a page in
Layout view.

7. **Move the mouse pointer over the box until you see a Hand icon and then click the mouse button.**

   The floating box is now selected. Several pull-points appear on the sides of the box to indicate its selection.

8. **With the Hand icon showing on the side of the floating box, drag the box to any position on the page.**

   You can move the floating box anywhere on the page; when you find just the right place for it, release the mouse button, and the box stays put. The little yellow square, however, remains in the upper-left corner of the page window.

   When you drag the floating box to a different position on your Web page, notice that the values for the Left and Top positions in the Floating Box Inspector change accordingly. You can move the floating box to different positions on the page to get a clear idea of what values correspond to several locations on the page. If you change the Left and Top values in the Floating Box Inspector and press Enter or Return, the floating box jumps to that location. In the example shown in Figure 16-1, the Left value is set to 290 and the Top value to 120, as shown on both the Transform palette and the Floating Box Inspector.

The process of adding a floating box to your Web page involves little more than dragging an icon onto the page, but the benefits are enormous. The rest of the chapter tells you how floating boxes can provide your pages with dramatic and dynamic possibilities.

Adding Text to the Box

After you have your floating box set where you want it on the page, you can add some text to it. It's easy:

1. **In Layout view of the document window, place the mouse pointer arrow over the floating box and click the mouse button.**

   You should see the I-beam cursor that shows you where to start typing.

2. **Type your text in the floating box.**

   Notice that the floating box expands to accept the text. In the Floating Box Inspector, you can see the dimensions of the box change from the default 100-by-100 pixels to the size necessary to contain the text. You format text in a floating box just as you would if it were on a Web page — by using either the Type menu on the menu bar or the Text toolbar.

3. **Select the floating box so that you can see the pull-points on the side.**

   Little blue pull-points, or handles, should be in the corners and on each side.

4. **Place the mouse pointer — now shaped as a double-headed arrow — over the lower-left pull-point on the side of the floating box and push it up and to the left until it doesn't go further.**

   With this step, you remove the extra space between the text and the box wall so that the floating box perfectly fits the text.

Putting text into floating boxes is pretty much like putting it on a Web page. GoLive 6 generally uses the same tools for different aspects of the page, and in this case you don't have to figure out a whole new way of getting text where you want it.

Floating Graphics

Placing graphics into floating boxes is very similar to putting graphics into a table cell or directly on a page. So get your site set up, open your document window to Layout view, and proceed with the following steps:

1. **Choose Window⇨Inspector from the menu bar or undock the Inspector by clicking the Inspector tab at the side of the screen.**

   The Inspector palette appears on your screen.

2. **Choose Window⇨Floating Boxes from the menu bar or undock the Floating Boxes palette by clicking the Floating Boxes tab at the side of the screen.**

   The Floating Boxes palette appears on the screen.

3. **Choose Window⇨Objects from the menu bar or undock the Objects palette by clicking the Objects tab at the side of the screen.**

   The Objects palette appears.

4. **Click the Basic tab of the Objects palette.**

   Twenty icons appear on the Basic tab of the Objects palette.

5. **Drag the Floating Box icon (the third icon from the left) from the Objects palette to Layout view of the document window.**

   The floating box gravitates to the upper-left corner of the page.

6. **Drag the Image icon (fifth one from the left) from the Objects palette and place it inside the floating box.**

   The Floating Box Inspector becomes the Image Inspector as soon as you drop the Image icon into the floating box.

7. **Pull the point-and-shoot line from the Image Inspector to the Select Window icon on the toolbar to bring up the Site window and select the graphic file from the Files tab of the Site window.**

   As always, if you worry about the steadiness of your hand, you can also use the Browse button in the Image Inspector to select a graphic file. The image now appears in the floating box and stays there no matter where you move the box.

8. **In the Floating Box Inspector, replace the name *Layer* in the Name text field with a name that better reflects the graphic you added to the floating box.**

   The new name then appears on the Floating Box palette. (I named mine *bee*. Originality is not required.)

Whenever you move a floating box with an image in it, watch the Hand cursor. If it appears, the whole floating box and image in it move together. However, if the arrowhead cursor with the box next to it appears, it means that it is on the graphic alone. If you attempt to move the floating box at this point, you pull the image out of the box instead.

Hide-and-Go-Seek Boxes

You can create dramatic effects with floating boxes by controlling their visibility. When a floating box is hidden, all its contents are hidden as well. You can create conditions to make boxes appear and disappear. The conditions can be automatic (based on a timing, for example) or triggered by a certain action taking place (such as a mouse click). To initially hide a floating box, simply deselect the Visible check box in the Floating Box Inspector, as shown in Figure 16-2.

Figure 16-2:
The Float-
ing Box
Inspector
indicates a
hidden box
when the
Visible
check
box isn't
selected.

Figure 16-2:
The Float-
ing Box
Inspector
indicates a
hidden box
when the
Visible
check
box isn't
selected.

After you have hidden a box, making it reappear is simply a matter of creating an action to make it happen. For example, you can make a button, add it to your Web page, and set it up so that clicking the button toggles visibility on and off.

Begin with a floating box you have hidden by deselecting the Visible check box in the Floating Box Inspector (refer to Figure 16-2). Before starting this operation, create or download a graphic image that can be used as a button. Any graphic will do. Put the graphic in the root folder of the site. With your page and site open, continue with the following steps:

1. **Choose Window⇨Inspector from the menu bar or undock the Inspector by clicking the Inspector tab at the side of the screen.**

   The Inspector palette appears on your screen.

2. **Choose Window⇨Objects from the menu bar or undock the Objects palette by clicking the Objects tab at the side of the screen.**

   The Objects palette appears.

3. **Choose Window⇨Floating Boxes from the menu bar or undock the Floating Boxes palette by clicking the Floating Boxes tab at the side of the screen.**

   The Floating Boxes palette appears on the screen.

4. **Drag the button graphic image from the site window to any position on the page in Layout view.**

   The Inspector becomes the Image Inspector. Keep the button selected for the next step.

5. **Click the Link tab of the Image Inspector and click the Link icon (the chain link) on the Link tab.**

   The (Empty Reference!) message appears in the URL window.

6. **Type a pound sign (#) to replace the** (Empty Reference!) **message.**

   The pound sign is a stand-in for the URL, but it effectively makes the graphic a hot spot, which means that you can add an action to it.

7. **Choose Window⇨Actions from the menu bar.**

   The Actions palette appears on the screen.

8. **Select the Mouse Click item in the Events column.**

   The action is set up to occur when a mouse click takes place.

9. **Click the New Item button (right next to the Trash icon) in the action.**

   The palette is now set to add an action from the Action pull-down menu.

10. **Choose Action⇨Multimedia⇨ShowHide from the Actions palette.**

    The Multimedia menu includes control over floating-box visibility. On the right side of the Actions palette, two pull-down menus appear, named Floating Box and Mode.

11. **From the Actions palette pull-down menu named Floating Box, choose the name of the floating box that you want to be visible and invisible.**

    You see the name of your floating box, or the name *Layer*. However, if you have several floating boxes on your page, you'll wish that you had renamed them to something more descriptive.

12. **From the Action palette, choose Mode⇨Toggle.**

    You could have selected Hide or Show rather than Toggle. Hide can only hide the floating box, and Show can only reveal a hidden floating box. But Toggle does both. (See Figure 16-3 for the final settings.)

Figure 16-3:
The Actions palette is set up for the visibility toggle for the Floating box named Spector.

Your Web page now has a button that lets the viewer toggle between showing and hiding the floating box.

Rather than go nuts trying to remember where you put your hidden floating boxes when working in Layout view, use the Floating Box palette to make them visible during development. To do so, choose Window➪Floating Box to get the Floating Box palette on-screen. Click the pencil icon on the Floating Box palette next to the name of the floating box. The box appears on your screen, and the eye on the Floating Box palette turns red, indicating that the box is really hidden (or that it has been keeping too many late nights).

Making the Floating Boxes Fly

You can make any or all your floating boxes move around on your Web page. Movement can begin when your page opens or when a person viewing the Web page clicks or rolls over a hot spot connected to an action. One of the better features in GoLive is the Record button in the Floating Box Inspector. Using this button makes adding movement to your floating boxes simple and intuitive.

1. **Begin in Layout view with a visible floating box containing text or a graphic image (or both) in place.**

   I created a floating box with the word *Fly* in it.

2. **Choose Window➪Inspector from the menu bar or undock the Inspector by clicking the Inspector tab at the side of the screen.**

   The Inspector appears on your screen.

3. **Choose Window➪Floating Boxes from the menu bar or undock the Floating Boxes palette by clicking the Floating Boxes tab at the side of the screen.**

   The Floating Boxes palette appears on-screen.

4. **Select the floating box by clicking the box's outline.**

   The Inspector becomes the Floating Box Inspector.

5. **On the Animation pull-down menu at the bottom of the Floating Box Inspector, choose Curve.**

   Linear is the default you see on pull-down menu. By choosing Curve, you make the movement of your floating box smoother.

6. **Click the Record button so that it is in the On position and can record the movement of your floating box. (It's right next to the Key Color text window.)**

   When the Record button is on, it appears to be indented.

7. Drag the floating box over the path you want it to travel.

Make the path as convoluted as you like — GoLive writes all the code for you.

8. When you reach the ending position for your Flying Box, release the mouse button.

The Record button pops to the Off position. You see a gray line tracing the path your floating box just took, as shown in Figure 16-4.

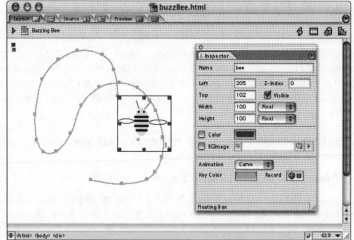

Figure 16-4:
The path of
a floating
box from
Layout view.

When you load your page into a browser, you can see your floating box follow the path you made for it. A floating box flying on your page gets the viewer's attention and, if done judiciously, can make a dramatic and interesting beginning for an index page. (You can also watch the flight of your floating box by viewing your Web page in Preview mode.)

Getting on the Timeline

You may not think that much of anything happens when a Web browser launches a standard Web page. You type in the URL address, press Enter, and the Web page appears. Take the time to think about it, however, and you can see that when a standard Web page is launched, its elements meet certain preset conditions. For example, perhaps all elements are meant to be visible and to stay put on the page.

To put it another way, "being visible" and "staying put on the page" are the default conditions applied to a standard Web page. But everyone knows that defaults are there to be changed; nothing on a Web page is set in stone. If you change the conditions (from being visible to being invisible and from staying put on the page to jumping all over the page), you add the distinctive dynamism of Dynamic HTML to your Web page.

You can set up the timing for a change in the default conditions of your Web page with the help of the GoLive Timeline Editor. It uses keyframes placed on a timeline as triggers for changing certain conditions and enables you to see and control every step of working with animations, visibility, and depth. The *keyframes* are those frames associated with a position on the Web page or an action. (Those dots on the trail of the floating box shown in Figure 16-4 indicate where a keyframe is located.)

You open the Timeline Editor from Layout view by clicking the icon that looks like a piece of film — the second icon from the left between a scroll icon and dynamic content icon — in the upper-right corner of the Layout window.

Pages with floating-box movement paths (refer to Figure 16-4) are shown in sequential, linear arrangement in the Timeline Editor. Each little dot on the movement path is a keyframe on the timeline (see Figure 16-5).

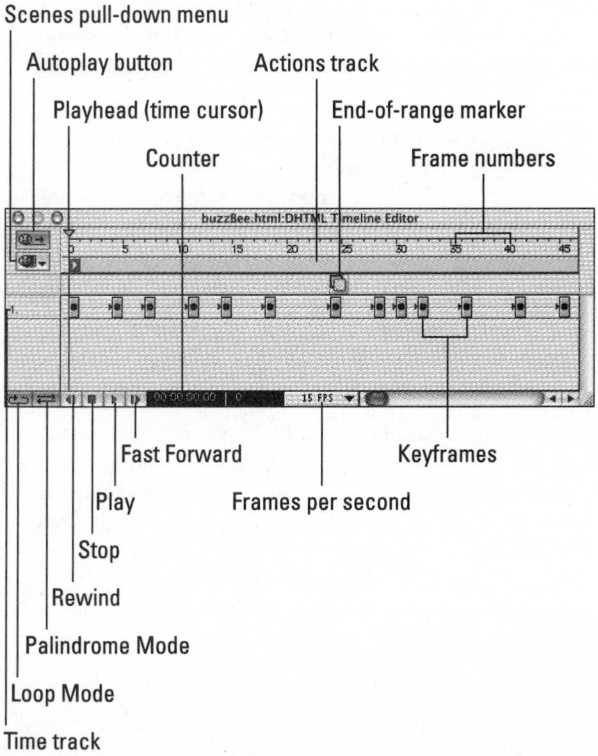

Figure 16-5:
The Timeline Editor with a single track for a single floating box.

Scenes pull-down menu
Autoplay button
Playhead (time cursor)
Counter
Actions track
End-of-range marker
Frame numbers

buzzBee.html:DHTML Timeline Editor

Fast Forward
Play
Stop
Rewind
Palindrome Mode
Loop Mode
Time track
Keyframes
Frames per second

Don't confuse the Timeline Editor in this chapter and the Timeline window in Chapter 15 — they're different. Other than each being a timeline with tracks, they are not similar. The following are key elements in the Timeline Editor:

✔ **Time track:** Each floating box has its own Time track. Time tracks make up the rows in the Timeline Editor. An arrow appears in the left column of the Time track for the selected floating box.

✔ **Time cursor:** The Time cursor looks like a vertical line topped by a triangle — a playhead. This line extends from top to bottom through the Time tracks, and you can drag it from left to right across the screen. As you drag the Time cursor left and right, you can watch the Layout view window and see what your objects are doing. At the bottom of the Timeline Editor are the playback buttons; pressing the Play button moves the Time cursor from left to right in the correct time proportions.

✔ **Frame:** Each hash mark on the timeline at the top of the Timeline Editor represents a frame. Think of each frame as a frame in a movie. At the bottom of the Timeline Editor, you see the default speed set to 15 FPS — that's 15 frames per second. You can change this default setting to speed up or slow down the actions.

✔ **Keyframes:** A *keyframe* is a frame that marks a change in direction or status of a property of the floating box. Properties include position, depth, and visibility. All those little marks on the path line shown in Figure 16-4, for example, represent keyframes. The Timeline Editor helps you keep track of all the keyframes for a floating box by marking keyframes on the timeline as little boxes with circles in them (refer to Figure 16-5).

✔ **Action track:** The row above the Time tracks is the Action track. Different built-in actions can be placed on the Action track to effect changes to properties associated with the page. For example, you may want to insert an action to change the background color of the page temporarily.

✔ **Scenes:** When your page opens, you may want to have all objects on your page perform a particular set of actions, such as appear and move around the screen. However, at another point, you may want your objects to do a completely different set of activities, such as move behind another floating box, where they're hidden from view.

If you think of all the visual happenings you create for your Web page as a short movie, you can imagine that one set of activities becomes one scene of your movie and the next set of activities becomes the next scene. GoLive 6 thinks in such film terms, too. The Scenes button appears in the upper-left corner of the Timeline Editor and shows the image of both a film reel and a single frame of film. Clicking the down arrow on this button opens the Scenes pop-up menu, where you can name and add all the scenes you want.

✔ **Loop and Palindrome Controls:** In the lower-left corner of the Timeline Editor screen, you can see two buttons graced with the images of a racetrack arrow and two opposing arrows. The racetrack arrow is the Loop button. When it is selected, the movement on the page repeats itself continuously. The opposing arrows represent the Palindrome button; when it is selected in conjunction with the Loop button, the actions run backward and forward. The default condition is *not* a loop.

Adding Actions in Movement

The Timeline Editor's many features may seem overwhelming at first, but with practice you soon get the hang of using them. A concrete example of how to use the Timeline Editor never hurts, either. Suppose that you want an invisible floating box to appear at a certain time after the page initially loads. If you coordinate the sudden appearance of your floating box with the action of another object, you can create the impression that the action of one object causes the appearance of the other.

Figure 16-6 shows the path of a floating box that contains a stylized bee image. Another floating box contains the image of a flower and is initially hidden on the page. When the Processing box hits the area with the hidden flower, the flower box "magically" becomes visible.

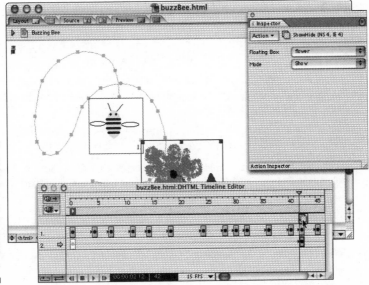

Figure 16-6:
The Timeline
Editor,
keyframes,
and the
action on
Action
Track.

First, draw and save (as a GIF, JPEG, or PNG file) a graphic bee and flower in your favorite graphic program, and then follow this next set of steps:

1. **Begin in Layout view with two floating boxes on your open Web page, with your bee image in one and the flower image in the other.**

   Make sure that you have a visible floating box and an invisible one. Each floating box should contain a graphic image. See the preceding sections for instructions on how to create floating boxes with contents (text and images, for example) and changeable visibility (visible or invisible).

2. **Choose Window⇨Inspector from the menu bar or undock the Inspector by clicking the Inspector tab at the side of the screen.**

   The Inspector appears on your screen.

3. **Choose Window⇨Floating Boxes from the menu bar or undock the Floating Boxes palette by clicking the Floating Boxes tab at the side of the screen.**

   The Floating Boxes palette appears on-screen. Be sure that the invisible floating box icon has an "eye" on the Floating Boxes palette. If it does not, you cannot see the invisible floating box! Just select the invisible floating box by clicking its name on the Floating Box palette and then click the eye next to it on the palette.

4. **Open the Timeline Editor by clicking the Timeline icon in the upper-right corner of the Layout view window.**

   The Timeline icon looks like a few frames of film and is located between the Scroll and Dynamic Links icons. The Timeline Editor appears on your page.

5. **Select the visible floating box and choose Curve from the Animation pull-down menu of the Floating Box Inspector.**

6. **Click the Record button in the Floating Box Inspector and then drag the visible floating box to make a movement path that touches the invisible floating box.**

   In the Timeline Editor, you see a number of keyframes created on the Time track of the object for which you just created a path.

7. **Drag the Time cursor back and forth until Layout view of the document window shows the visible floating box just touching the invisible floating box.**

   You can see where they intersect in Layout view. If the corners overlap a little, you can be sure that they intersect.

8. **Select the invisible floating box by clicking its name on the Floating Box palette.**

   Make sure that the Lock icon on the Floating Box palette is *not* selected and active. (If it is not, it locks the floating box and doesn't allow you to make changes.) The Time track of the selected floating box has an arrow in the leftmost column of the track, as shown in Figure 16-6.

9. **On the Time track for the selected (invisible) floating box, insert a keyframe at the Time cursor position you set in Step 7 by placing the mouse pointer on the Time cursor position and pressing Ctrl+click (in Windows) or ⌘+click (on the Macintosh).**

   A keyframe appears on the Time track for the invisible floating box, as shown in Figure 16-6. The little box icon below the new keyframe is the temporary cursor that appears while you're inserting the keyframe. The cursor indicates that you have taken the correct steps to this point.

10. **Immediately above the new keyframe on the Action track, Ctrl+click (in Windows) or ⌘+click (on the Macintosh).**

    A question-mark icon appears on the Action track, indicating that the keyframe is ready to accept an action. The Inspector becomes the Actions Inspector, and an Actions pull-down menu icon appears near the top of the Actions Inspector.

11. **Choose Multimedia⇨ShowHide from the Actions pull-down menu in the Actions Inspector.**

    A Show/Hide icon appears on the Action track. The Actions Inspector shows two pull-down menus — one for a floating box and the other for the mode. The modes in Show/Hide are Show, Hide, and Toggle.

12. **From the Floating Box menu, choose the name of the invisible floating box you want to show (the flower). From the Mode menu, choose Show.**

    As soon as the floating box reaches the keyframe on the timeline on the Action track where the Actions icon appears, the event is launched. In this case, the event causes the invisible floating box to become visible (that is, to show).

With these steps, you place a marker on the Action track so that when the visible floating box comes to the Action marker in the timeline (which is invisible on a Web page), the property of the selected object changes the visibility from invisible floating box to visible. Figure 16-6 shows what the page and Timeline Editor look like when the combination of elements comes together. The effect is something like a magic wand as the moving floating box touches the invisible floating box. Presto! It becomes visible.

By using a similar set of steps, you can change any other feature of a floating box in the Floating Box Inspector. For example, you can change the depth of a floating box so that it passes on top of rather than underneath another floating box.

You can achieve a fun, eyeball-grabbing effect by changing background colors to reveal a hidden message on your Web page. Just type some message (like **Wow!**) in the same color as your original background color. When you change the background color to contrast with the message color, the words jump out. Changing back to the original background color hides the message again.

Part V
The Part of Tens

The 5th Wave By Rich Tennant

"Mary-Jo, come here quick! Look at this special effect I learned with the new GoLive software."

In this part . . .

Are you ready to create a dazzling Web page but find that you can't decide on the right look? Do you want to uncover the best features of GoLive 6 and take advantage of them quickly? Look no further, my friend, for you're about to enter The Part of Tens. This traditional element of all *For Dummies* books spells out what I consider the best tips on designing a Web page.

In this part, you find out the do's and don'ts of good Web page design, such as "Don't use camouflage as a background image on your page if you want people to be able to read your text!" This part gets you thinking ahead of time about the common mistakes Web page designers make, such as using so many fonts that their pages look like a kaleidoscope. Cluttering the background is another common mistake Web page designers make. Some folks just don't think about those kinds of things and fill the background of their pages with cute little teddy bears. They don't realize that e-mail and other contact information is lost among those critters.

Part V also tells you why GoLive 6 is the best thing since sliced bread. I identify what I consider the best ways to use ten fantastic GoLive features to create classy-looking Web pages. It's the kind of information that inquiring minds want and need to know, and it's all right here in The Part of Tens. Don't hesitate. Don't think twice! Get wise and get smart.

Chapter 17

The Ten Best Features of GoLive 6

● ●

In This Chapter

▶ Laying out on a grid

▶ Using the diagram

▶ FTPing without pain

▶ Working the Workgroup Server

▶ Pointing and shooting and getting it right

▶ Cascading style sheets made easy

▶ Locking in those Web color combinations

▶ Previewing before you post

▶ Getting friendly with the Objects palette

▶ Changing the Inspector's identity

● ●

The most difficult part of writing this book was narrowing the best GoLive 6 features to ten. I like virtually every feature, but an endless list isn't much help to you. When I first began using GoLive, I was struck by a number of features I hadn't seen in other HTML site-development tools, and a number of these features make my top ten.

Layout on a Grid

My first and still-favorite GoLive feature is the grid. Using a grid eases the process of putting together a Web page so much that I shudder at the thought of going back to either watching all the parts of my page flying all over the place or trying to get them to behave by creating my own tables for the bits and pieces.

Whatever you do with GoLive, don't neglect using the grid! You need to use the grid to take advantage of the Align palette. With objects all over the grid, you can align, space, and place your page components quickly by using the Align palette on the grid. (All right, so I sneak in the Align palette as another favorite, but it does complement the grid.)

Diagram It!

GoLive 6 makes you think *site* and not just *page*. It gets you started with a broader attitude by providing different ways you can look at your site. The tools to see and develop your site include the Navigation and Links view windows, the Site Diagram window, and the In & Out Links Inspector. All these tools, along with the Site window and all its views, make life a breeze when you seriously have to make a Web site. By providing a graphical view of your site as well as its links, you can better decide which alternatives in your design work best. The thumbnail or icon images with lines showing the links between pages put the site designer in a position to better visualize whether the site-design goals have been accomplished and all the pages and links that need to be in the site are where they belong. (You can also see whether some pages or links need to be removed.)

Painless FTP

The GoLive file-transfer options help you get your sites on and off the Web host without going crazy. By integrating the FTP (File Transfer Protocol) into the Site window, transferring files no longer requires guesswork. By design, GoLive 6 uses the Site window to show all files in the root folder. Because the site has been developed in the Site window, transferring sites to a host server is simply a matter of clicking a button on the toolbar to send the site as a whole to the server. Because GoLive treats your work as a *site* rather than as a collection of loose pages, all the relative links are maintained during transfer. So, when you tweak a page to improve it, your whole site doesn't collapse when you send in your modified page.

Divvying up the Work with Workgroup Server

If you're working on a group project, you'll love the Workgroup Server, which comes with GoLive 6. You can turn your computer into a server and develop a team project without ever having to leave your office. Working with a dispersed group in your office or with developers in Katmandu and Timbuktu, you can all create, edit, and share tasks on the same Web site. The Workgroup Server helps you keep from stepping on each other's work and lets you all see how the project is proceeding.

Keeping Organized with Point-and-Shoot

At first, I thought that point-and-shoot was just a fun way to make links to pages, graphics, and other media. However, using point-and-shoot forces me to pay attention to all the elements in my site. If my page or other media isn't in the Site window, the point-and-shoot feature doesn't work. (The point-and-shoot line just sort of wobbles and returns to the button when the target isn't where it belongs.) Intuitively, point-and-shoot establishes a link between the Web page and other pages and media located in the root folder. Because the point-and-shoot procedure works *only* with pages and media in the root folder, you're more likely to spot a problem at the point of developing the site where the problem resides. Later, you do not need to fumble through all the pages and media in your site to locate a problem. I know of no other application that has a point-and-shoot feature, and I like it.

Cascading Your Style Sheets

With the new GoLive 6 CSS palette, creating and applying Cascading Style Sheets (CSS) in GoLive is simpler than ever. If you do nothing else with this book, go over the material on how to set up and use CSS with GoLive 6. Using CSS not only gives you the ability to control text formatting, but it also saves bandwidth because you don't have to use graphic substitutions for other than the most simple text formatting provided in standard HTML.

Working with Color Combinations

When I found that I could drag the mouse pointer from the Color palette across the page and match a color with a graphic on the page, I was sold! Without a doubt, the color-matching feature of the Color palette is worth the price of the application. Combined with the color wells, drop-down swatches, and site color collections, GoLive 6 is unparalleled when it comes to handling colors.

In addition to all the other color features of GoLive 6, a little-used Custom palette is available on the Palettes color tab of the Color palette. Put your favorite color combinations on your own Custom palette once, and GoLive 6 stores them permanently.

Previewing Before You Post

Another favorite feature in GoLive 6 is Preview view in the document window. Not only does this feature save you time galloping between GoLive and the browsers, but you can also view your page as it appears on different platforms and different browsers and browser versions — including cellphones. If you've ever created a page on a Macintosh and then viewed it on the Windows platform, you may have been surprised by "BIG text" or some other formatting that wasn't quite what you had in mind. Likewise, a page in Microsoft Internet Explorer can look very different in Netscape Navigator. By having a preview of both different platforms and browsers, GoLive 6 saves you the time of browser and platform jumping. It's a simple, elegant, and incredibly useful tool.

Making the Objects Palette Your Pal

To be honest, when I first started using the Objects palette, I wasn't quite comfortable with it. However, now I find it a practical and simple way to organize a huge number of features that you can put on your pages or your site. Rather than have to fish through menus, submenus, and sub-submenus to find the features you need, the Objects palette provides a well-organized collection of them at your mouse-tip. (That's like a mouse's fingertip.) Familiarizing yourself with the icons is easy because the name flashes at the bottom as you drag the mouse across the icons.

Changing the Inspector to Just What You Need

I swear, the Inspector is magic. As a context-sensitive tool, there's nothing to look up or dig up. No matter what part of the page or site you're working with, the Inspector knows what's what and presents you with all the options for a selected object. The page can get a little crowded with different palettes, but the Inspector keeps changing into different tools, including ones that have their own subset of tabs. It's like a very bright golf caddy who hands you *just the right club* when you need it.

Chapter 18

The Ten Best GoLive 6 Design Tips

. . . .

In This Chapter

▶ Plan twice, publish once

▶ Talent borrows, genius steals!

▶ Design good navigation

▶ Consider your audience

▶ Keep a simple elegance

▶ Choose your colors

▶ Rule out the rules

▶ Set the tone with fonts

▶ Beautify your page with balance

▶ Paint your text with CSS

. . . .

*N*ot coming from an artistic or design background, I have had to struggle to get my Web pages looking good. The most important realization I had was that good design doesn't happen by chance or because you know all about computers. I read everything I can on design, and I use every tip I can. Moreover, the learning never ends.

Plan Twice, Publish Once

I have one thing to say to those who think that they can make up a design as they go along: *Forget about it!* Creating a design on the fly is like trying to get dressed on the drive to work. The time you spend planning pays you back tenfold compared to the time you take undoing a poor design. If you carefully plan your design (and GoLive 6 provides plenty of design tools) before launching your site, you have a better-looking site and spend less time making it so. After you have a good design and design components, GoLive helps you duplicate those design elements throughout your site. In this way, you do it right the first time rather than waste time undoing a rush job.

Talent Borrows, Genius Steals!

If you see a Web design you like, *copy it!* You don't have to duplicate it exactly, but study it carefully and use the navigation system, page design, or color scheme that appeals to you. Chances are that some of the best Web sites on the World Wide Web snaked more than a few ideas themselves! All good designers flatter fellow designers by pilfering ideas. It's part of an elaborate moral code. (Hey, I don't make the rules. I just follow them.)

Design Good Navigation

An important element of design in Web sites is a good navigational system. Working on your own Web site, it's easy to become so familiar with all the nooks and crannies that you may forget that a Web surfer who views your site may not have a clue how to find pages. A user must always know where she is in a site and how to get to a home or core page. A clear exit point is another important feature of good navigation. If a user feels trapped in your site, she won't come back. Therefore, be sure to provide a clearly marked exit page with a fond farewell and some final goodies or tips.

Another important element of good navigational design is consistency. If one page has one navigational system and another has a different one, the user could quickly come to believe that she has left your site. Use GoLive components to help maintain navigational consistency.

Consider Your Audience

Good design is good communication, so be aware of your audience. Design your page so that it communicates who you are and that you understand who your audience members are. If the group you're addressing is a group with whom you're familiar, such as a club or civic organization or a certain type of business, design your communication so that you address them the same way you would at a conference or convention. Speak the audience's language, and if you don't know their primary interests and concerns, find out. In some cases, you may even want to consider a bilingual or multilingual site if your audience speaks more than a single language. Remember it's literally a *World Wide* Web, and so is your potential audience.

Keep a Simple Elegance

Some of the best designs are simplicity exemplified. In all things, simplicity is clarity, beauty, and intelligence. Ironically, designing a simple site probably takes more time than designing a complex one. If you (or your client) want everything "up front," where the Web surfer can see it, no one may see anything. A simple "front door" page with an intriguing invitation to enter the site is a far better design than a cluttered one where disparate messages call the viewer's attention in all directions at once and there's no focus.

Choose Your Colors

Two important considerations should guide your choice of colors. First, you need to understand (or at least consider) the relationship between colors and what your Web site represents. On a more obvious level, if your client's corporate colors are blue (as in Big Blue — IBM) and your client's competition sports red, you probably don't want to generate much red in your site. Culturally, colors have different meanings as well. Japan associates the color white with funerals, whereas Americans associate white with weddings. (Yes! There *is* a difference.)

A second consideration in the choice of colors has to do with color schemes. If you see a Web site with an attractive color scheme, use GoLive's ability to borrow the color set for your site. If you haven't worked with color schemes and don't yet know much about them, educate yourself. Better yet, take a look at Leslie Cabarga's books *The Designer's Guide to Global Color Combinations* (HOW Design Books, 2001) and *The Designer's Guide to Color Combinations* (North Light Books, 1999) — both books provide the color values in CMYK, and *Global Color* in RGB values as well.

Rule Out the Rules

Rarely do you need horizontal rules on your Web page. (That's the <HR> tag for you code jockeys.) Rules separate a page a bit too much. If you have lots of items on a single page and you want to separate them by using rules, why put them on the same page? The world won't have a silicon shortage because you use an extra page. Use paragraph indents or double spaces rather than rules because rules extinguish continuity and connection on a page. (I don't even tell you where GoLive keeps them. You have to dig them up yourself.)

Set the Tone with Fonts

How you use fonts is one of the most important elements of design. Fonts themselves are designs. Look at pages in books, magazines, and (especially) at the opening titles in movies. Fonts are everywhere. They convey every emotion humans experience and tell the viewer in an instant the feeling of a page. Choose your fonts carefully, and rarely use more than two fonts on a page. As a general rule, use the sans serif fonts — such as Arial, Helvetica, and Verdana — for headers and the serif fonts — like Times, Georgia, New York, and Palatino — for the body font. (Verdana [sans serif] and Georgia [serif] are good, general-purpose fonts for the Web because they were designed for Web pages.) Because the Web has so few reliable fonts (ones you can be sure all computers see the same way), don't shy away from using graphic fonts for headers. If you need an art deco font for a header on your page, don't risk 95 percent of the computers on the Internet not seeing it correctly — put it in a graphic.

Beautify Your Page with Balance

A well-balanced page hides its balance, and an unbalanced page advertises its imbalance. When you drive your car on balanced and properly aligned tires, you feel nothing. But if your tires are out of balance, your car wobbles noticeably. I've seen enough wobbly pages to make me carsick. *Balance* in a Web page refers to the positioning of its elements in a harmonious relationship with one another. Moving a large child forward on a teeter-totter achieves balance when a large child and a small child ride together. The same can be said for a well-balanced Web page. Position large items at the bottom and toward the center, and put smaller items upward and outward. As with considering other elements of design, balance is a quality that needs study and practice.

Lining up everything in the middle of the page and centering your text *is not* balance. Just thought you'd want to know.

Paint Your Text with CSS

Cascading Style Sheets (CSS) are easy to create and apply with GoLive 6, and using CSS removes the severe limitations placed on page design by the original HTML styles. Use CSS to control the size, shape, color, background, margin, indent, and all the other elements surrounding text. Use elegant indents to begin paragraphs rather than a thumping-big horizontal rule and a canyon of space that separates one thought from the next. Highlight text and design your text as a complement to the overall design of your pages and site.

Chapter 19

The Ten Most Common GoLive 6 Web Page Mistakes

....

In This Chapter

▶ Dancing baloney

▶ Big, fat graphics

▶ A Web page is not a book

▶ Lost in the background

▶ "This looks like a ransom note"

▶ "No indents, please — I'm a Web page"

▶ "Uh, they moved and didn't tell us"

▶ Who cut the graphics with a chain saw?

▶ But it works on my browser!

▶ "Gee, it looked fine on my computer"

....

*W*eb pages and sites can be a minefield of booby traps if you don't navigate them carefully. You must be aware of not only technological limitations but also the design and navigational elements of a page. This chapter describes my little shop of horrors for Web sites and pages.

Dancing Baloney

The first rule in designing Web pages is Do Not Annoy The Viewer. *Dancing baloney* describes the animated pests that inhabit a Web page and draw the viewer's attention away from the content. Usually, a dancing-baloney page designer is a rank amateur who puts up his first animated GIF innocently and is as pleased as punch with his technological breakthrough. Pesky ads that blink at you while you're trying to find content on a page are common now. (Those ads pay the bills!) However, a grown-up Web page designer putting blinking graphics or text on a page is akin to moving into a cheap hotel room with a neon sign forever announcing its presence. Animated elements on a page draw attention, and if you must use animated materials on your page, slow it down so that the viewer doesn't beat a hasty retreat to another, calmer site.

Big, Fat Graphics

The larger a file, the more time it takes to load. The more time it takes to load, the more likely the Web surfer will boogie off to a faster site. Assume that the viewer has the slowest modem speed during peak Internet use hours, and you're safe. If a graphics file is larger than 50K (and less than 30K is even better), think about reducing both its size and weight by using any tool you can. After all, what good is a big, fat graphic when no one stays around to look at it? (The same goes for a bunch of little graphic files.)

A Web Page Is Not a Book

You're now reading a book. A Web page is not a book. Scientists using Canadian rats found that it takes the rats three times as long to read a Web page as it does to read a book page (and even less time than that to eat the page). If your page scrolls on for several screens, the viewer won't be amused and you won't get your content across. As a general rule, I don't like to make my pages any more than two screen scrolls long for a page viewed on a 14-inch monitor. Rather than use the long scroll, use a good navigational system. (Add some graphics to that long page, and you've got a long, long load.)

Lost in the Background

I once saw a Web page that used camouflage for a background. I never found out what the page was about because I couldn't read the text. Another site was so sweet that I got a cavity. It used a bed of roses for a background. Furthermore, by using a pink font, the designer made sure that no one got her message. It astounds me that people use those types of backgrounds and expect people to be able to guess what the page is all about. What's even more dumbfounding is that software companies that sell Web-design tools happily provide these backgrounds for free. One of my favorites is a gritty sandpaper or a high-relief wood background that you can get with just about any Web-page development program. That background does a great job of making text disappear. *Use your head.* If you can't make out a single word on your gravel-encrusted background, nobody else can either. Use background graphics on your pages judiciously and remember that you probably really don't need a graphic background.

"This Looks Like a Ransom Note"

Just because you have numerous fonts available doesn't mean that you have to use them all on your page. Your figuring out that choosing Type⇨Font from the menu bar in GoLive 6 unleashes all the fonts in your computer doesn't mean that you have to employ the riches of your fontdom. First, only a handful of fonts show up on everyone's computer, and second, your page is probably really ugly. As a general rule, stick to two, possibly three, fonts. Use the same font set consistently on both your pages and sites. (Usually, a sans serif font, like Verdana, works well for headers, and a serif font, like Georgia, works well for body text.) If you have a specialized font, such as one designed for a logo, save it as a graphic so that everyone sees the same thing.

"No Indents, Please — I'm a Web Page"

One of the most useful ways to separate paragraphs is by using a simple indent. However, few Web pages contain this graceful yet effective demarcation. Page designers usually prefer either the horizontal rule or a thumping double space. Truly consider using paragraph indents in your body text. The indent provides the information that a new paragraph has begun, but does not separate it from the preceding paragraph. The indent provides continuity and uncoupling at the same moment. (CSS makes it easy!)

"Uh, They Changed the Address and Didn't Tell Us"

Want to send a Web surfer scurrying? Hook her up to a nonexistent page. One Web-page designer responsibility is periodically checking to make sure that a link still exists. If a link no longer exists, remove the link or change it.

Often, and wisely so, a page design calls for a frame set. A *frame set* enables a designer to send viewers to an external link and use one of the frames for a navigation tool to keep the user in her own site. When a broken link occurs in a frame set, it looks like something is wrong with your own site and may turn off users.

Who Cut the Graphics with a Chain Saw?

When using graphics, especially transparent GIFs, watch out for jagged edges. Well-designed sites can look awful if the edges of the graphics (especially on curves and angles) appear to have been ripped from a page. Most software applications that prepare graphics for the Web nowadays have an anti-aliasing feature. *Anti-aliasing* smoothes the edges by blurring them a bit. The blurs are nowhere near as noticeable as the jagged sides of the graphic images. Be acutely aware of using graphic fonts that have not been anti-aliased.

"But It Works on My Browser!"

If a page looks great on one browser, it may not look so great on another. You must consider two things as far as browsers are concerned. First, and most obvious, look at your site with both Netscape Navigator and Internet Explorer. If a tasteful marquee scrolling your message across the screen is a major feature of your site, you'll be delighted with it in Internet Explorer. However, in Netscape Navigator, the scrolling marquee is stuck like a duck on a frozen pond. Some features work in one browser, but not in the other. Second, different versions of the browsers work differently. Newer versions generally pick up the older versions of HTML and JavaScript in Web pages. However, if your pages are involved in some fancy footwork with the latest CSS and JavaScript, you had better check them out on some older browsers. This way, you're aware of what minimum version the user needs.

"Gee, It Looked Fine on My Computer"

On your computer with twin 48-inch monitors, a dedicated T3 line, and a processor measured in jillihertz (that's a jillion cycles per second), your pages all look great and load in a blink. However, you have to be realistic if you want to extend your Web reach beyond your own office. Most users still have 14- or 15-inch monitors (including all iMacs) and use phone lines rather than high-speed links. GoLive lets you prepare for different monitor sizes and even how the page looks like on another platform. If you want to reach the widest possible audience, create pages that can be read on their systems, not on yours. And now with the Internet available on cell phones, remember to preview your site on the GoLive 6 cell phone preview.

Index

• *J* •